FOR JOANNA,
TEODOR AND
STEFAN

D1482787

"TIME AND SPACE
DO NOT EXIST"
AUGUST STRINDBERG

1ST EDITION
UNITED KINGDOM

dennis wojda

566

FRAMES

borderline press

WHO IS WHO IN THE BOOK

THE AUTHOR

FAMILY ON
MOTHER'S SIDE

1. HALINA – MOTHER
2. WŁADYSŁAWA – GRANDMOTHER
3. SERGEI – GRANDFATHER
4. KATARZYNA – GREAT GRANDMOTHER
5. JANEK – GREAT GRANDFATHER
6. STEFANIA – GREAT GRANDMOTHER
7. FYODOR – GREAT GRANDFATHER
8. JANEK'S BROTHER
9. JANEK'S BROTHER
10. KATARZYNA'S MOTHER,
    GREAT GREAT GRANDMOTHER
11. JANEK'S MOTHER,
    GREAT GREAT GRANDMOTHER (MS. DANISZEWSKA)
12. JANEK'S FATHER,
    GREAT GREAT GRANDFATHER (MR. DANISZEWSKI)

FAMILY ON
FATHER'S SIDE

13. CZESŁAW – FATHER
14. AUNT JADZIA
15. AUNT KRYSTYNA
16. JANINA – GRANDMOTHER
17. ALEKSANDER – GRANDFATHER
18. MR. PIEŃKOWSKI
    – GRANDMOTHER'S BROTHER
19. MARIA PIEŃKOWSKA

I WAS BORN ON FRIDAY THE 13TH AT 15:35.

EXACTLY 40 YEARS AGO.

GAGA.

I MIGHT HAVE LOOKED LIKE THIS.

MY MUM GOT HER FIRST LABOR PAIN AT ABOUT 9 IN THE MORNING.

COME, QUICKLY!

SO SHE CALLED HER BEST FRIEND.

MY DAD WAS IN KALMAR AT THE TIME.
400 KM FROM STOCKHOLM.

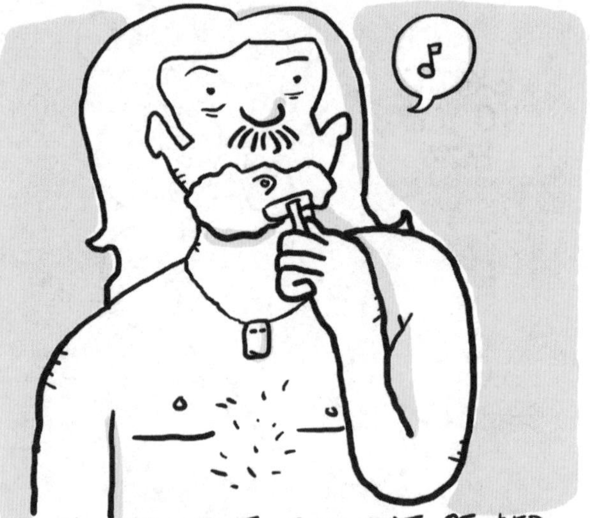

HE HAD JUST GOT OUT OF BED.

HE WAS DEAD TIRED FROM PLAYING DRUMS
ALL NIGHT. CONCENTRATING... NOT THINKING...

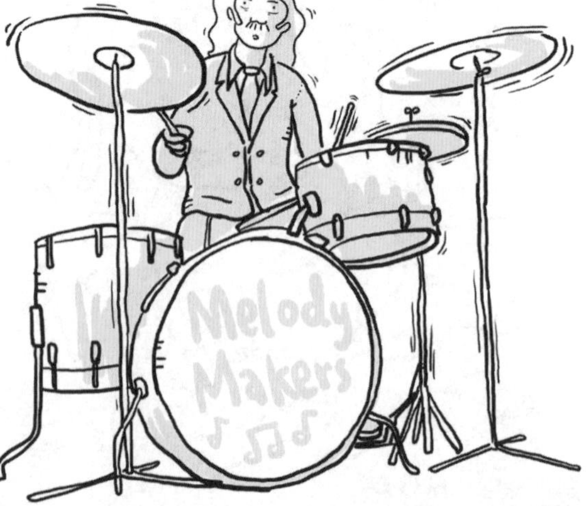
Melody
Makers

NOT EVEN OF ME.

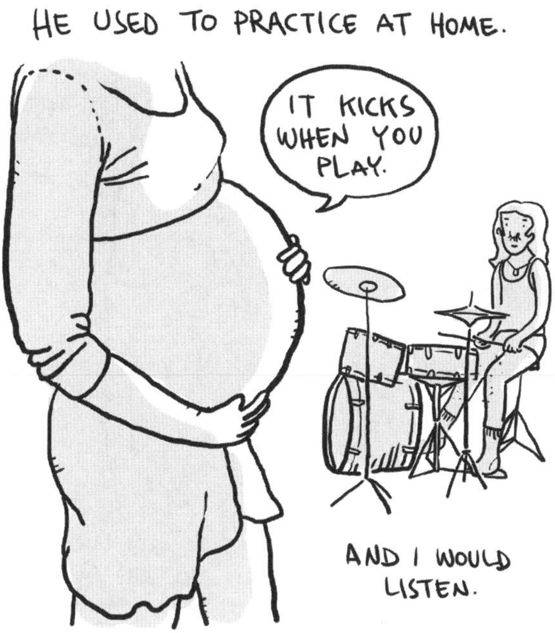
HE USED TO PRACTICE AT HOME.
IT KICKS WHEN YOU PLAY.
AND I WOULD LISTEN.

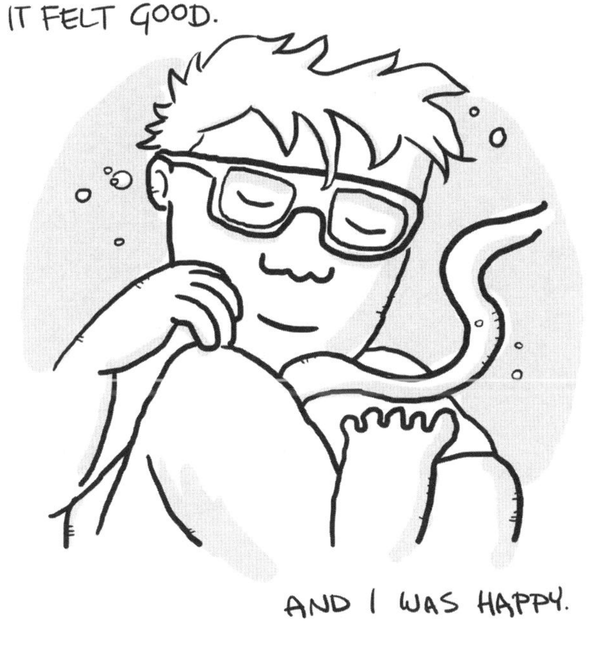
IT FELT GOOD.
AND I WAS HAPPY.

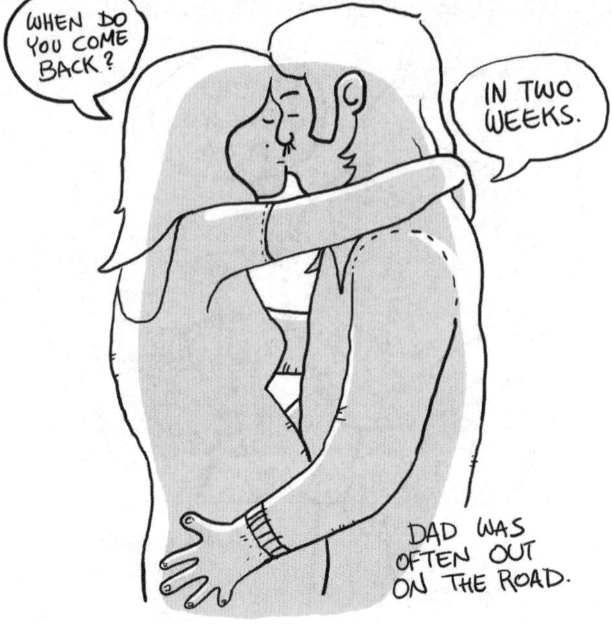
WHEN DO YOU COME BACK?
IN TWO WEEKS.
DAD WAS OFTEN OUT ON THE ROAD.

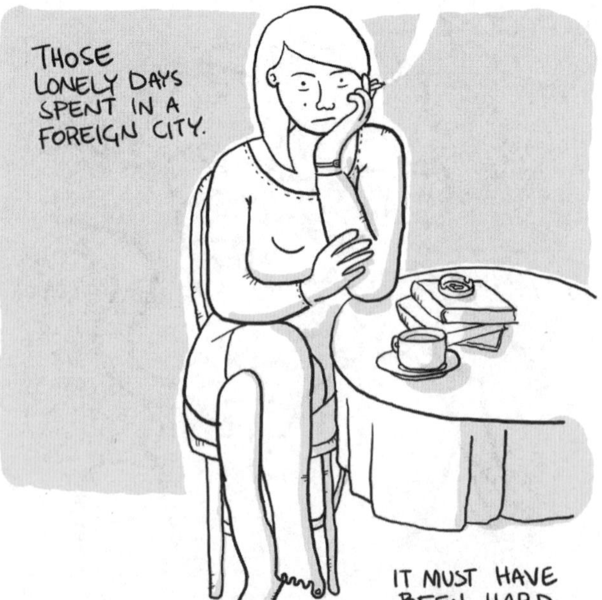
THOSE LONELY DAYS SPENT IN A FOREIGN CITY.
IT MUST HAVE BEEN HARD.

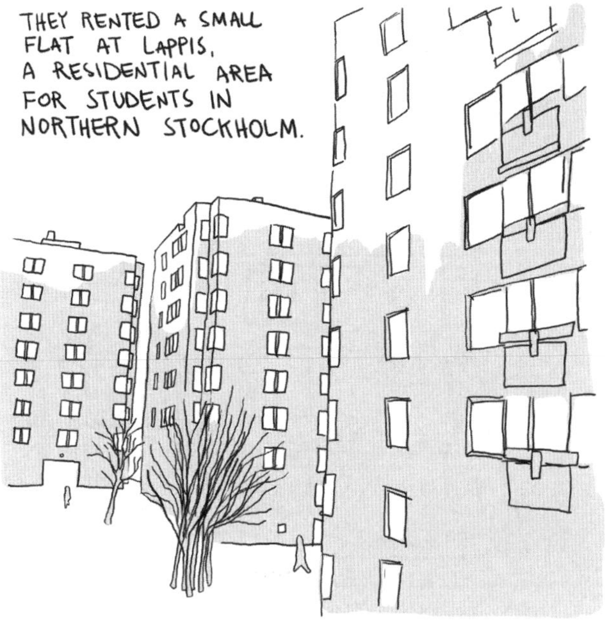
THEY RENTED A SMALL FLAT AT LAPPIS, A RESIDENTIAL AREA FOR STUDENTS IN NORTHERN STOCKHOLM.

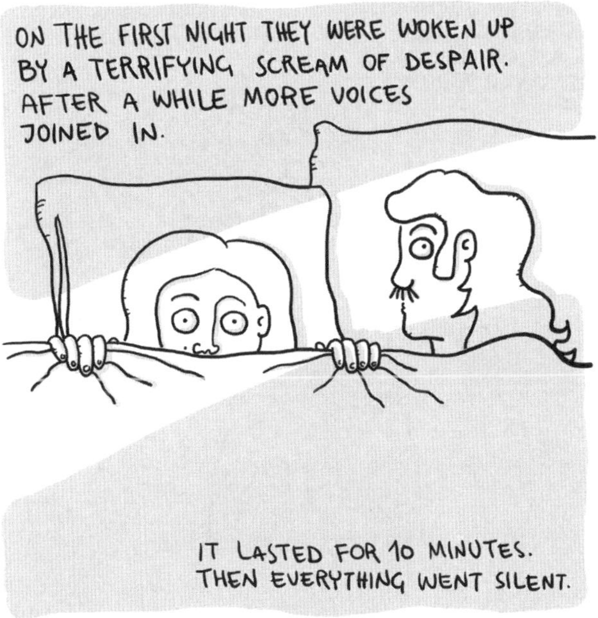
ON THE FIRST NIGHT THEY WERE WOKEN UP BY A TERRIFYING SCREAM OF DESPAIR. AFTER A WHILE MORE VOICES JOINED IN.
IT LASTED FOR 10 MINUTES. THEN EVERYTHING WENT SILENT.

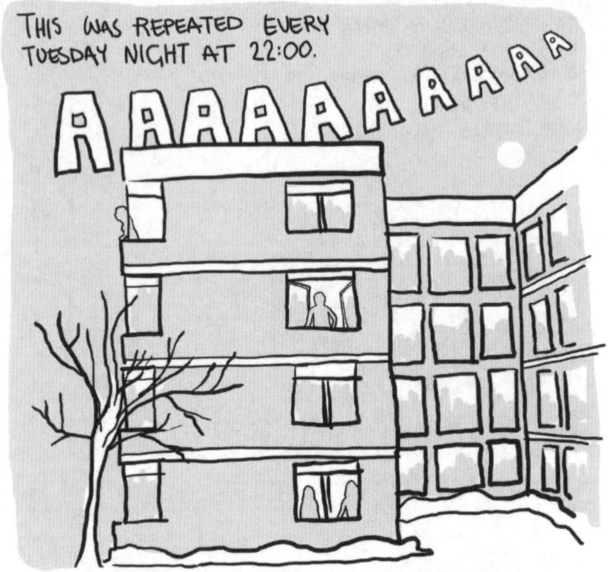
THIS WAS REPEATED EVERY TUESDAY NIGHT AT 22:00.
AAAAAAAAAAAA

IT WAS A SCREAM OF FRUSTRATION.
A STUDENT TRADITION AT LAPPIS.

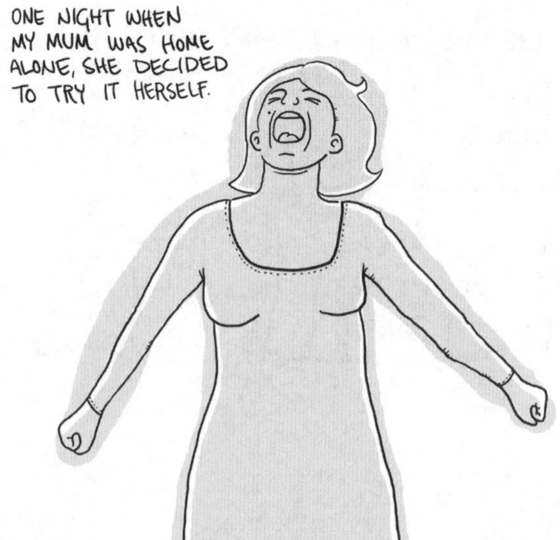
ONE NIGHT WHEN MY MUM WAS HOME ALONE, SHE DECIDED TO TRY IT HERSELF.

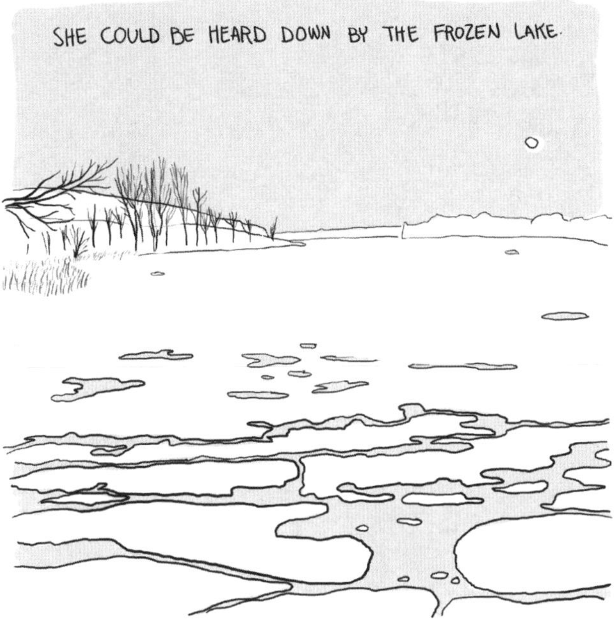
SHE COULD BE HEARD DOWN BY THE FROZEN LAKE.

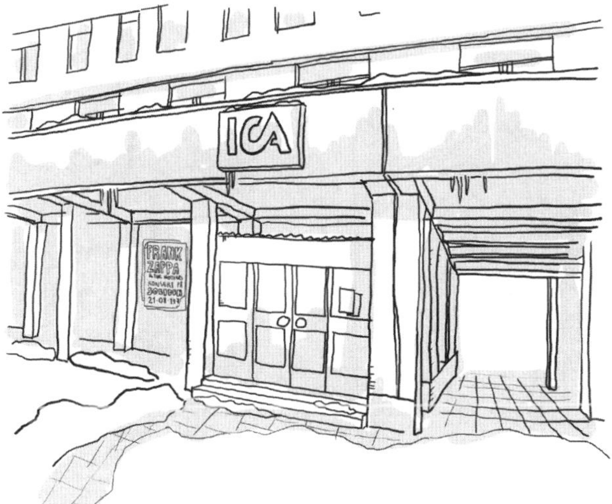
ICA
FRANK ZAPPA

AT THE CLOSED GROCERY STORE.

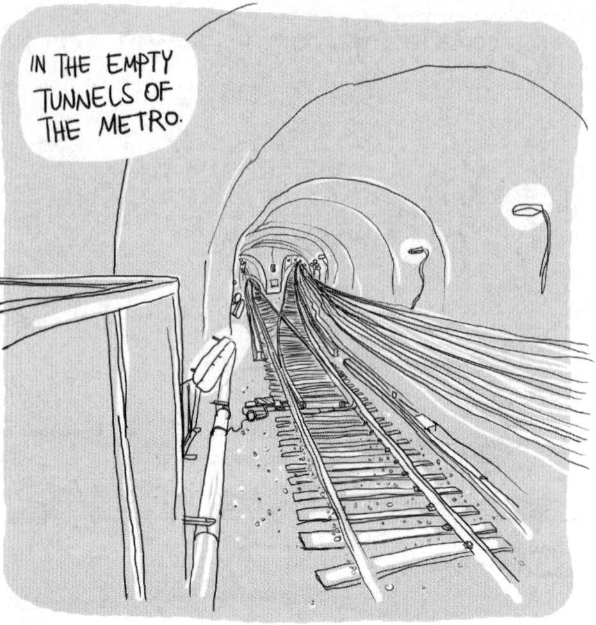
IN THE EMPTY TUNNELS OF THE METRO.

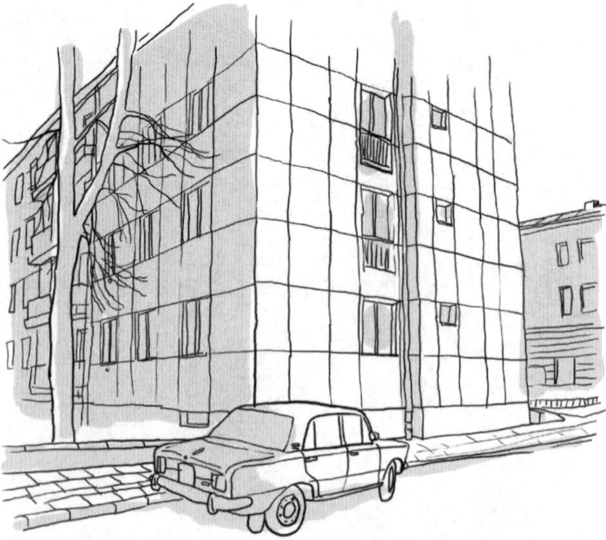

AT THE SAME TIME, FAR AWAY IN WARSAW, ON 15 ELEKTORALNA STREET.

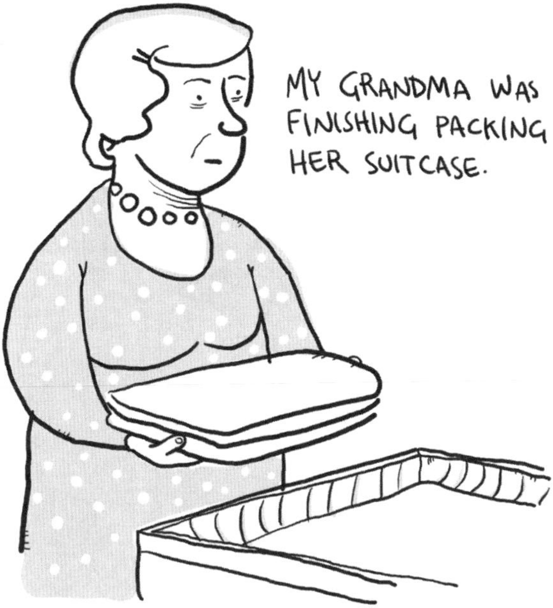
MY GRANDMA WAS FINISHING PACKING HER SUITCASE.

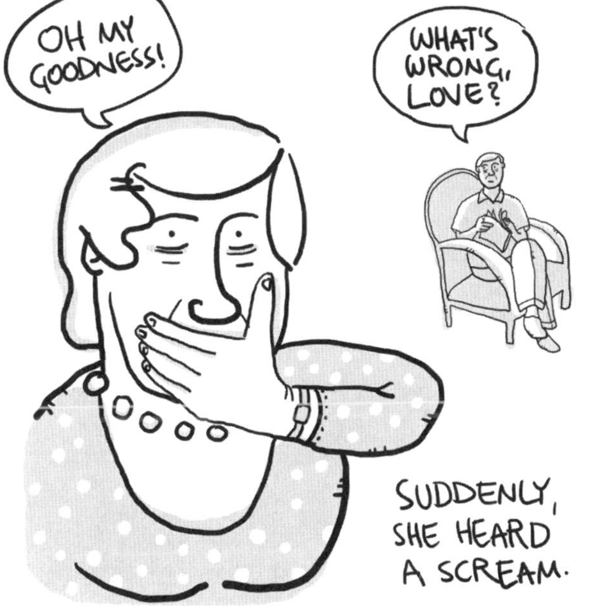
OH MY GOODNESS!
WHAT'S WRONG, LOVE?
SUDDENLY, SHE HEARD A SCREAM.

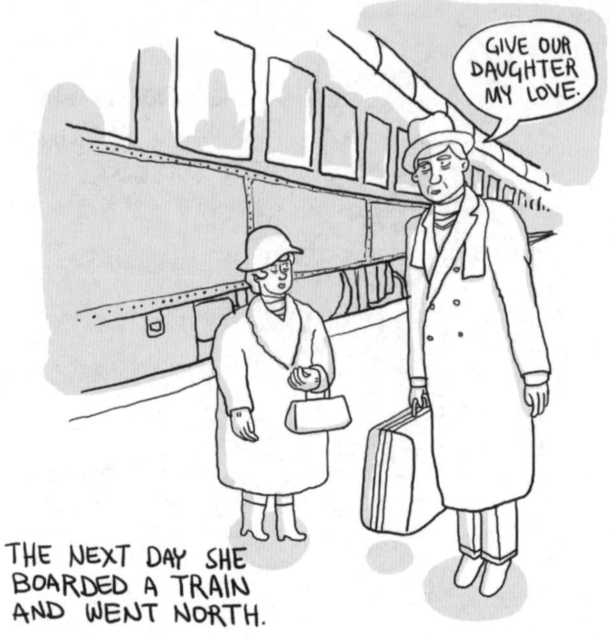
GIVE OUR DAUGHTER MY LOVE.
THE NEXT DAY SHE BOARDED A TRAIN AND WENT NORTH.

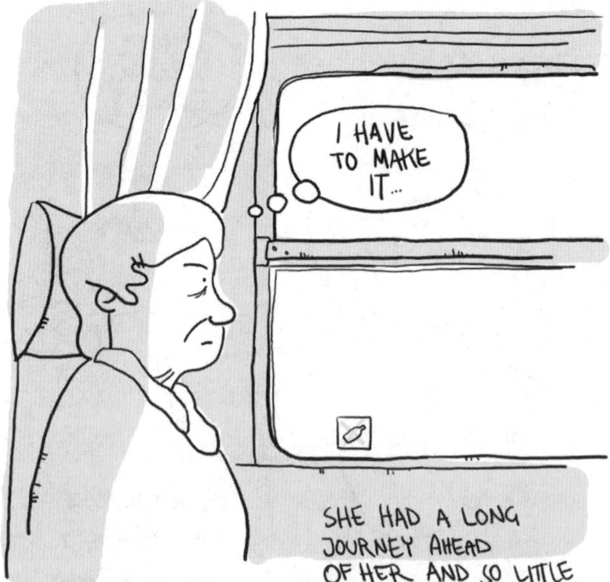
I HAVE TO MAKE IT...
SHE HAD A LONG JOURNEY AHEAD OF HER AND SO LITTLE TIME LEFT.

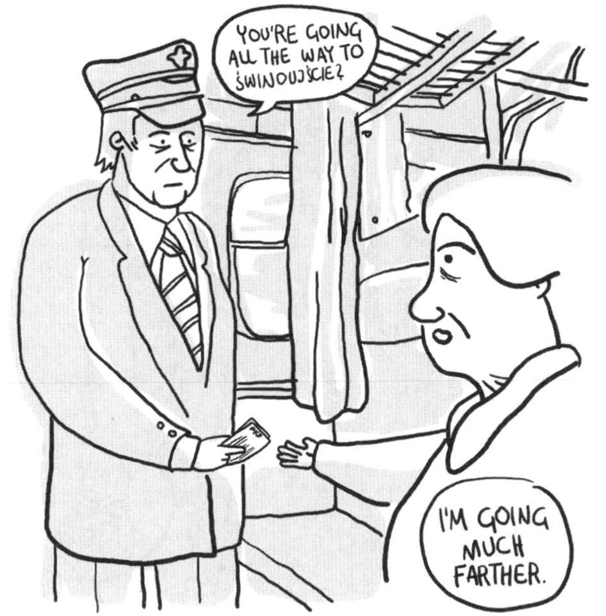
YOU'RE GOING ALL THE WAY TO ŚWINOUJŚCIE?
I'M GOING MUCH FARTHER.

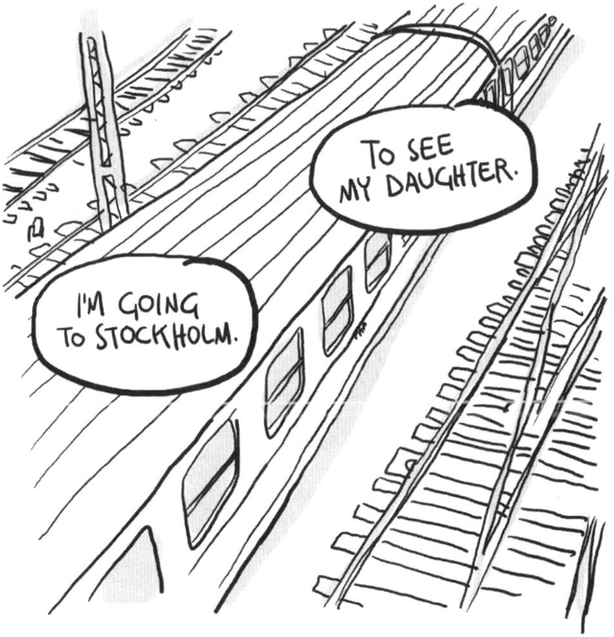
I'M GOING TO STOCKHOLM.
TO SEE MY DAUGHTER.

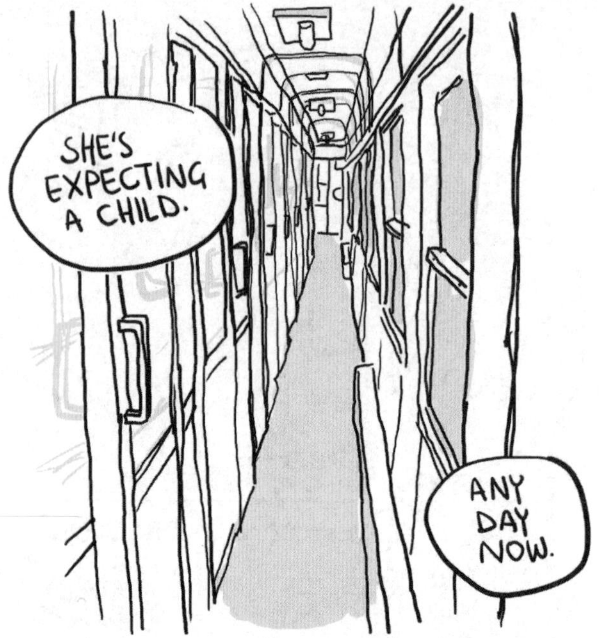
SHE'S EXPECTING A CHILD.
ANY DAY NOW.

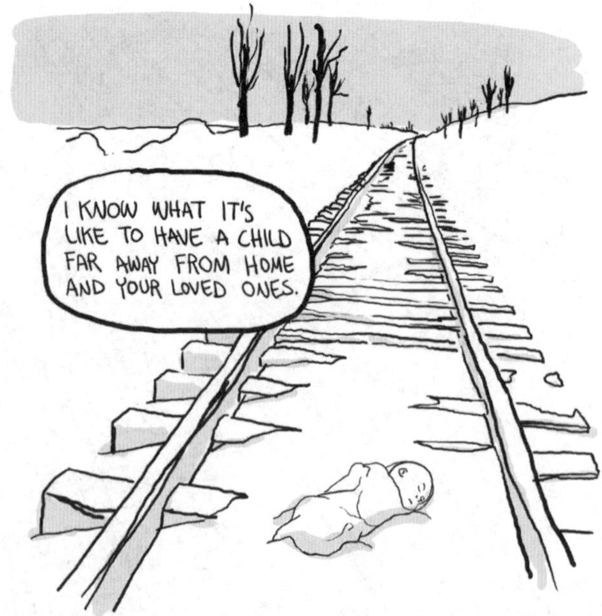
I KNOW WHAT IT'S LIKE TO HAVE A CHILD FAR AWAY FROM HOME AND YOUR LOVED ONES.

MY GRANDMA HAD FOUR CHILDREN. MY MUM WAS HER THIRD.

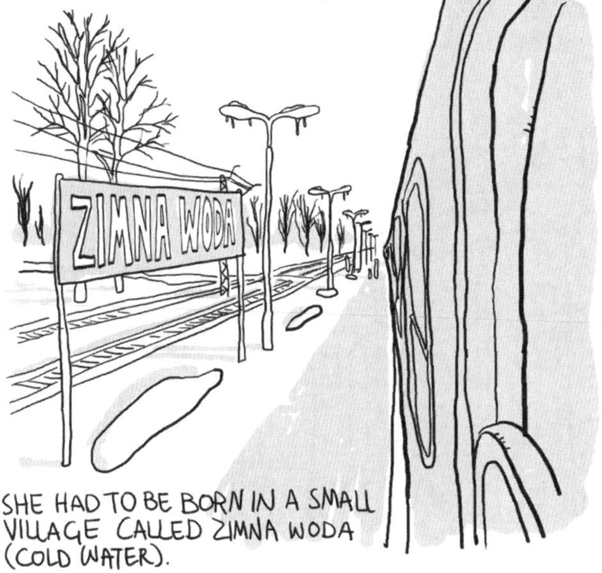
ZIMNA WODA

SHE HAD TO BE BORN IN A SMALL VILLAGE CALLED ZIMNA WODA (COLD WATER).

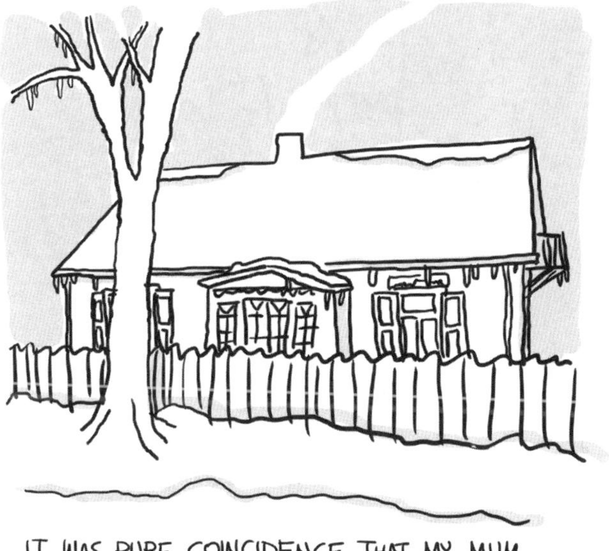

IT WAS PURE COINCIDENCE THAT MY MUM WAS BORN THERE, IN A COTTAGE IN THE MIDDLE OF A FOREST.

BEFORE THAT MY MUM'S FAMILY LIVED
CLOSE TO WARSAW'S OLD TOWN.
TODAY NOBODY REMEMBERS
WHERE EXACTLY.

ALL I'M CERTAIN OF,
THOUGH, IS THAT THE
SUMMER WAS HOT
AND THAT GRANDMA
HAD A NEW DRESS.

THERE WERE FRESH FLOWERS ON THE TABLE EVERY DAY.

MY MUM'S OLDER SISTERS HAD
BEAUTIFUL BRAND NEW SHOES.

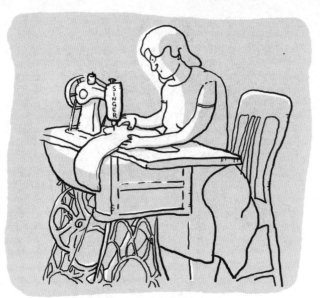

DURING THE EVENINGS GRANDMA
WOULD MAKE CLOTHES FOR THE NEW BABY.

MY GRANDPA HAD
SOMEHOW MANAGED
TO FIND A CRADLE.

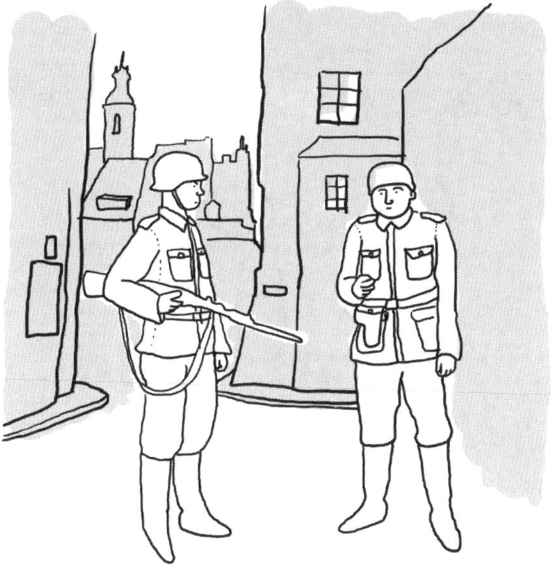

GERMAN SOLDIERS WERE PATROLLING THE STREETS.

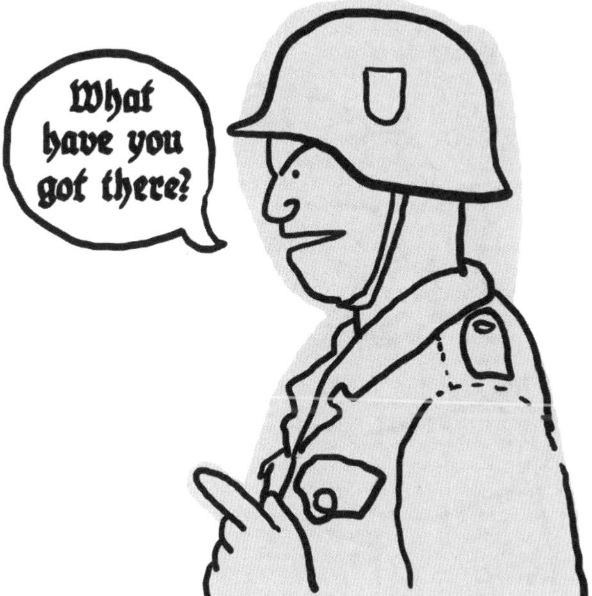
What have you got there?

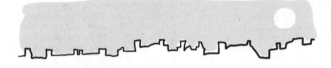

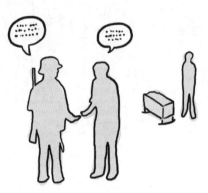

GRANDPA WAS FLUENT IN GERMAN. HE WAS ABLE TO TALK HIS WAY OUT OF TROUBLE.

I WAS SO AFRAID YOU WOULD GET ARRESTED.
IT'S ALLRIGHT. I GAVE THEM SOME MONEY.

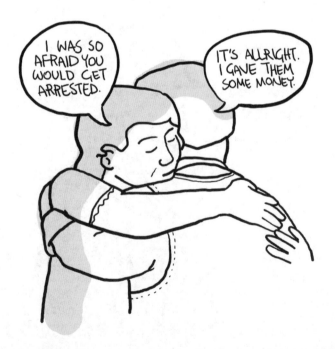

LIKE ALL CITIZENS IN OCCUPIED POLAND, GRANDPA HAD A "KENNKARTE" ID.

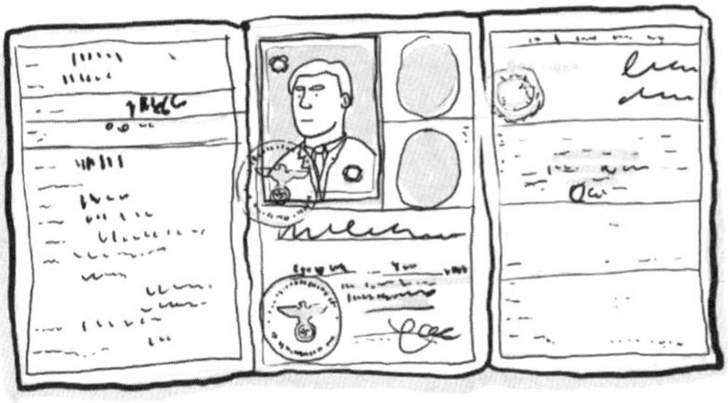

THE DIFFERENCE WITH HIS WAS IT WAS FORGED.

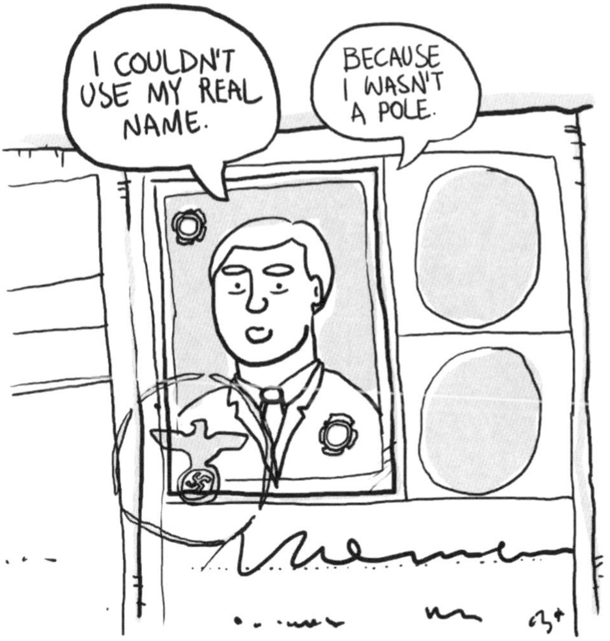
I COULDN'T USE MY REAL NAME.
BECAUSE I WASN'T A POLE.

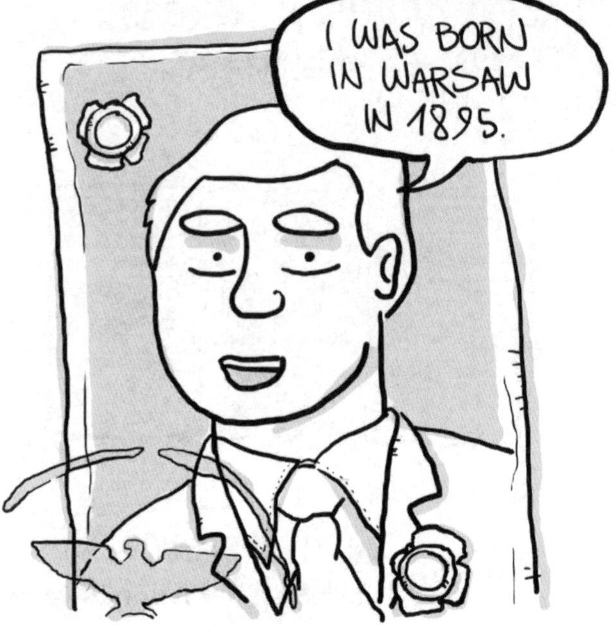
I WAS BORN IN WARSAW IN 1895.

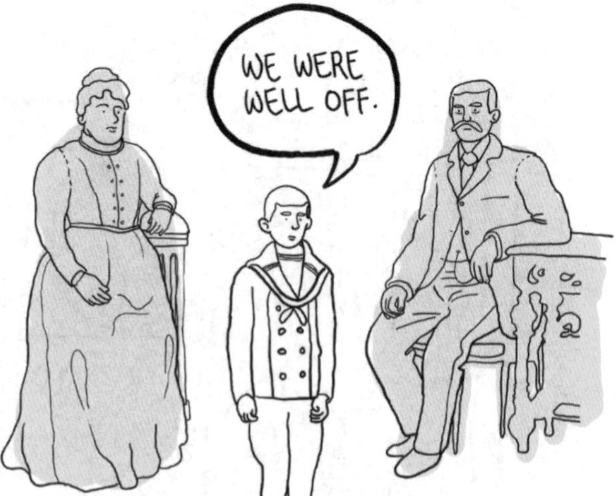
WE WERE WELL OFF.

MY GRANDPA'S FAMILY WAS QUITE WEALTHY.

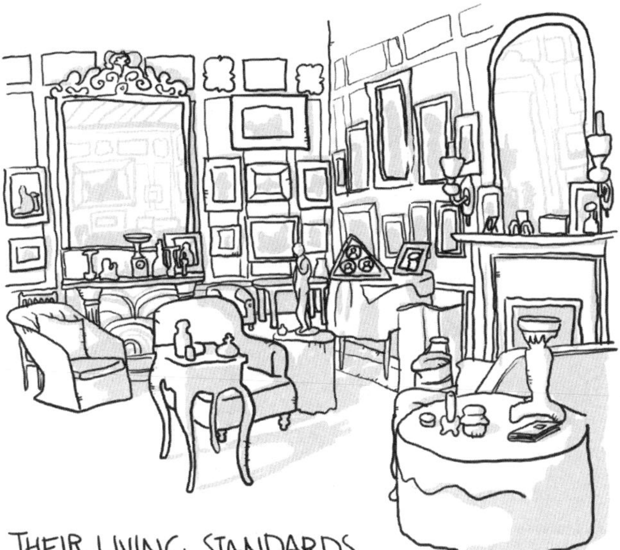

THEIR LIVING STANDARDS WERE FAR ABOVE AVERAGE BACK IN THOSE DAYS.

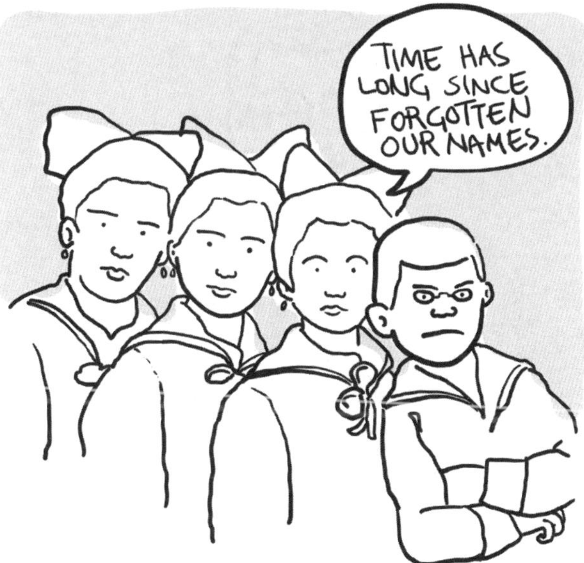
TIME HAS LONG SINCE FORGOTTEN OUR NAMES.

THE FAMILY WAS LARGE BUT NO ONE SEEMS TO REMEMBER JUST HOW LARGE.

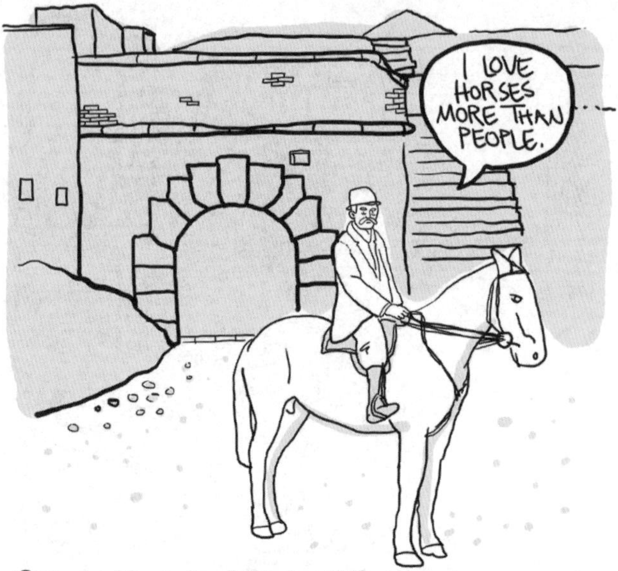
I LOVE HORSES MORE THAN PEOPLE.

GRANDPA'S DAD WAS A VETERINARY IN THE RUSSIAN IMPERIAL ARMY.

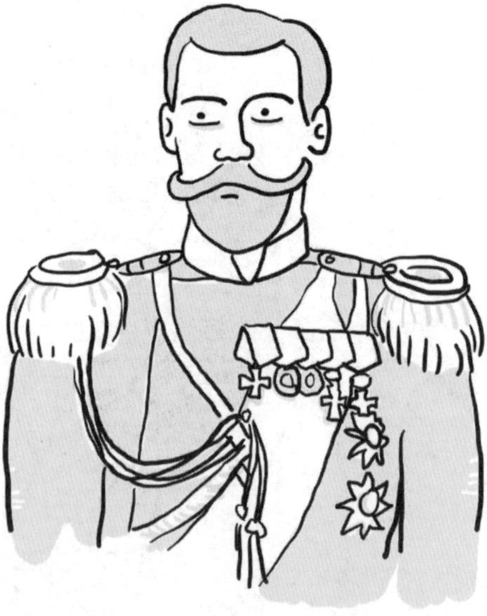

HIS EMPLOYER'S NAME WAS NICHOLAS II ALEXANDROVICH ROMANOW.

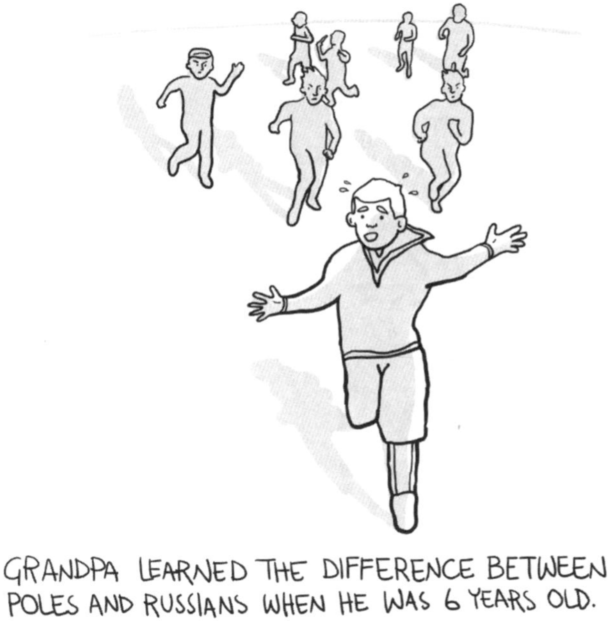
GRANDPA LEARNED THE DIFFERENCE BETWEEN POLES AND RUSSIANS WHEN HE WAS 6 YEARS OLD.

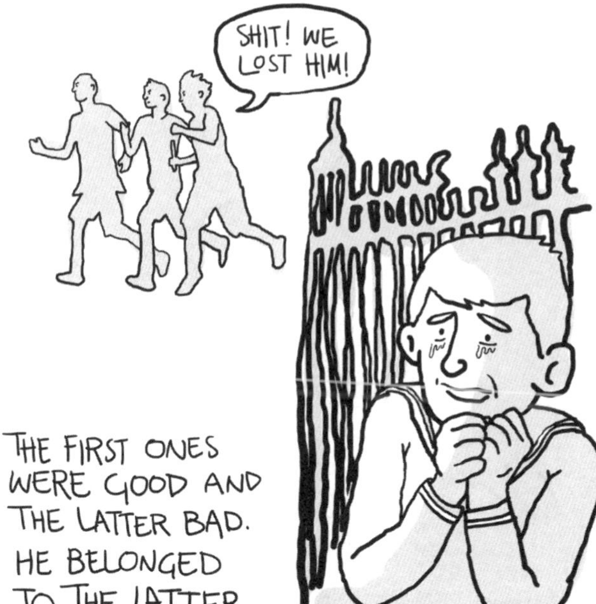
SHIT! WE LOST HIM!
THE FIRST ONES WERE GOOD AND THE LATTER BAD. HE BELONGED TO THE LATTER.

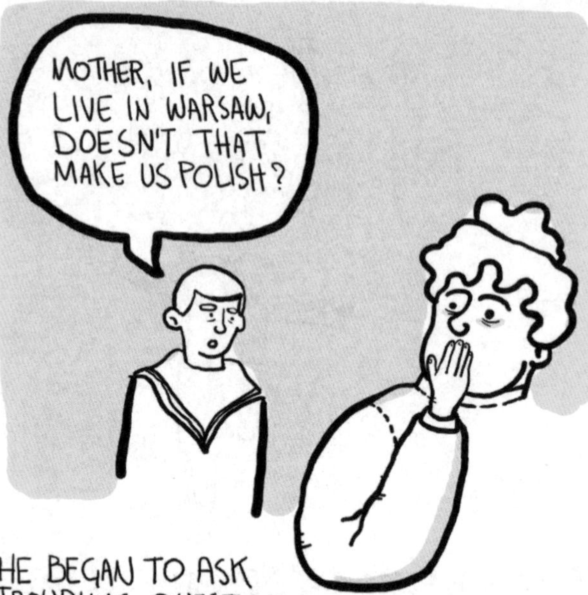
MOTHER, IF WE LIVE IN WARSAW, DOESN'T THAT MAKE US POLISH?

HE BEGAN TO ASK TROUBLING QUESTIONS.

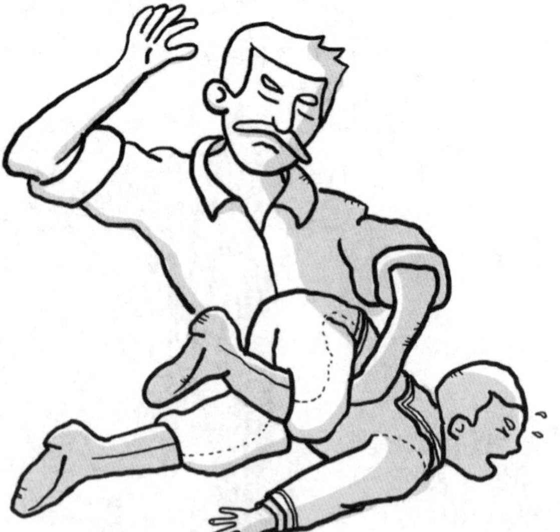

QUESTIONS HIS FATHER COULDN'T TOLERATE.

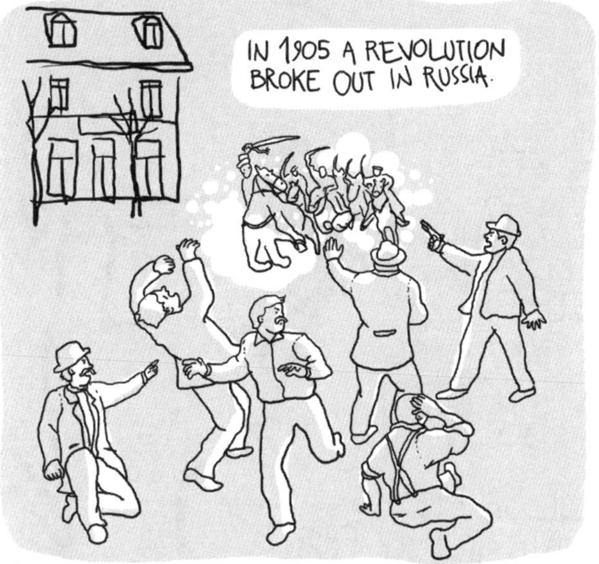
IN 1905 A REVOLUTION BROKE OUT IN RUSSIA.

WARSAW WASN'T SPARED FROM THE TURMOIL AND BLOODY STREETWARS THAT FOLLOWED.

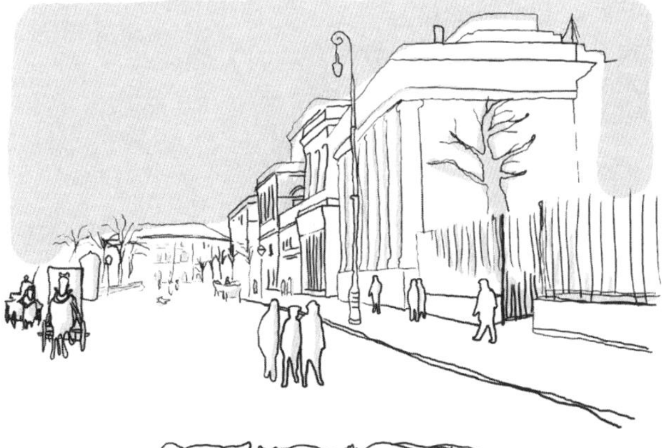

MY GRANDPA WAS 6 YEARS OLD AND HE THOUGHT IT WAS THE END OF THE WORLD.

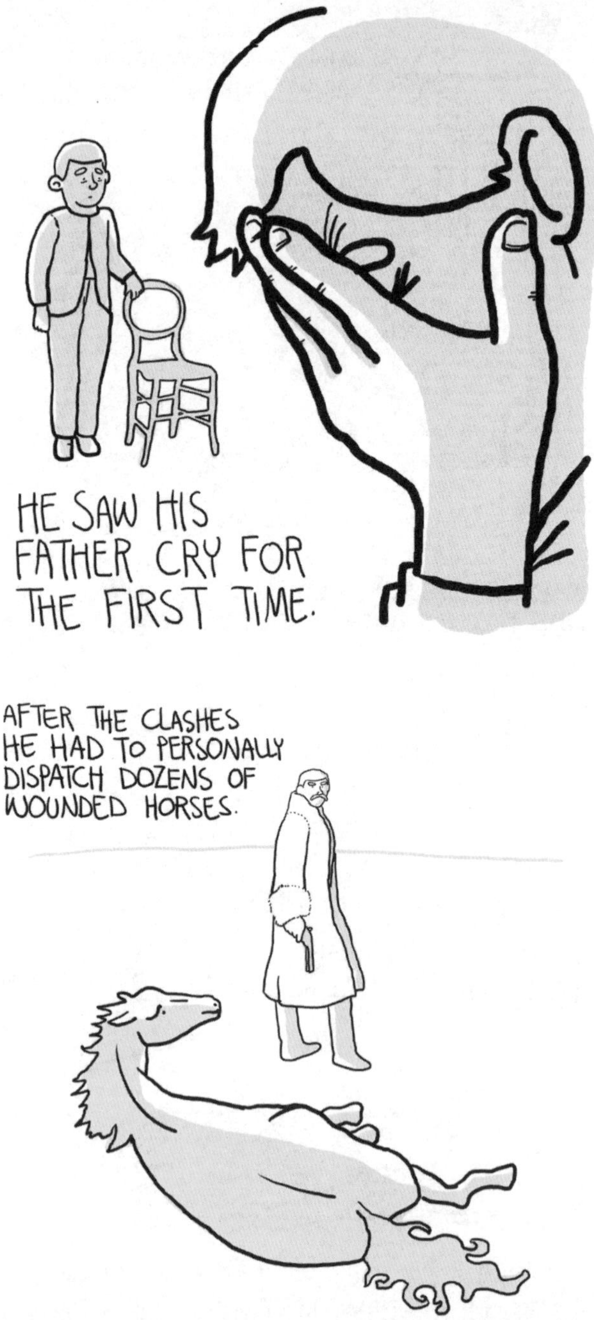
HE SAW HIS FATHER CRY FOR THE FIRST TIME.
AFTER THE CLASHES HE HAD TO PERSONALLY DISPATCH DOZENS OF WOUNDED HORSES.

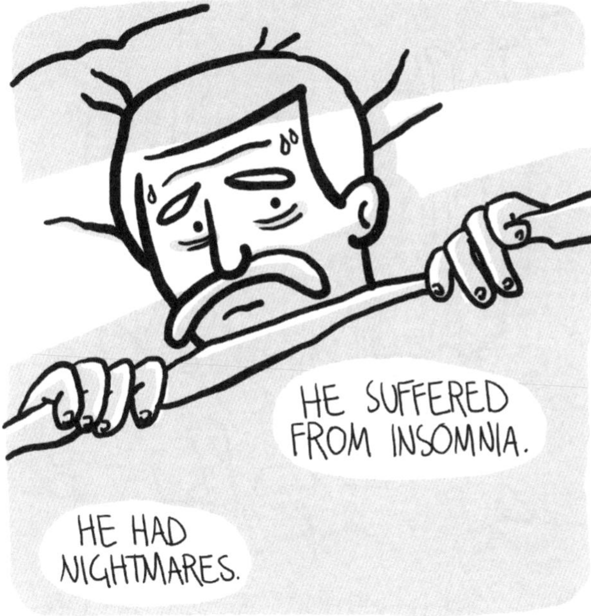
HE SUFFERED FROM INSOMNIA.
HE HAD NIGHTMARES.

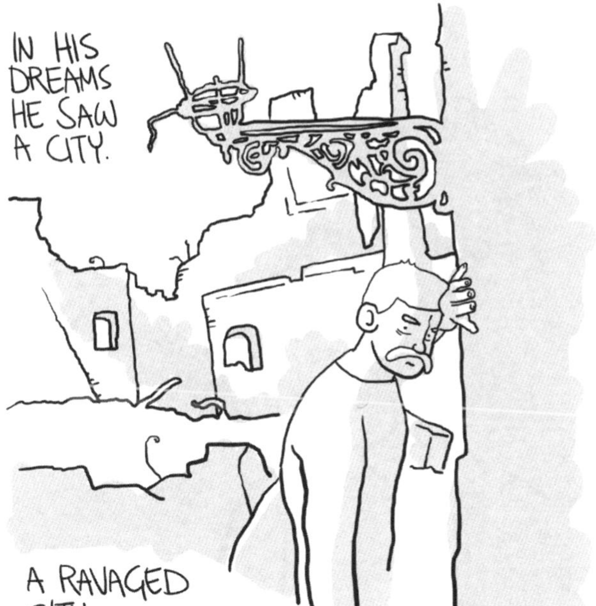
IN HIS DREAMS HE SAW A CITY.
A RAVAGED CITY.

ABANDONED, WITHOUT A SIGN OF LIFE.

EVERY NIGHT HE'D PAY THIS STRANGE PLACE A VISIT.

IT SMELLED
OF FEAR.

AND DEATH.

HE KNEW THEY WERE WATCHING HIM ALL THE TIME.

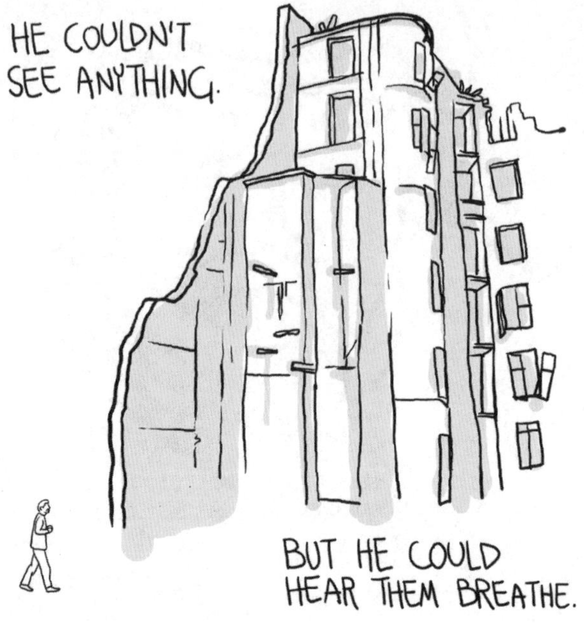
HE COULDN'T SEE ANYTHING.
BUT HE COULD HEAR THEM BREATHE.

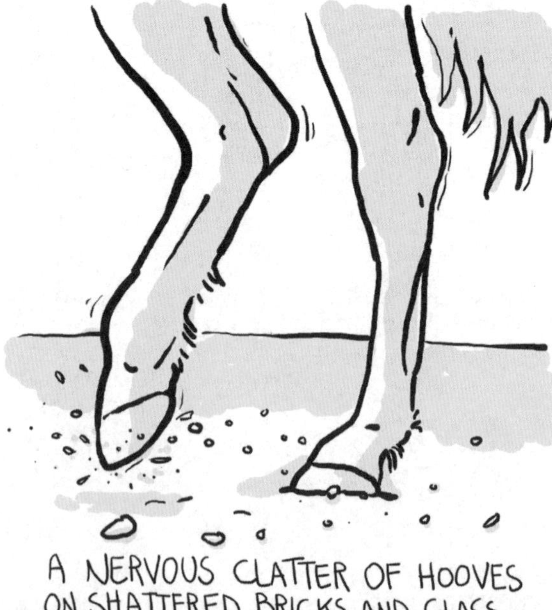
A NERVOUS CLATTER OF HOOVES ON SHATTERED BRICKS AND GLASS.

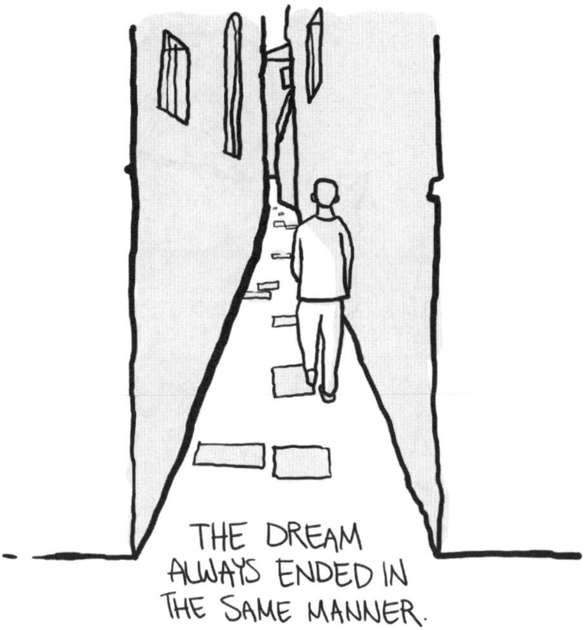
THE DREAM ALWAYS ENDED IN THE SAME MANNER.

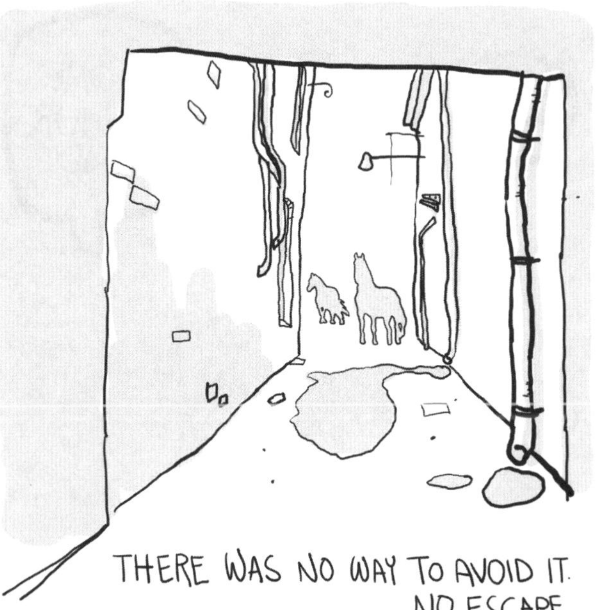
THERE WAS NO WAY TO AVOID IT.
NO ESCAPE.

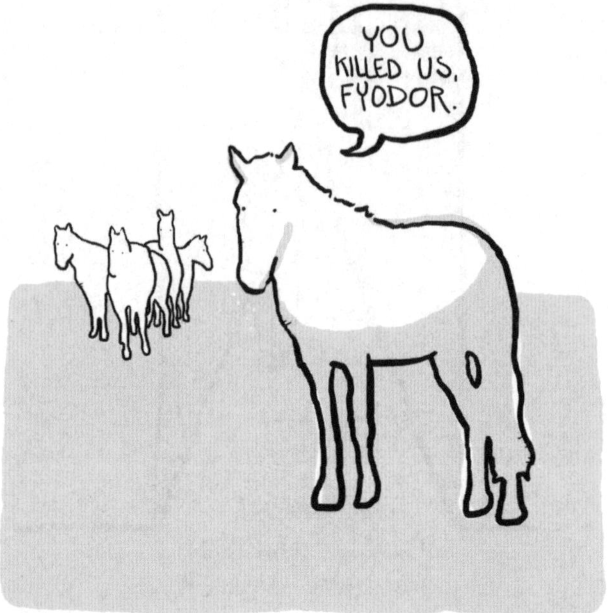
YOU KILLED US, FYODOR.

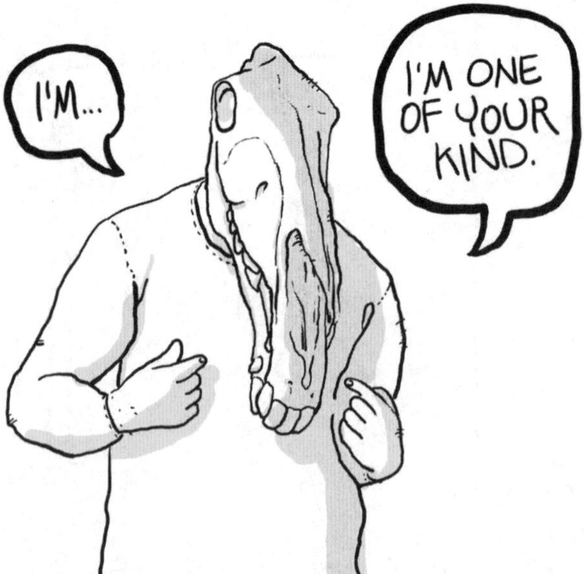
I'M...
I'M ONE OF YOUR KIND.

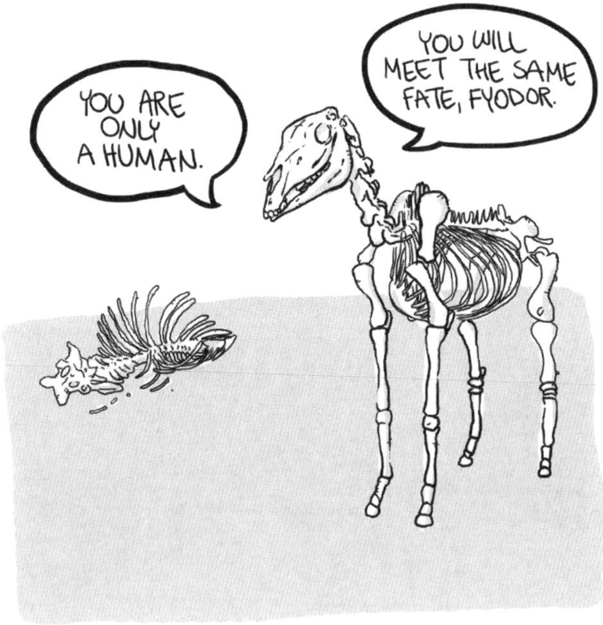
YOU ARE ONLY A HUMAN.
YOU WILL MEET THE SAME FATE, FYODOR.

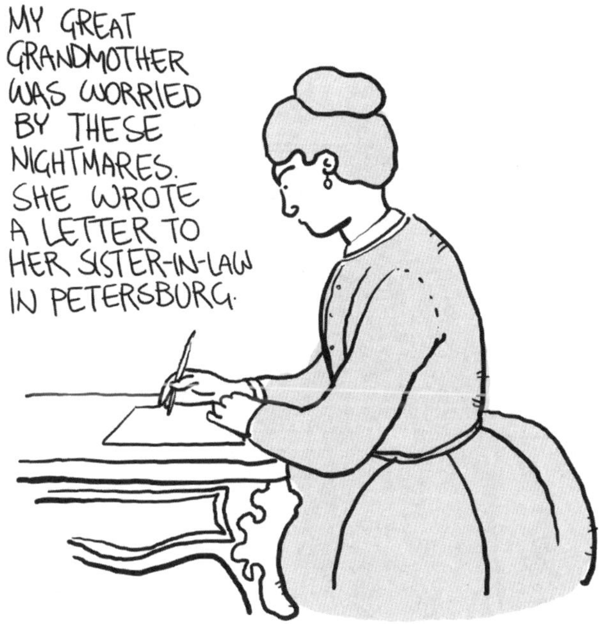
MY GREAT GRANDMOTHER WAS WORRIED BY THESE NIGHTMARES. SHE WROTE A LETTER TO HER SISTER-IN-LAW IN PETERSBURG.

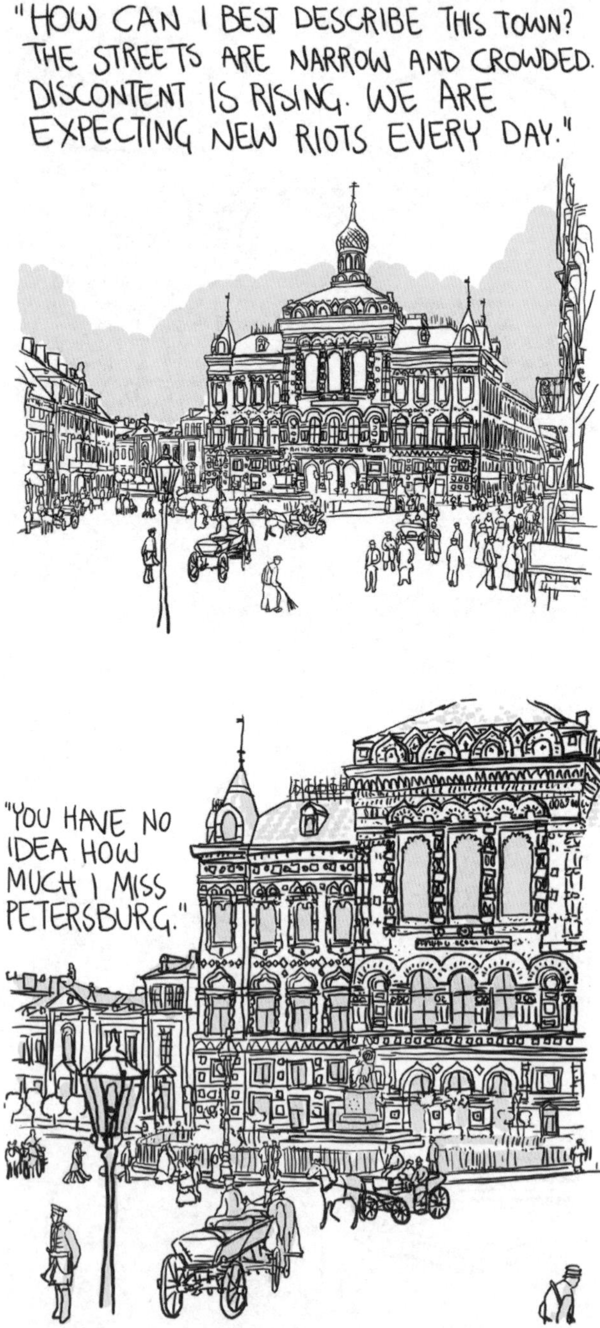
"HOW CAN I BEST DESCRIBE THIS TOWN? THE STREETS ARE NARROW AND CROWDED. DISCONTENT IS RISING. WE ARE EXPECTING NEW RIOTS EVERY DAY."
"YOU HAVE NO IDEA HOW MUCH I MISS PETERSBURG."

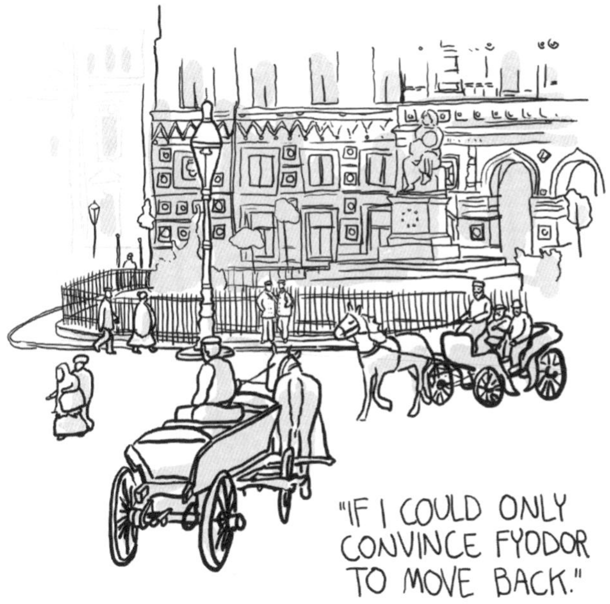
"IF I COULD ONLY CONVINCE FYODOR TO MOVE BACK."

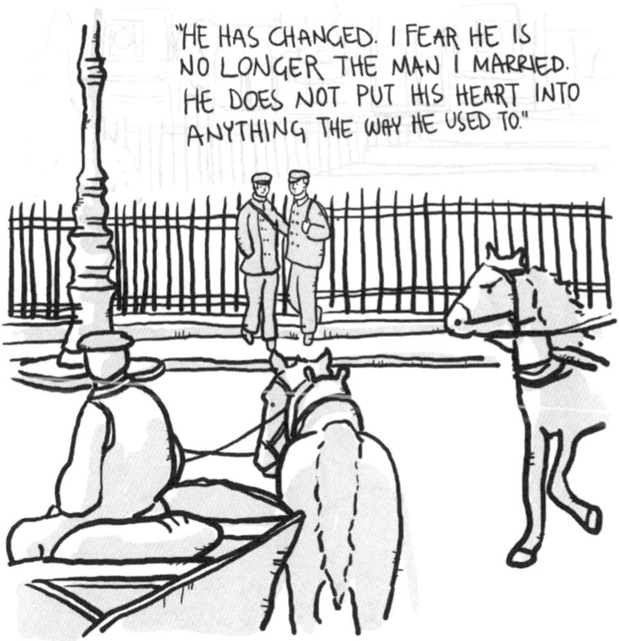
"HE HAS CHANGED. I FEAR HE IS NO LONGER THE MAN I MARRIED. HE DOES NOT PUT HIS HEART INTO ANYTHING THE WAY HE USED TO."

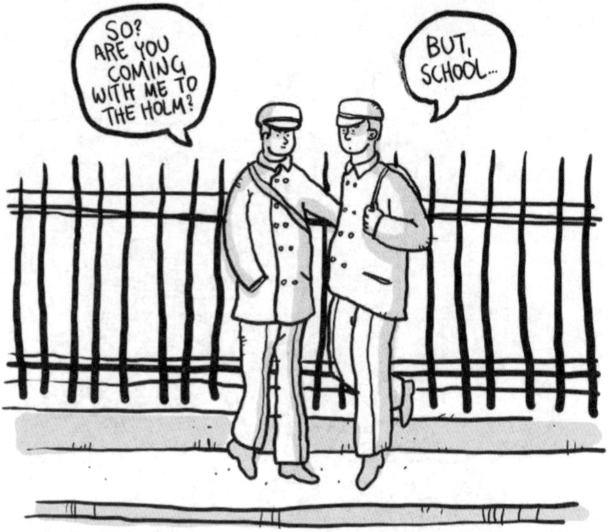
SO? ARE YOU COMING WITH ME TO THE HOLM?
BUT, SCHOOL...

"THIS HAS A BAD INFLUENCE ON THE CHILDREN. MOSTLY ON SERGEI. WHAT WILL BECOME OF THE BOY?"

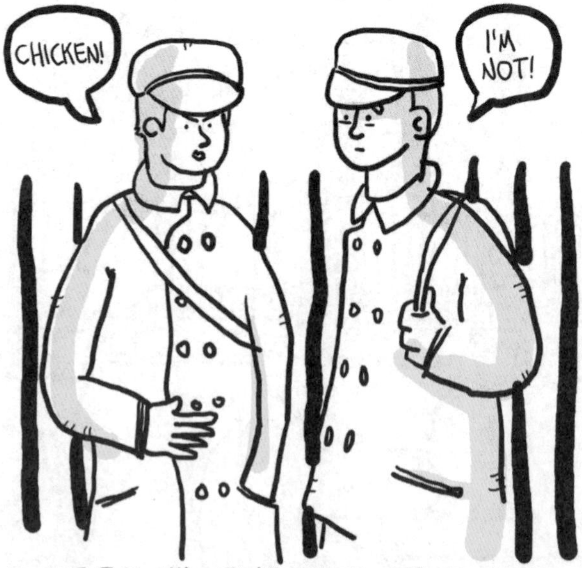
CHICKEN!
I'M NOT!

IN THE END MY GREAT GRANDMOTHER FORGOT TO SEND THE LETTER TO HER SISTER-IN-LAW.

MY GREAT GRANDMOTHER'S CONCERNS
ABOUT HER SON WERE JUSTIFIED.

HE WAS ALWAYS SKIPPING SCHOOL
AND FAILED HIS EXAMS.

ON WARM SUNNY DAYS HE'D RATHER GO
WITH HIS PALS TO THE SASKA KEPA BOROUGH.

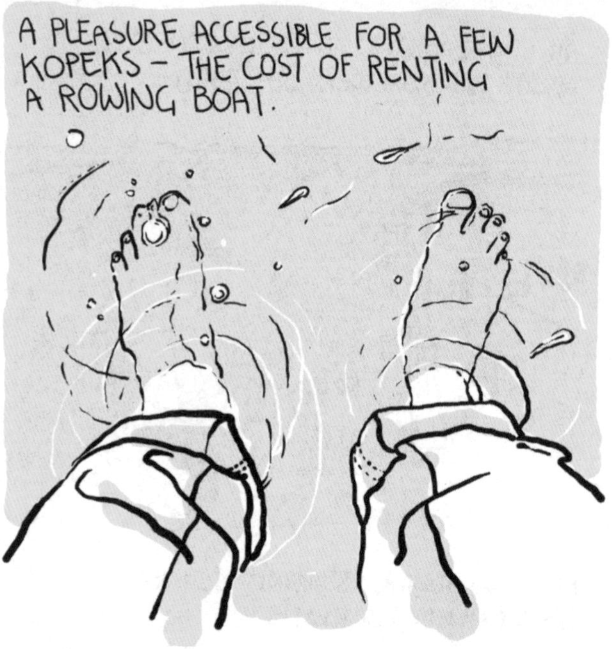
A PLEASURE ACCESSIBLE FOR A FEW KOPEKS – THE COST OF RENTING A ROWING BOAT.

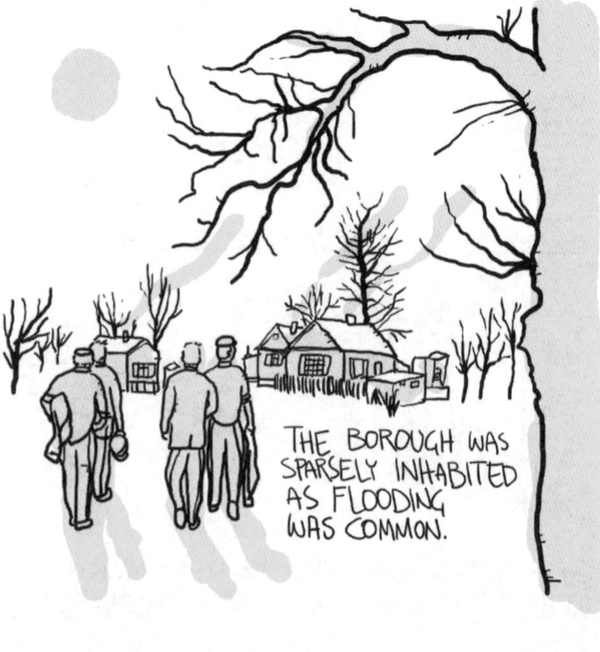
THE BOROUGH WAS SPARSELY INHABITED AS FLOODING WAS COMMON.

PEOPLE FROM WARSAW LOVED TO COME HERE
TO RELAX AND TO GET AWAY FROM THE BUSY CITY.

FOOD AND DRINKS
COULD BE BOUGHT
AT THE LOCAL
FARMS.

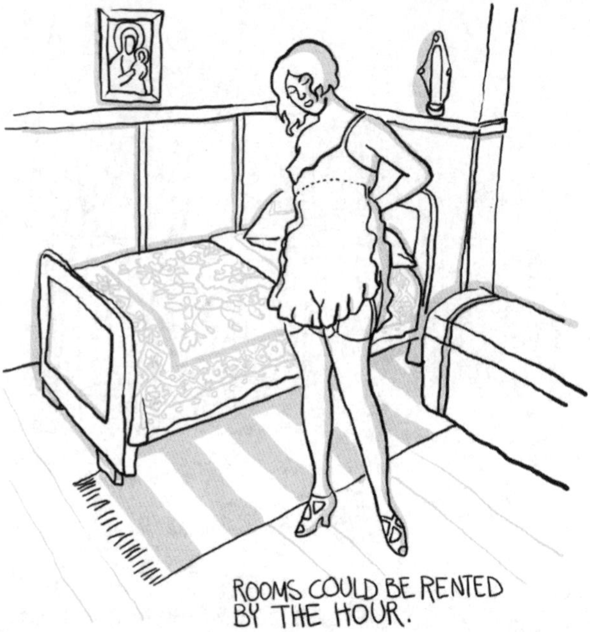
ROOMS COULD BE RENTED BY THE HOUR.

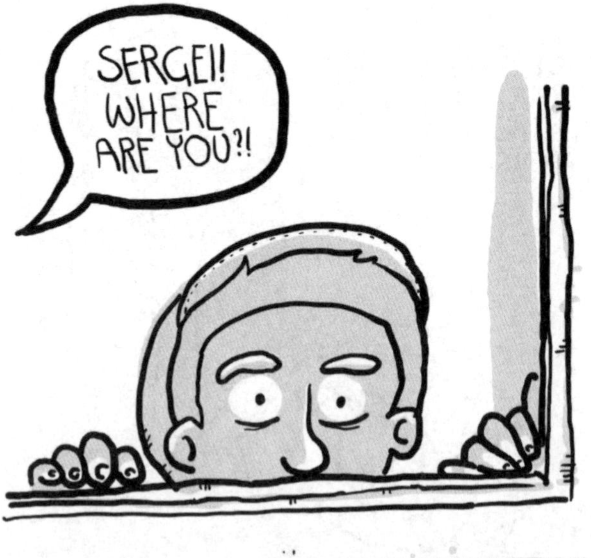
SERGEI! WHERE ARE YOU?!

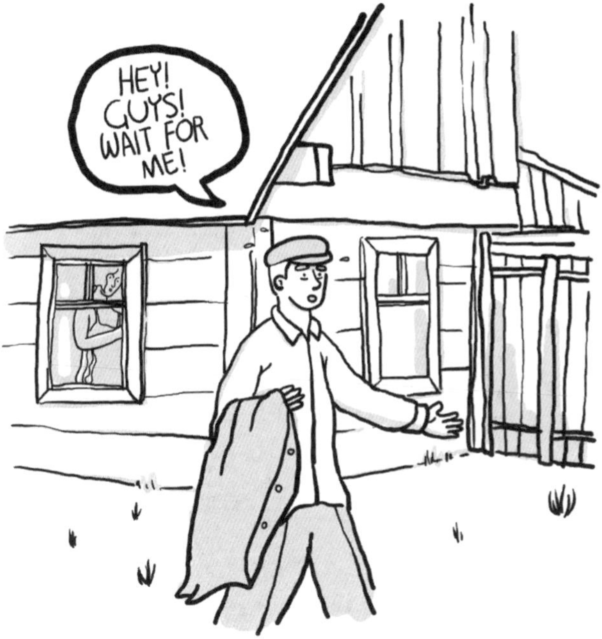
HEY! GUYS! WAIT FOR ME!

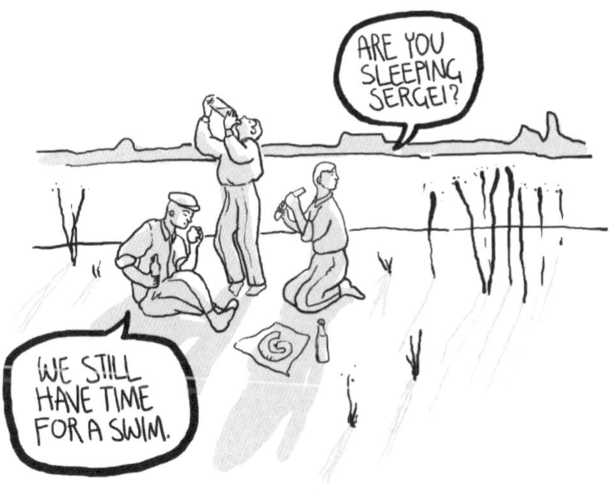
ARE YOU SLEEPING SERGEI?
WE STILL HAVE TIME FOR A SWIM.

GRANDPA OFTEN RETURNED TO THOSE DAYS IN HIS THOUGHTS.

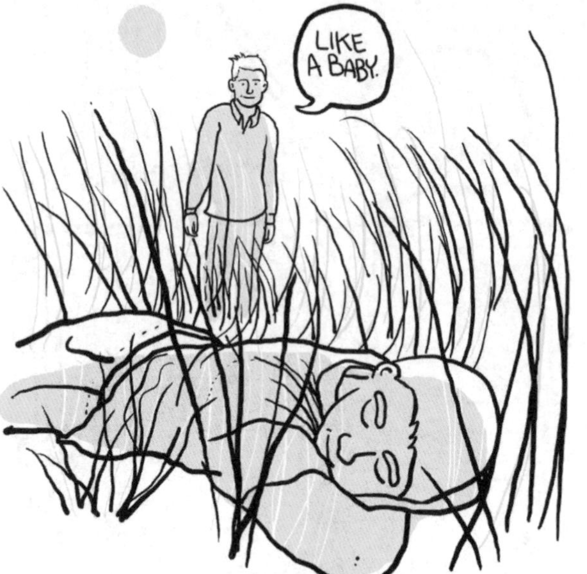
LIKE A BABY.

HIS DAYS WERE PEACEFUL AND CAREFREE.

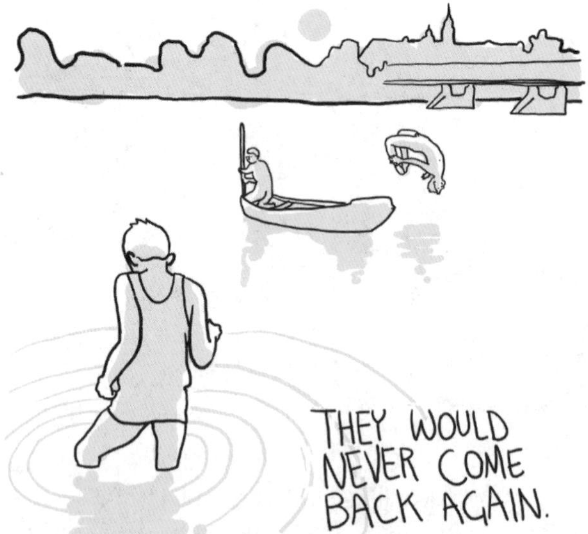

THEY WOULD NEVER COME BACK AGAIN.

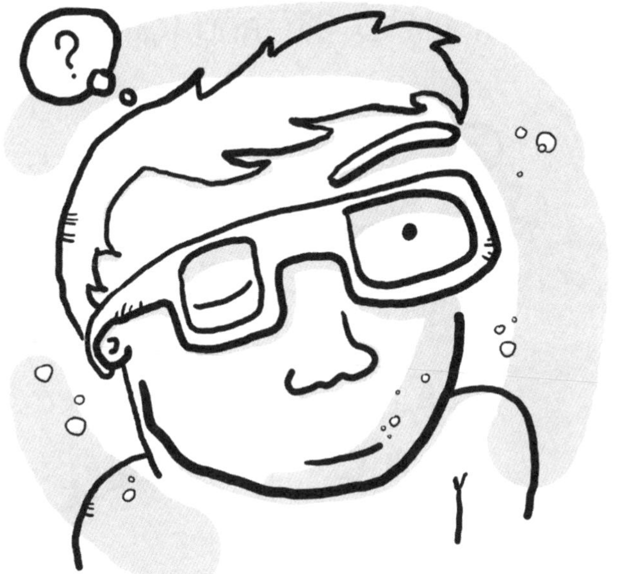
?

SUDDENLY I FELT SOMEONE'S TOUCH.

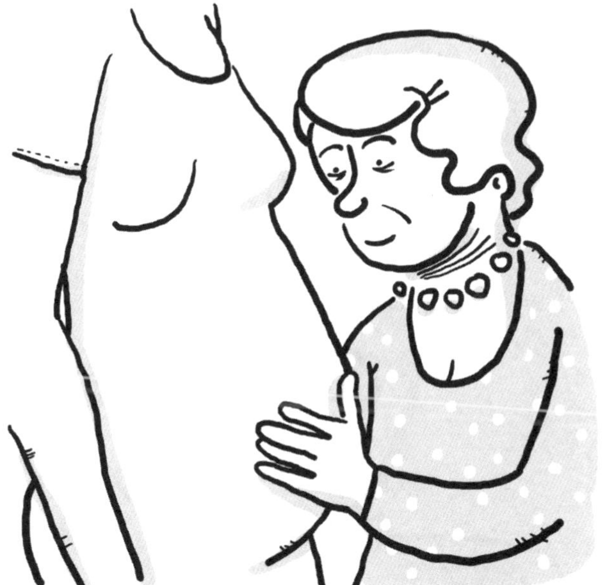

THE TOUCH OF MY GRANDMA.

HER HAND WAS DRY AND WRINKLED.

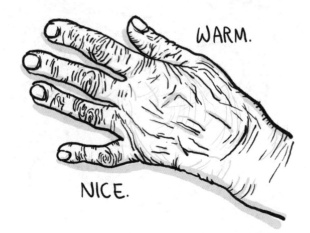

WARM.

NICE.

TREMBLING.

SHE LEANED IN
CLOSE AND
WHISPERED.

HEY, BOY...

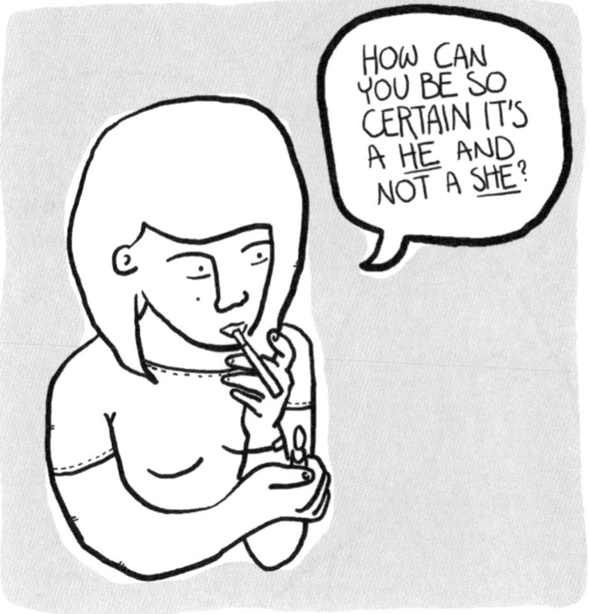
HOW CAN YOU BE SO CERTAIN IT'S A HE AND NOT A SHE?

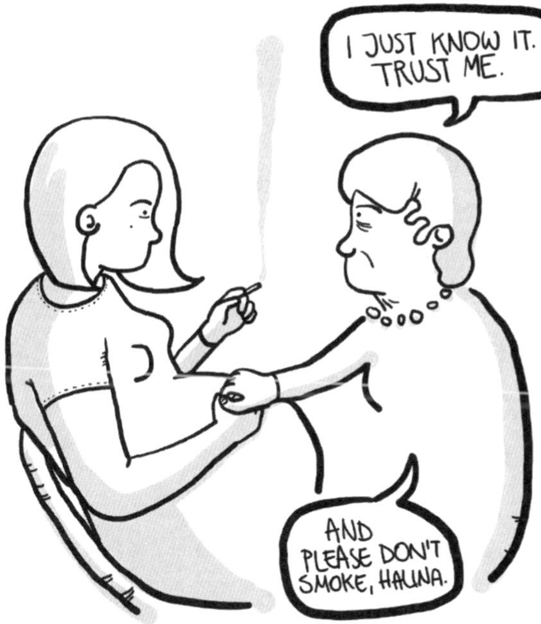
I JUST KNOW IT. TRUST ME.
AND PLEASE DON'T SMOKE, HALINA.

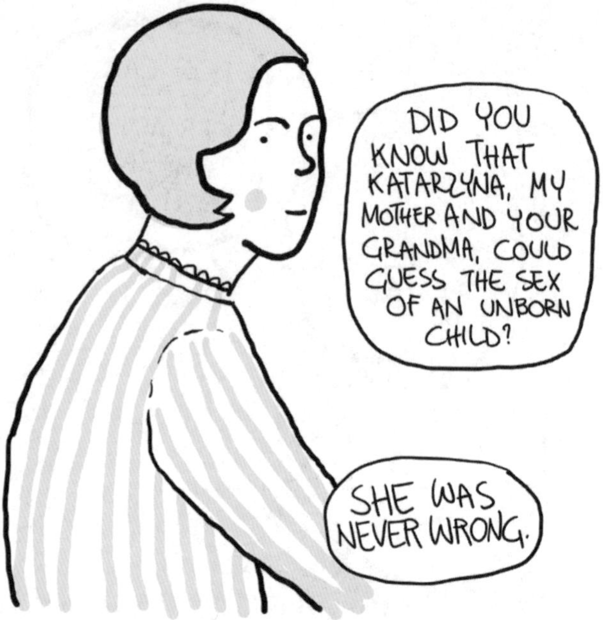
DID YOU KNOW THAT KATARZYNA, MY MOTHER AND YOUR GRANDMA, COULD GUESS THE SEX OF AN UNBORN CHILD?
SHE WAS NEVER WRONG.

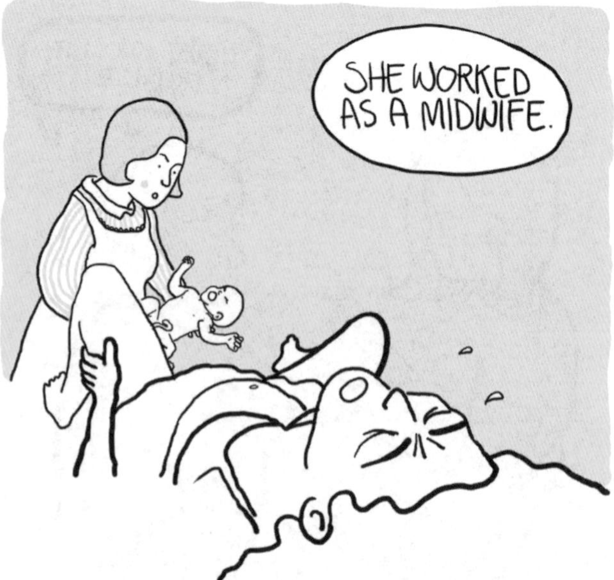
SHE WORKED AS A MIDWIFE.

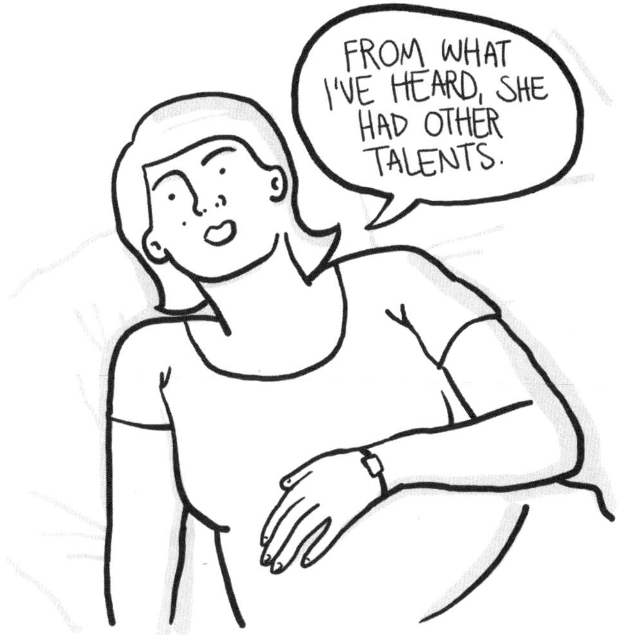
FROM WHAT I'VE HEARD, SHE HAD OTHER TALENTS.

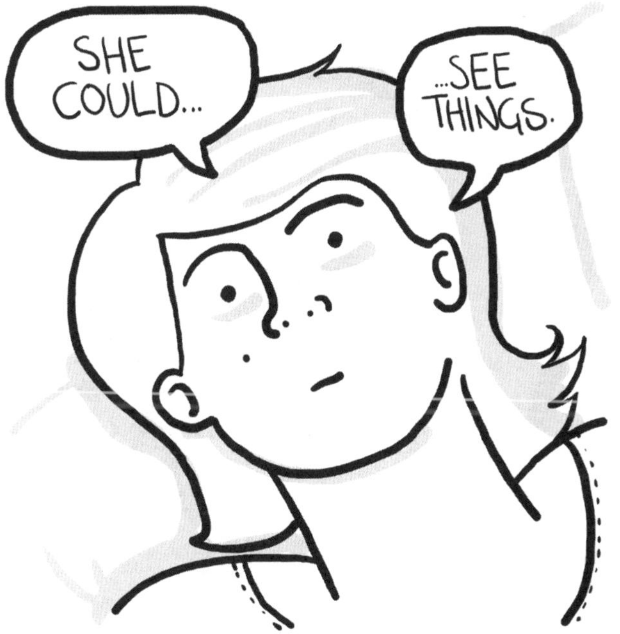
SHE COULD...
...SEE THINGS.

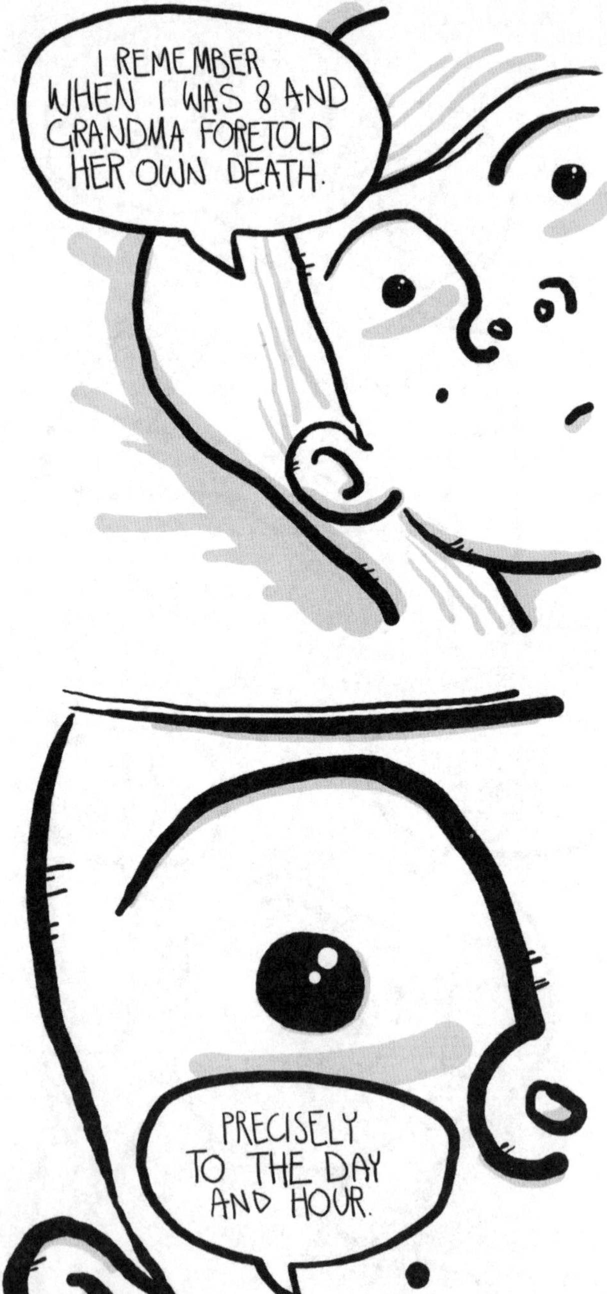
I REMEMBER WHEN I WAS 8 AND GRANDMA FORETOLD HER OWN DEATH.
PRECISELY TO THE DAY AND HOUR.

WHEN HALINA WAS A LITTLE GIRL, HER BIGGEST TREASURE WAS A NOTEBOOK.

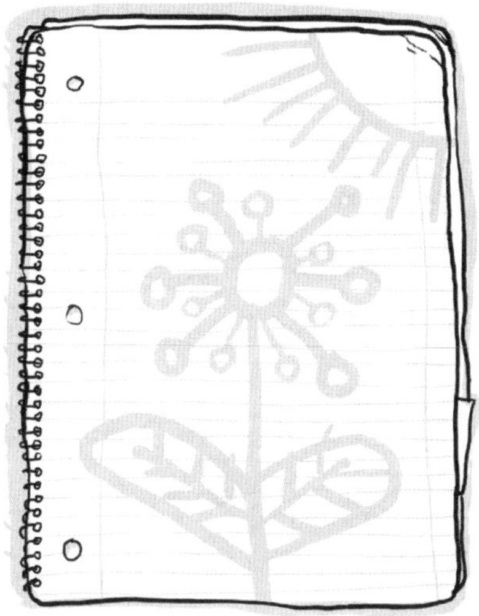

IN IT SHE DREW STORIES OF DRAGONS, KNIGHTS AND PRINCESSES.

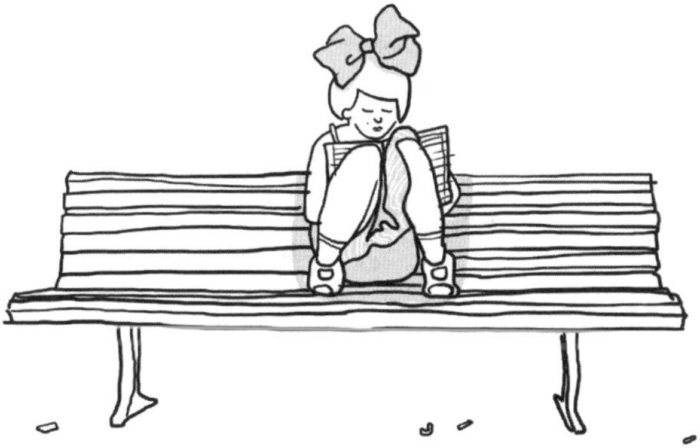

SHE WROTE DOWN HER POEMS AND MOST SECRET DREAMS.

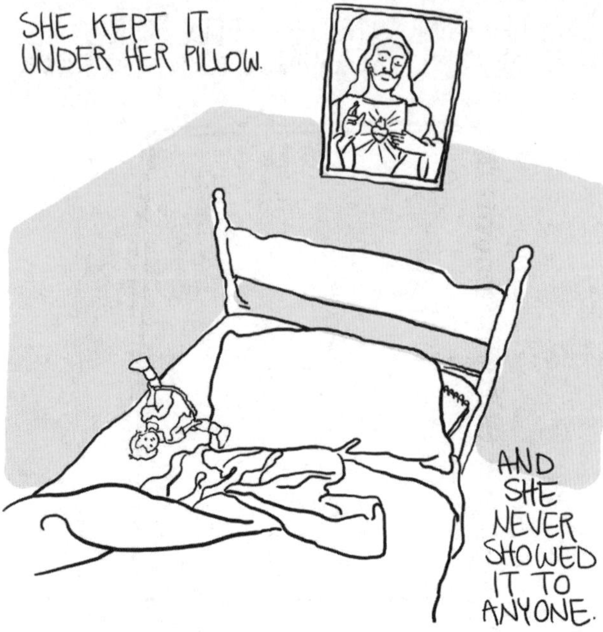
SHE KEPT IT UNDER HER PILLOW.
AND SHE NEVER SHOWED IT TO ANYONE.

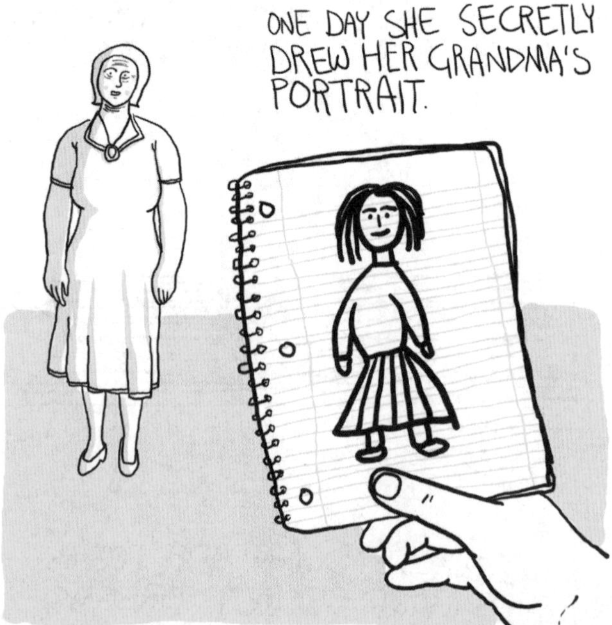
ONE DAY SHE SECRETLY DREW HER GRANDMA'S PORTRAIT.

SHE WAS QUITE OLD AND HAD LIVED THROUGH TWO WORLD WARS. MOST OF THE TIME SHE STAYED IN, SITTING AT THE WINDOW.

SHE WOULD WATCH MY MUM AND HER SIBLINGS, BUT HER MIND WOULD BE SOMEWHERE ELSE.

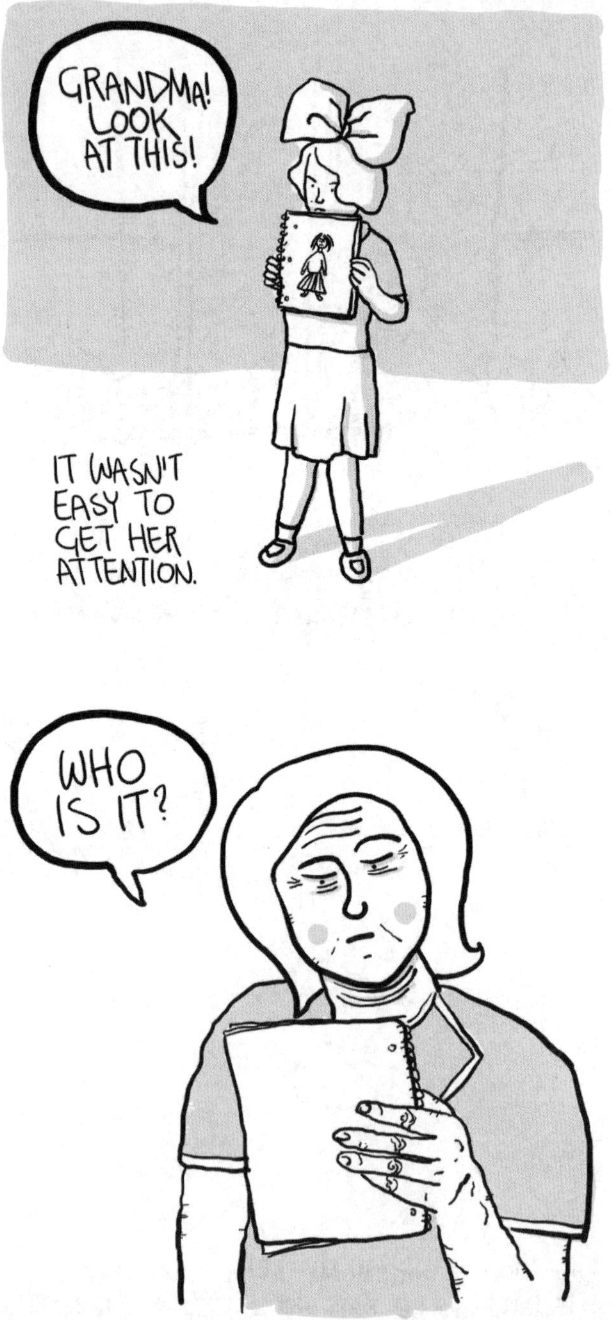
GRANDMA! LOOK AT THIS!
IT WASN'T EASY TO GET HER ATTENTION.
WHO IS IT?

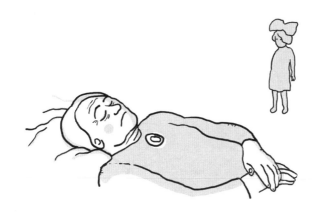

THREE DAYS LATER,
SHE PASSED AWAY
IN HER SLEEP.

YEARS LATER
MY MUM MADE
A DISCOVERY
WHEN GOING
THROUGH
SOME OLD
STUFF.

OH MY GOD!

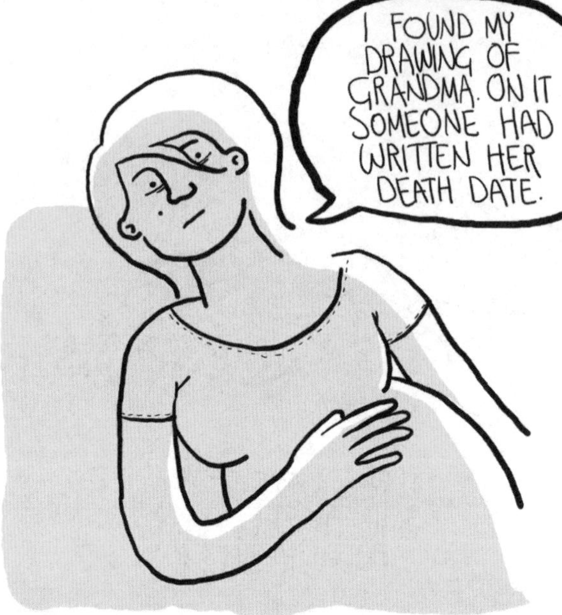
I FOUND MY DRAWING OF GRANDMA. ON IT SOMEONE HAD WRITTEN HER DEATH DATE.

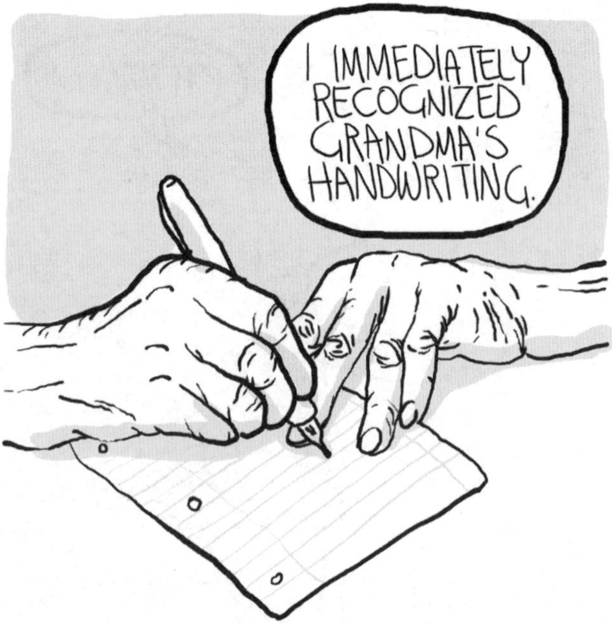
I IMMEDIATELY RECOGNIZED GRANDMA'S HANDWRITING.

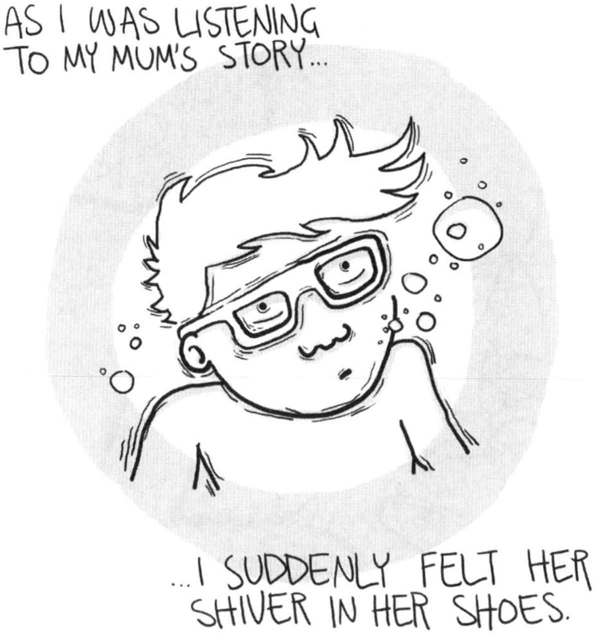
AS I WAS LISTENING TO MY MUM'S STORY...
...I SUDDENLY FELT HER SHIVER IN HER SHOES.

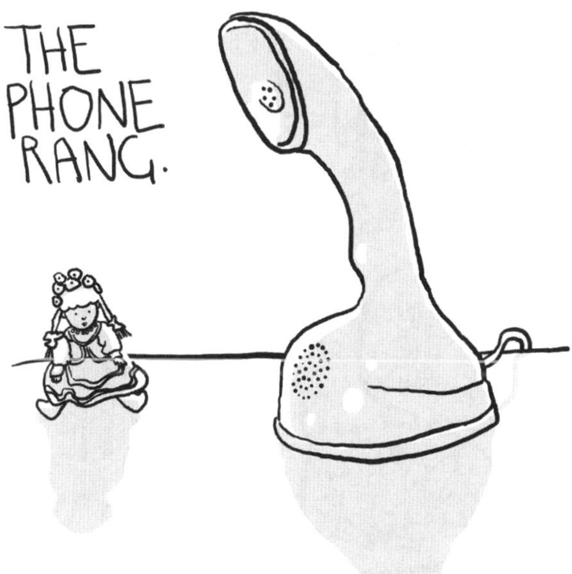
THE PHONE RANG.

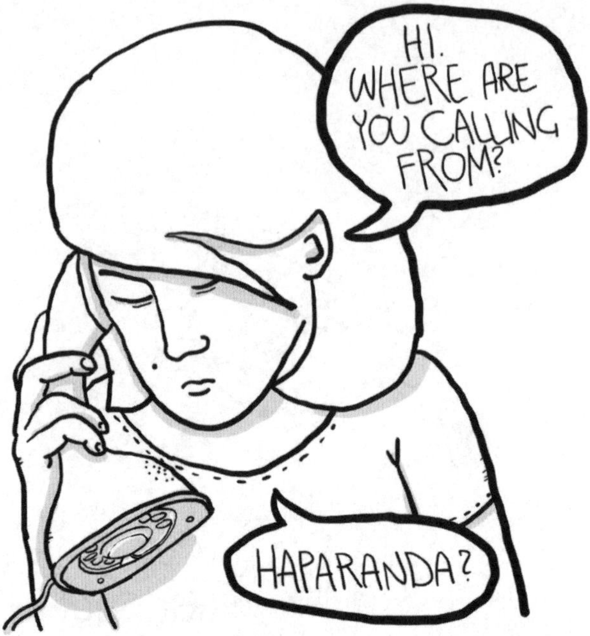
HI. WHERE ARE YOU CALLING FROM?
HAPARANDA?

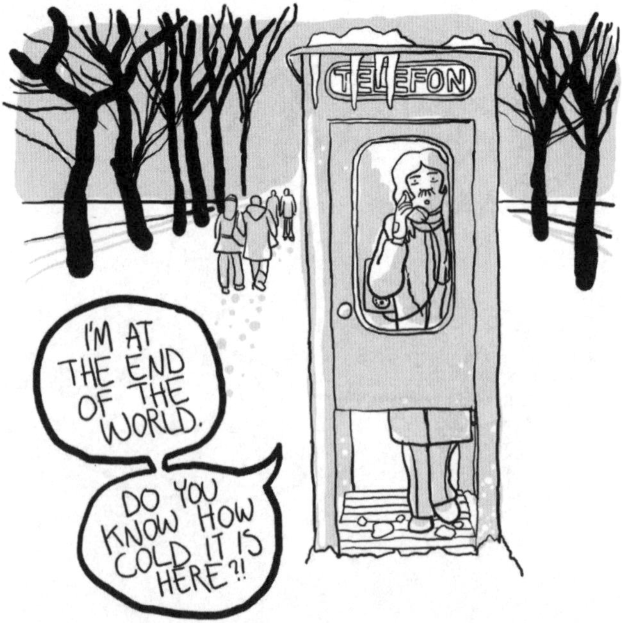
I'M AT THE END OF THE WORLD.
DO YOU KNOW HOW COLD IT IS HERE?!

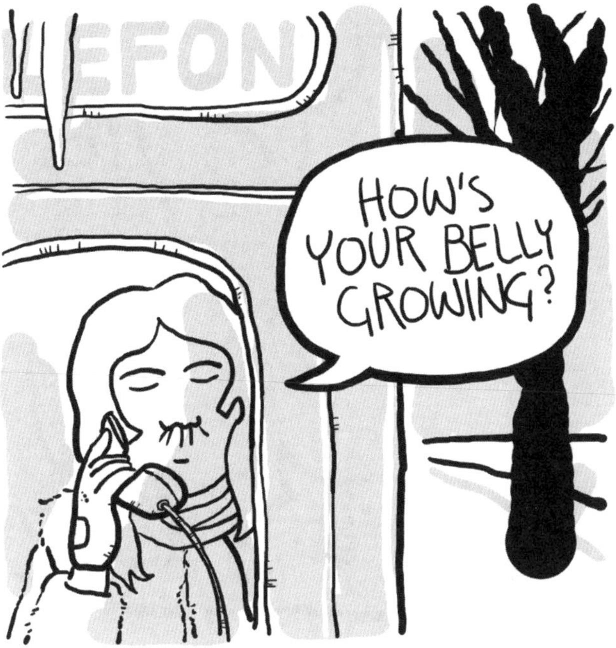
EFON
HOW'S YOUR BELLY GROWING?

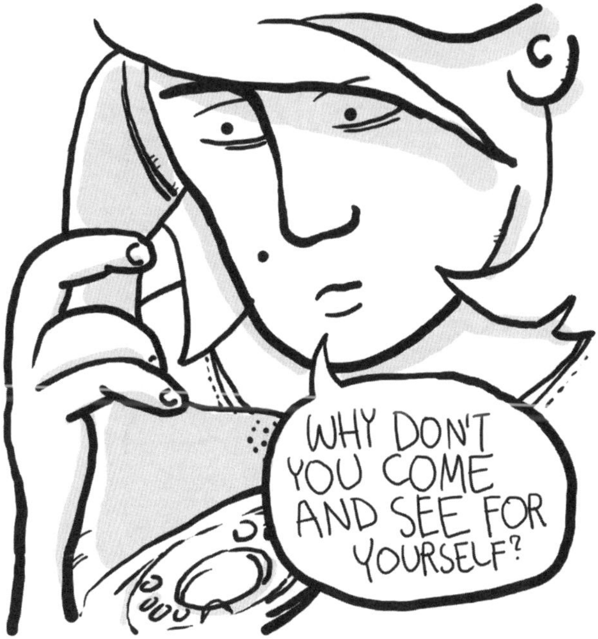
WHY DON'T YOU COME AND SEE FOR YOURSELF?

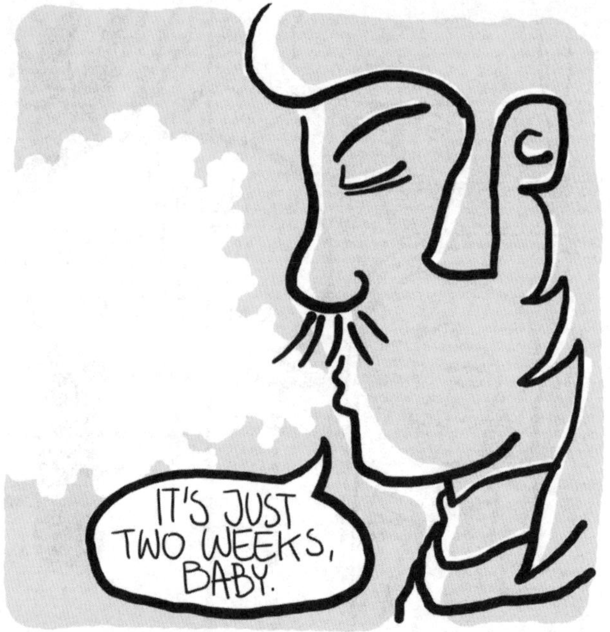
IT'S JUST TWO WEEKS, BABY.

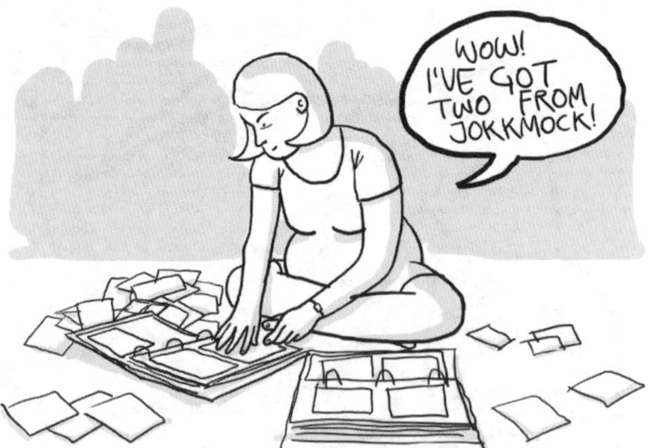
WOW! I'VE GOT TWO FROM JOKKMOCK!

MY DAD'S BAND PLAYED ALL OVER SWEDEN. HE ALWAYS SENT A POSTCARD FROM EACH NEW PLACE.

THE BAND WAS TRAVELLING IN MY DAD'S BLACK CADILLAC WITH THEIR INSTRUMENTS CRAMMED INTO A TRAILER.

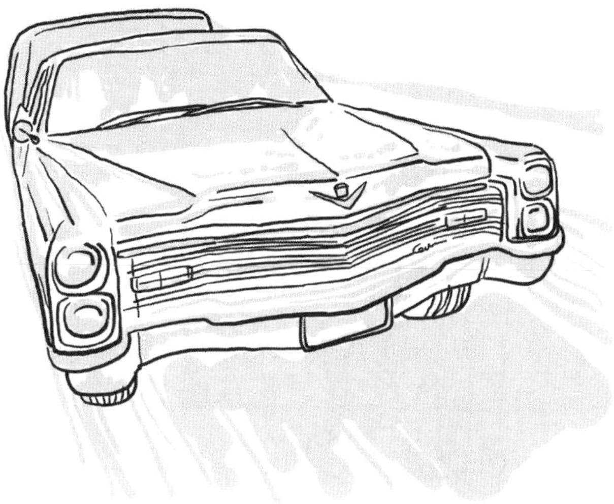

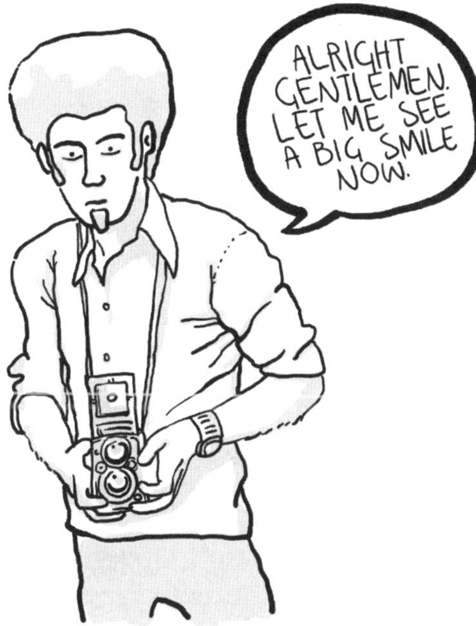
ALRIGHT GENTLEMEN. LET ME SEE A BIG SMILE NOW.

SHHH!
MAN, I'M SWEATING.
SHIT! I CAN'T STAND IT MUCH LONGER.

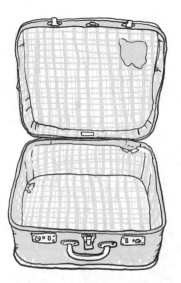

IT ALL STARTED IN 1967 WHEN MY DAD BOUGHT HIMSELF A SECONDHAND SUITCASE.

IN IT HE PACKED
TWO CLEAN WHITE SHIRTS.

A BUNCH OF
US DOLLARS
IN CASH.

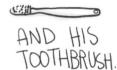

AND HIS
TOOTHBRUSH.

HE ALSO BROUGHT WITH HIM A PHOTO OF
MY MUM. ON THE BACK SHE HAD WRITTEN:

SHE WAS 24. HER HAIR WAS
DYED BLACK AND FLATIRONED.

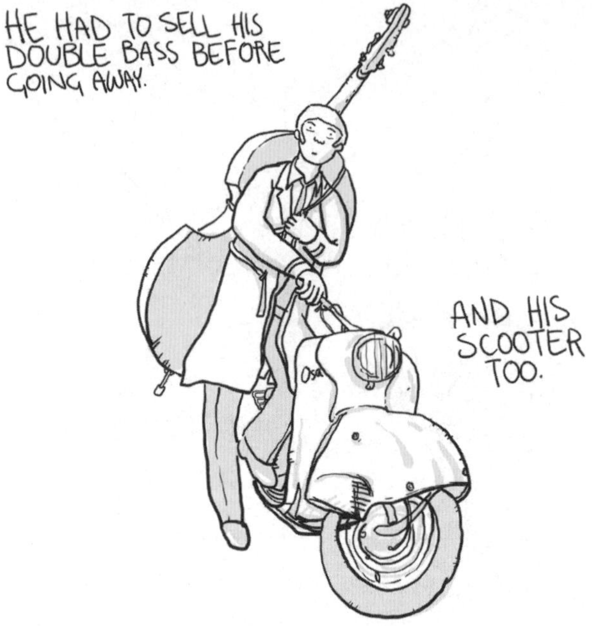
HE HAD TO SELL HIS DOUBLE BASS BEFORE GOING AWAY.
Osa
AND HIS SCOOTER TOO.

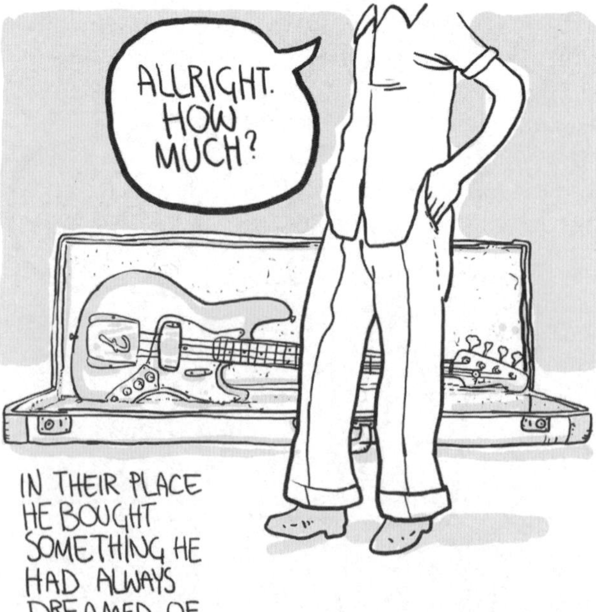
ALLRIGHT. HOW MUCH?
IN THEIR PLACE HE BOUGHT SOMETHING HE HAD ALWAYS DREAMED OF.

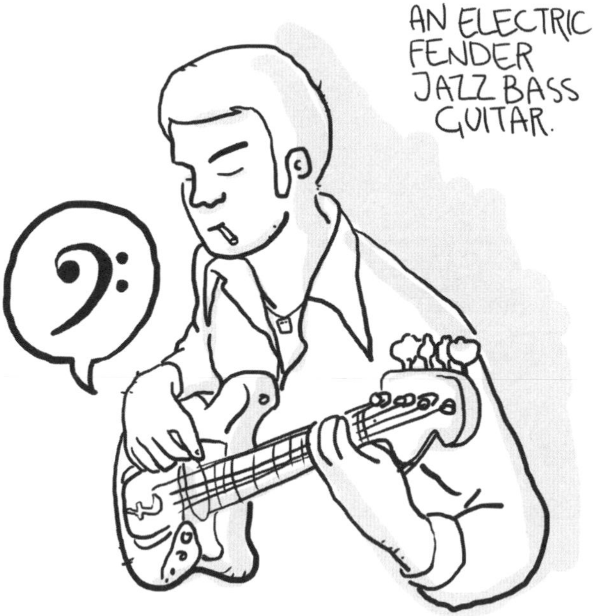
AN ELECTRIC FENDER JAZZ BASS GUITAR.

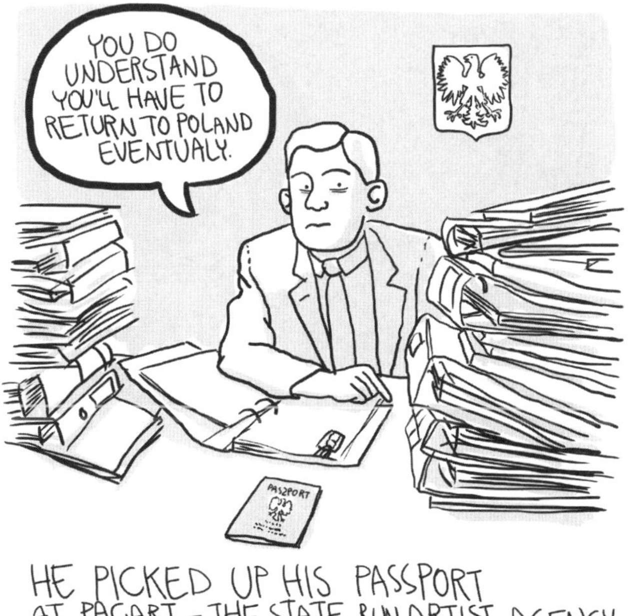
YOU DO UNDERSTAND YOU'LL HAVE TO RETURN TO POLAND EVENTUALY.
PASSPORT

HE PICKED UP HIS PASSPORT AT PAGART – THE STATE RUN ARTIST AGENCY.

THEN HE BOUGHT A ONE WAY TICKET.

HE NEVER
INTENDED
TO COME
BACK.

HE DREAMED OF GOING
TO AUSTRALIA.

BUT INSTEAD
HE CHOSE
SWEDEN.

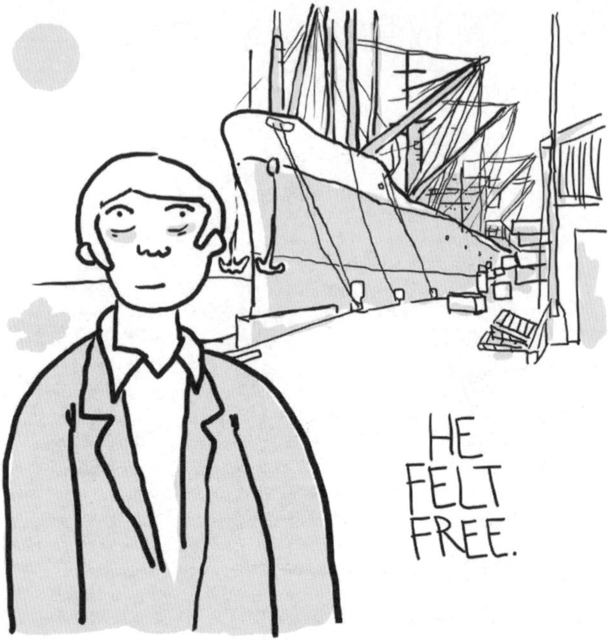
HE
FELT
FREE.

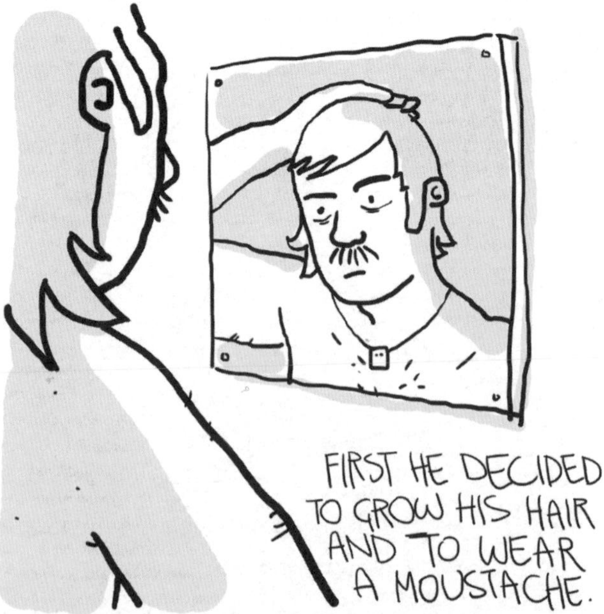
FIRST HE DECIDED
TO GROW HIS HAIR
AND TO WEAR
A MOUSTACHE.

HE BOUGHT HIMSELF AN AFGHAN FUR COAT IN THE MIDDLE OF THE SUMMER.

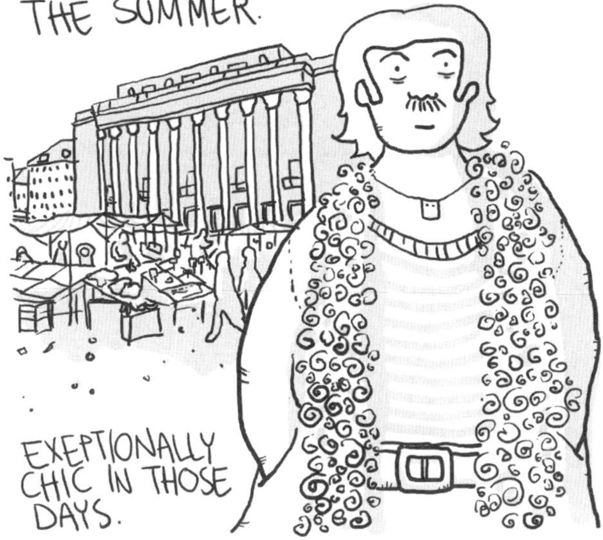
EXEPTIONALLY CHIC IN THOSE DAYS.

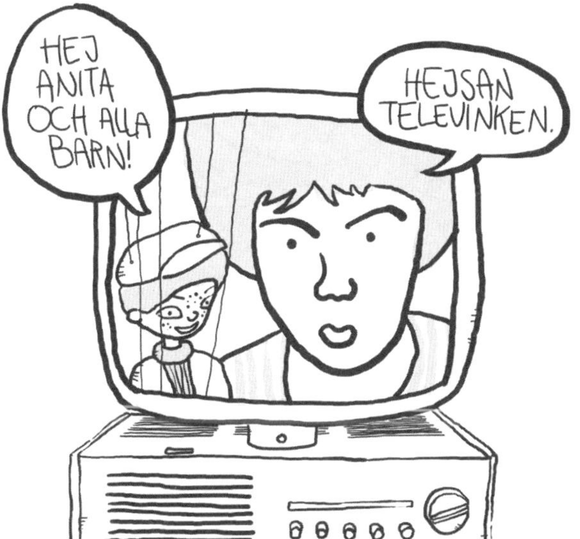
HEJ ANITA OCH ALLA BARN!
HEJSAN TELEVINKEN.

INSTEAD OF TAKING A SWEDISH COURSE HE LEARNED THE LANGUAGE BY WATCHING TV.

HIS FIRST JOB WAS AS A CLOAKROOM ATTENDANT IN A HOT NIGHTCLUB.

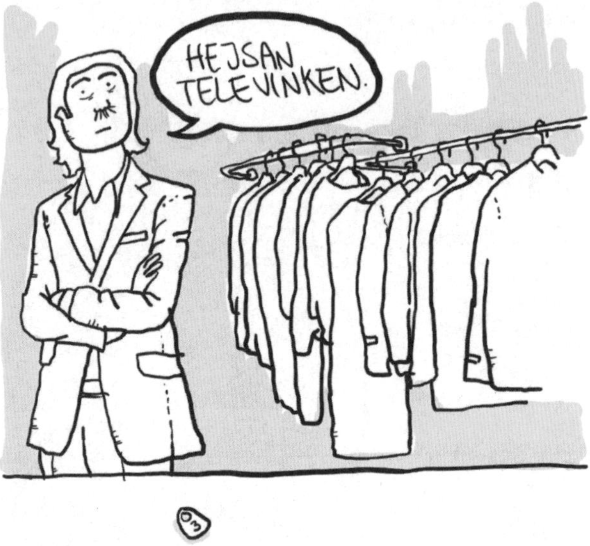
HEJSAN TELEVINKEN.

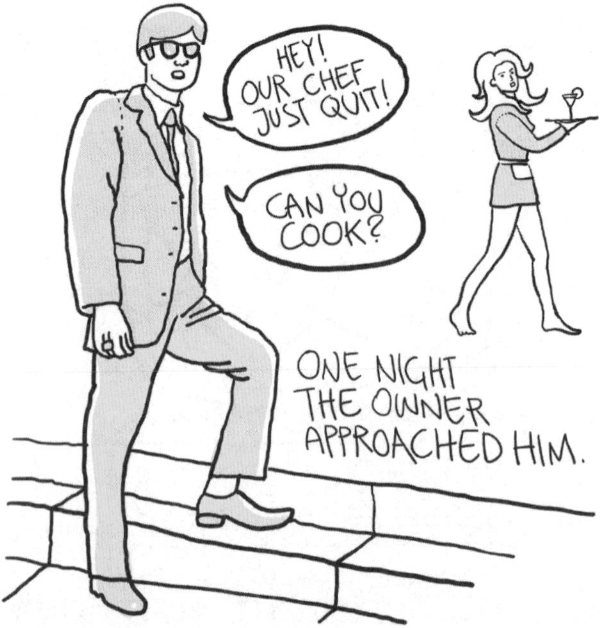
HEY! OUR CHEF JUST QUIT!
CAN YOU COOK?
ONE NIGHT THE OWNER APPROACHED HIM.

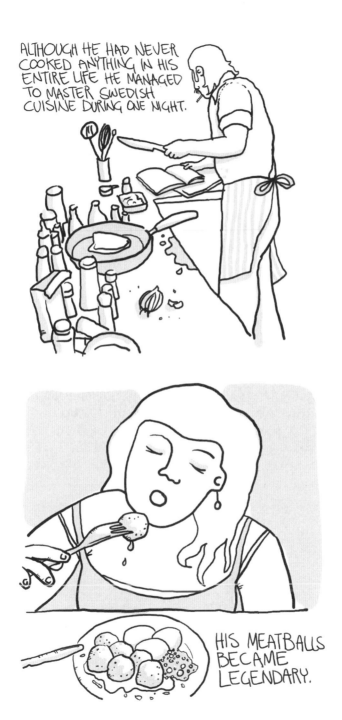

ALTHOUGH HE HAD NEVER COOKED ANYTHING IN HIS ENTIRE LIFE HE MANAGED TO MASTER SWEDISH CUISINE DURING ONE NIGHT.

HIS MEATBALLS BECAME LEGENDARY.

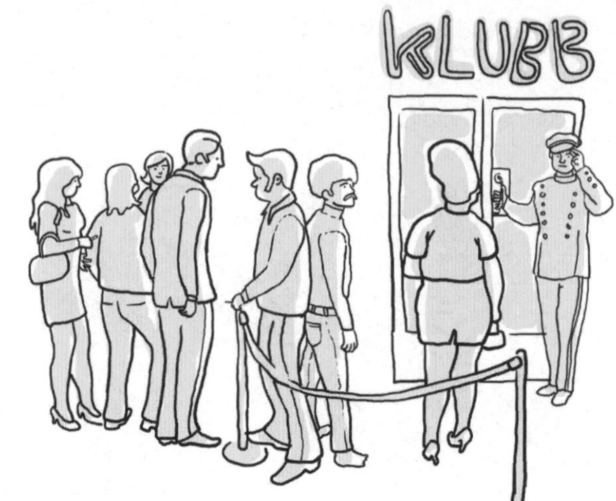
KLUBB

OVERNIGHT THE CLUB BECAME ONE OF STOCKHOLM'S HIPPEST.

NOBODY KNEW THAT THE REASON FOR THIS WAS A HERBAL BROTH FROM POLAND THAT MY DAD HAD USED AS AN INGREDIENT IN THE MEATBALLS.

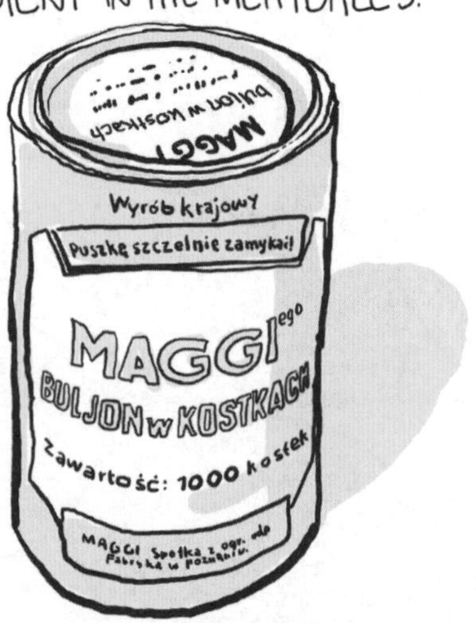
MAGGI
bulion w kostkach
Wyrób krajowy
Puszkę szczelnie zamykać!
MAGGI[ego]
BULJON w KOSTKACH
Zawartość: 1000 kostek
MAGGI Spółka z ogr. odp.
Fabryka w Poznaniu.

PEOPLE BEHAVED STRANGELY AFTER EATING THEM.

SOME OF
THEM GOT
HYSTERICAL.

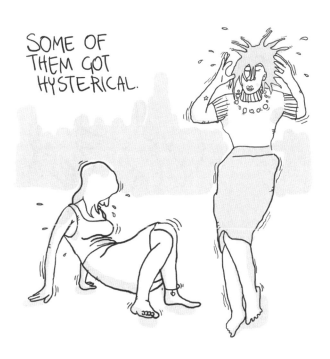

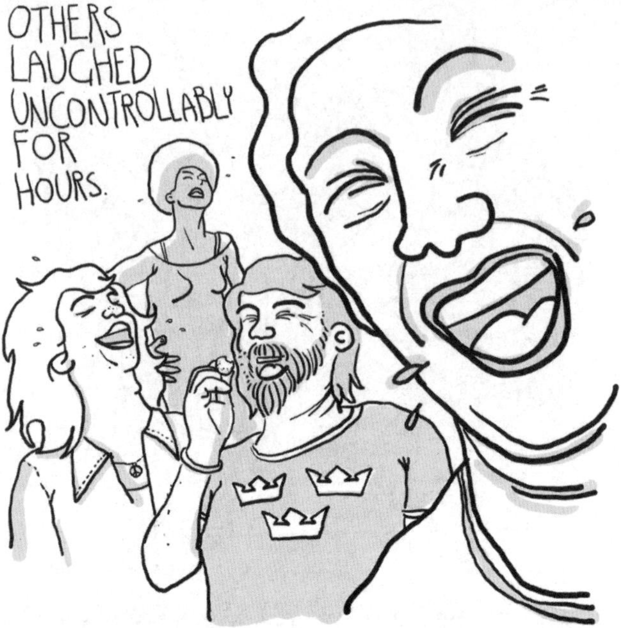
OTHERS LAUGHED UNCONTROLLABLY FOR HOURS.

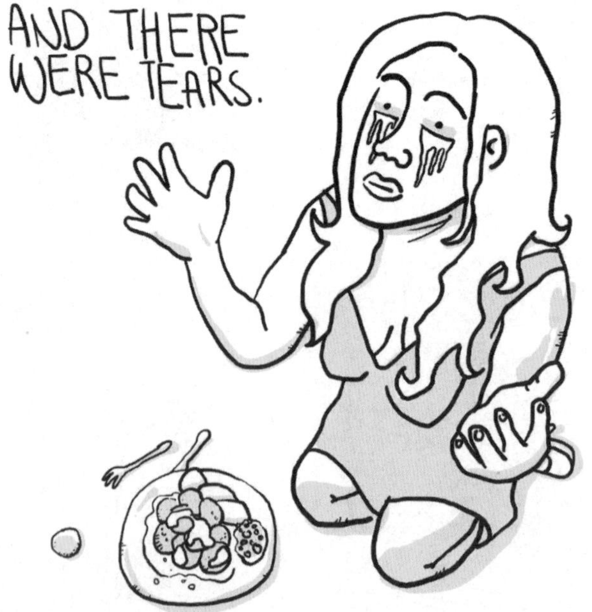
AND THERE WERE TEARS.

THEN THE POLICE GOT INVOLVED.

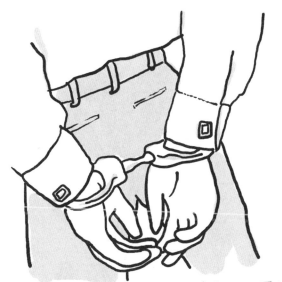

THEY TOOK THE CLUB OWNER TO THE POLICE STATION FOR QUESTIONING.

MY DAD'S BROTH WAS ANALYSED.

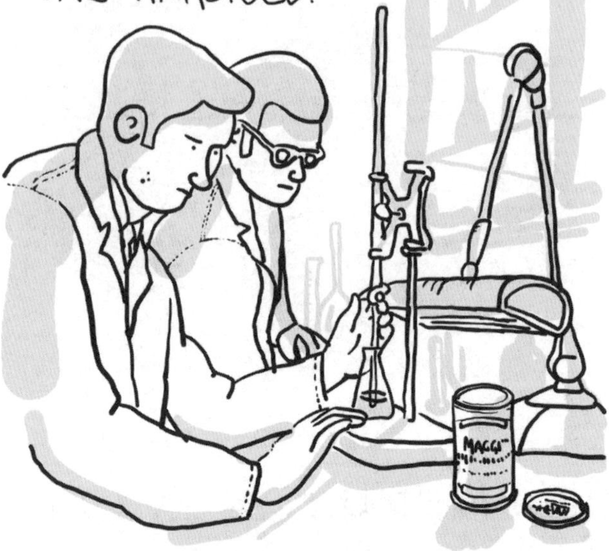
MAGGI

IT TURNED OUT IT CONTAINED AN EXTRACT FROM LOVAGE, A VERY RARE PLANT IN SWEDEN.

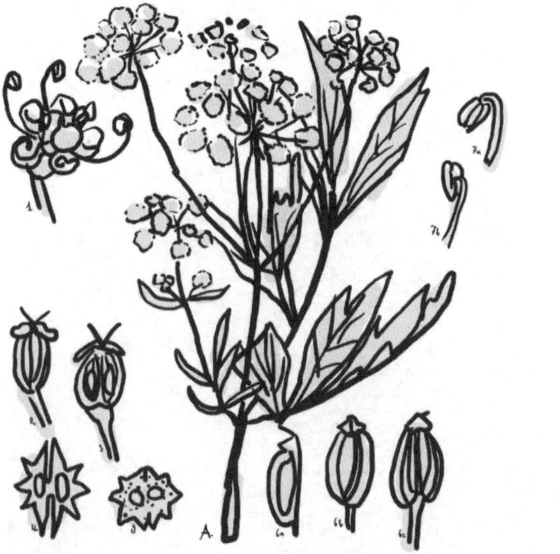
A.

AFTER HAVING CONSULTED A CERTAIN PROFESSOR FROM UPPSALA, AN EXPERT ON THE SUBJECT, THE POLICE LEARNED THIS WAS A PERSIAN APHRODISIAC.

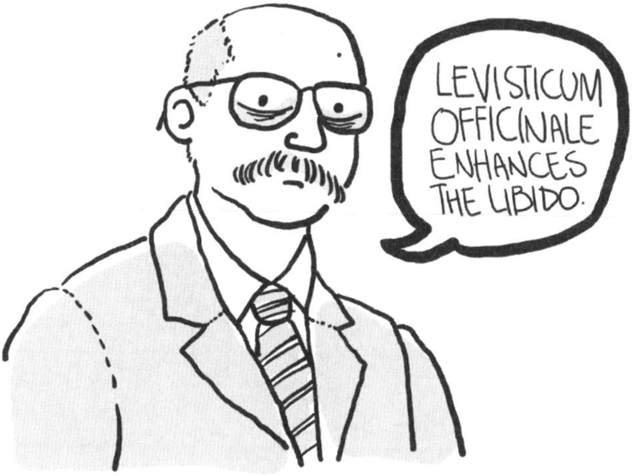
LEVISTICUM OFFICINALE ENHANCES THE LIBIDO.

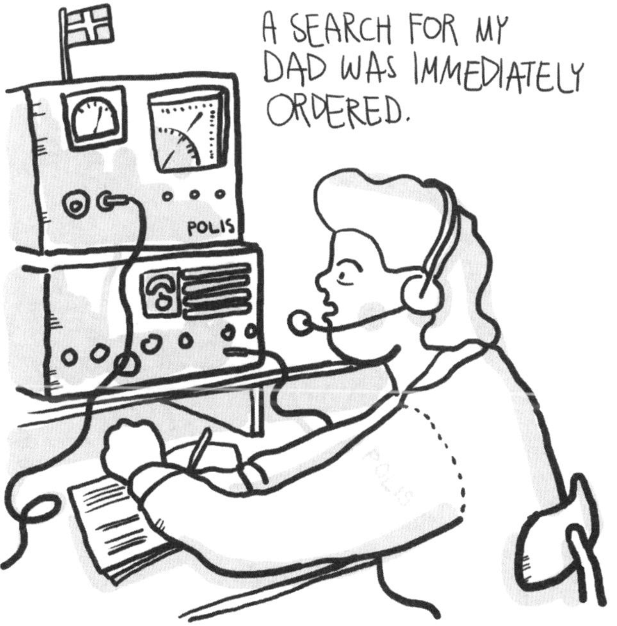
A SEARCH FOR MY DAD WAS IMMEDIATELY ORDERED.
POLIS

MEANWHILE, HE WAS AT HIS
FIRST ROCK CONCERT.

THE JIMI HENDRIX EXPERIENCE

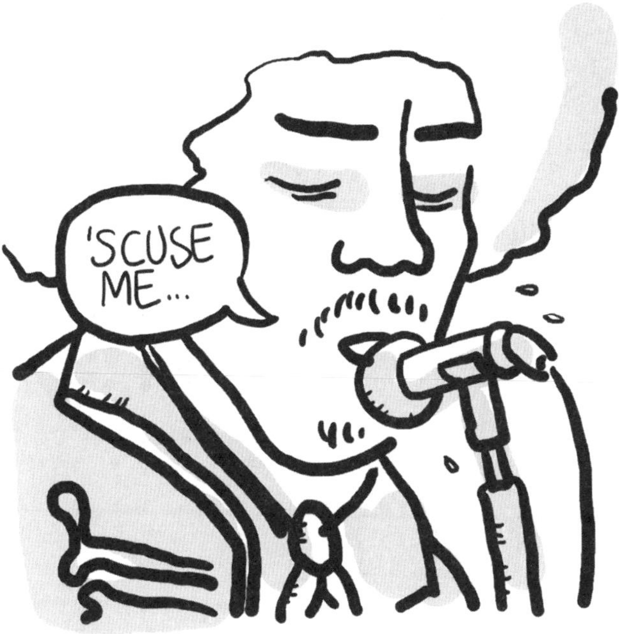
'SCUSE ME...

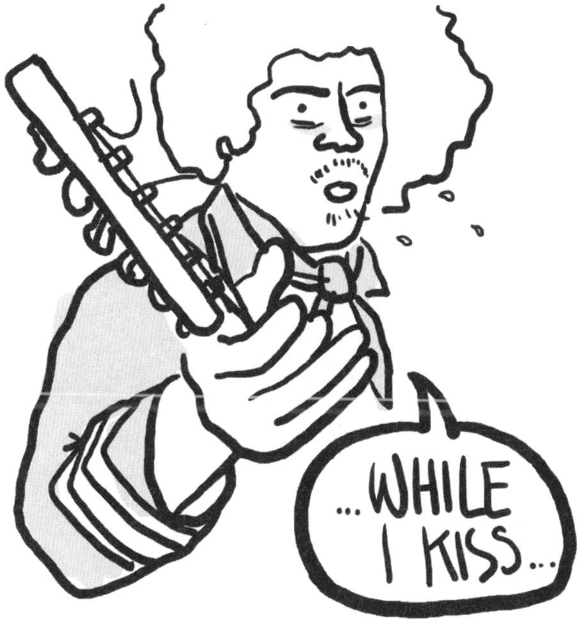
...WHILE I KISS...

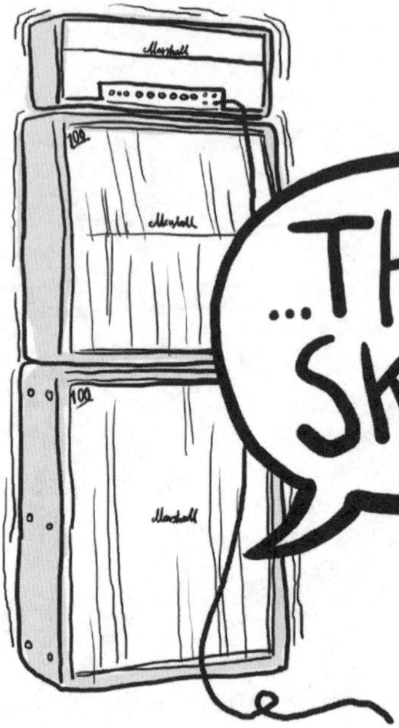
...THE SKY!!!

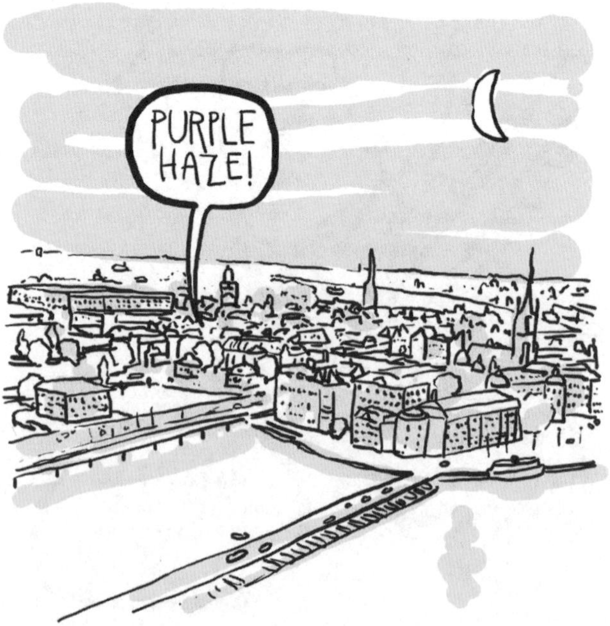
PURPLE HAZE!

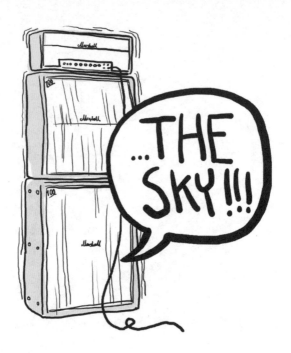

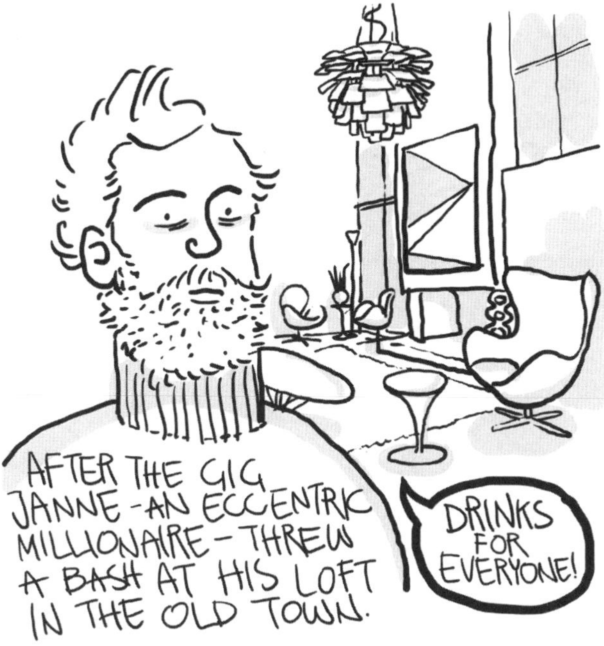
AFTER THE GIG JANNE - AN ECCENTRIC MILLIONAIRE - THREW A BASH AT HIS LOFT IN THE OLD TOWN.
DRINKS FOR EVERYONE!

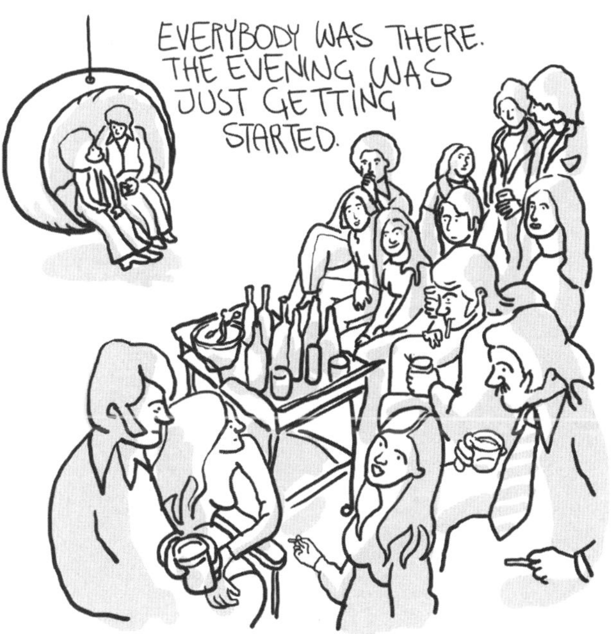
EVERYBODY WAS THERE. THE EVENING WAS JUST GETTING STARTED.

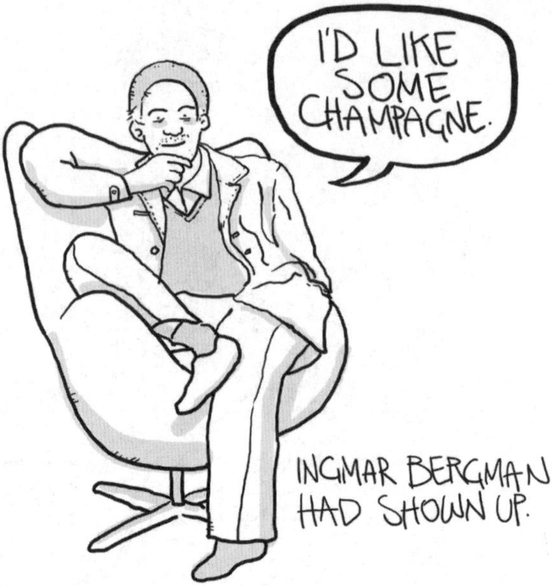
I'D LIKE SOME CHAMPAGNE.
INGMAR BERGMAN HAD SHOWN UP.

AND THE YOUNG ACTRESS LENA NYMAN.

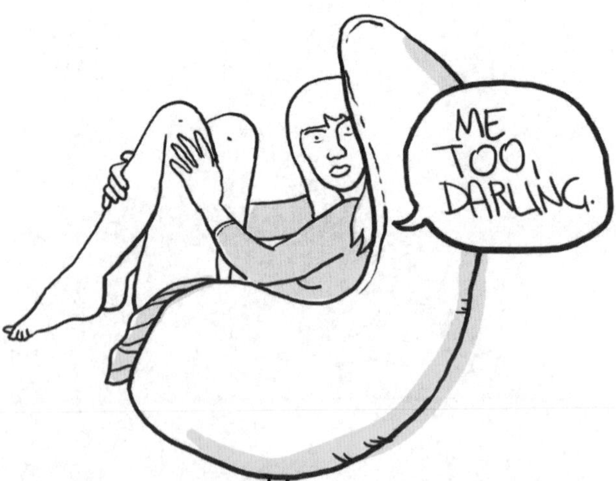
ME TOO, DARLING.

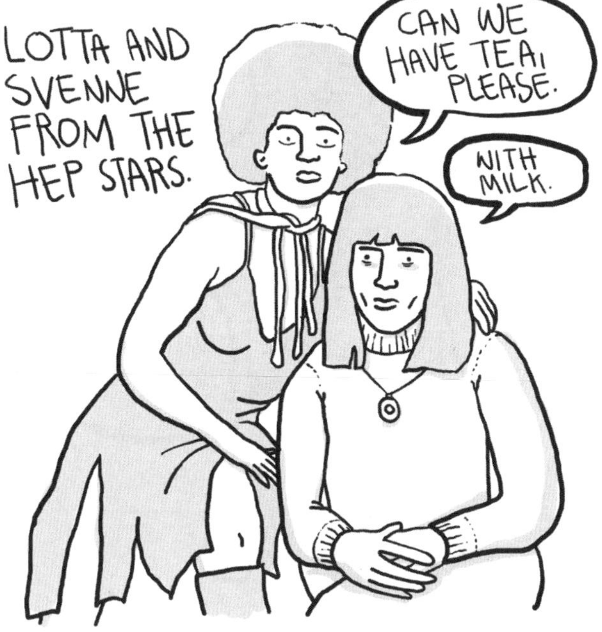
LOTTA AND SVENNE FROM THE HEP STARS.
CAN WE HAVE TEA, PLEASE.
WITH MILK.

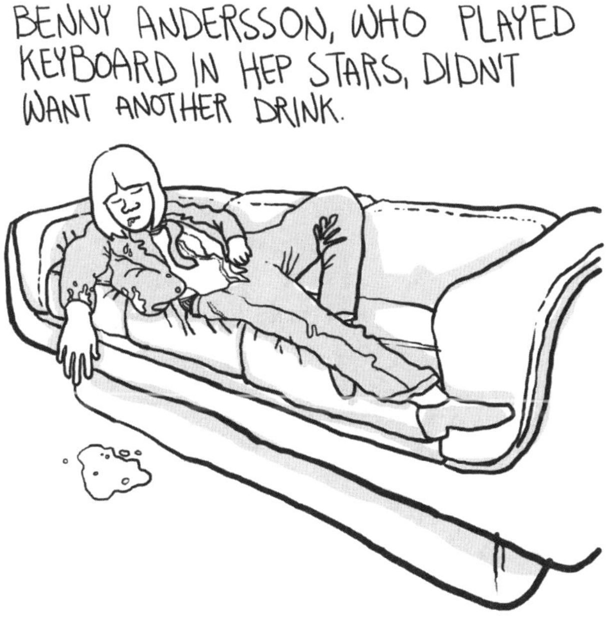
BENNY ANDERSSON, WHO PLAYED KEYBOARD IN HEP STARS, DIDN'T WANT ANOTHER DRINK.

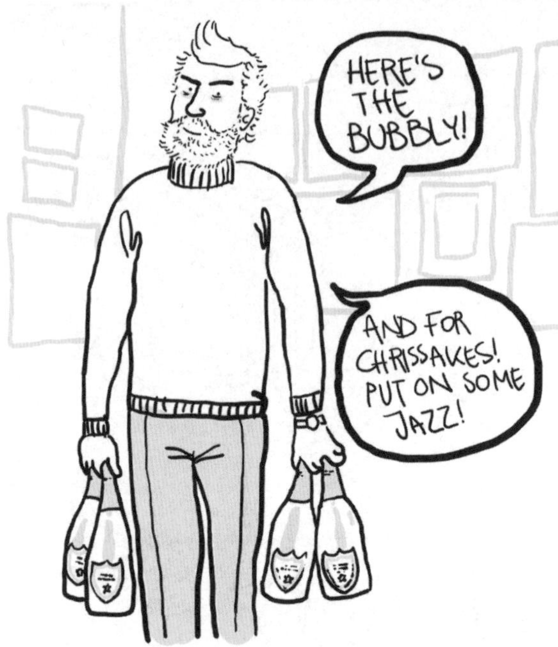
HERE'S THE BUBBLY!
AND FOR CHRISSAKES! PUT ON SOME JAZZ!

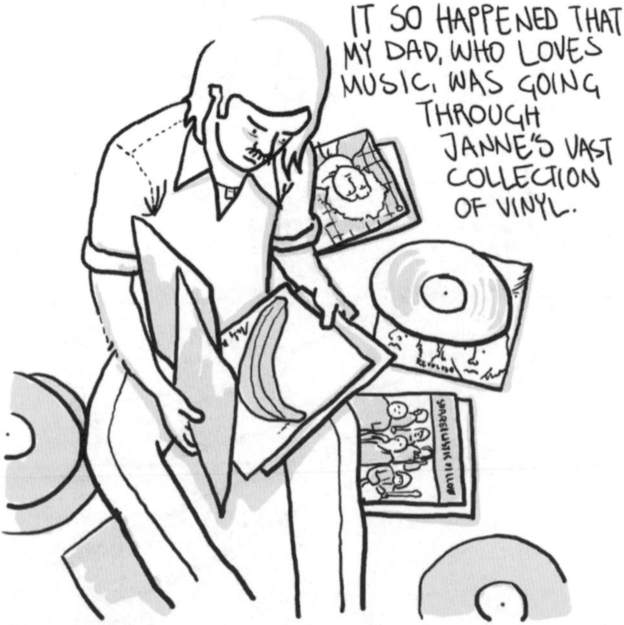
IT SO HAPPENED THAT MY DAD, WHO LOVES MUSIC, WAS GOING THROUGH JANNE'S VAST COLLECTION OF VINYL.

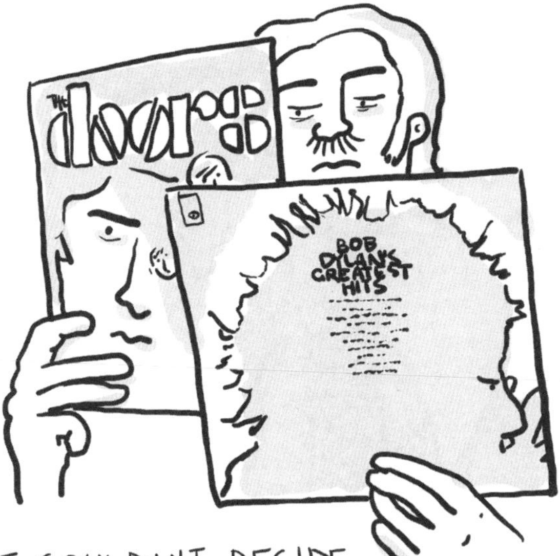
THE doors
BOB DYLAN'S GREATEST HITS

HE COULDN'T DECIDE
WHAT RECORD TO PLAY.

THEN
SUDDENLY...

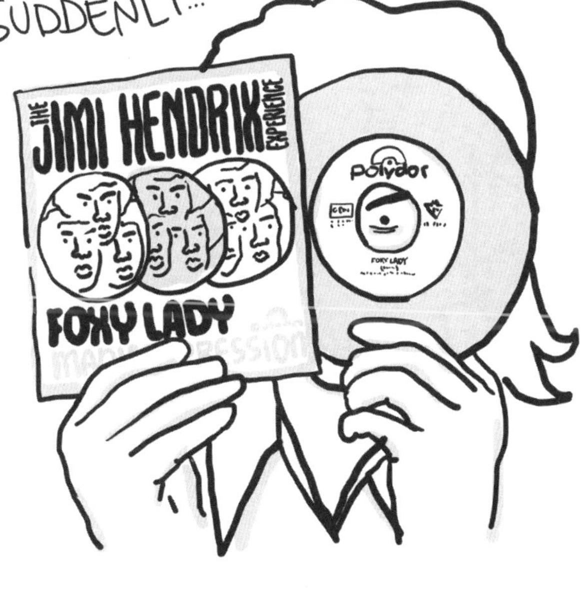
THE JIMI HENDRIX EXPERIENCE
FOXY LADY
Polydor
FOXY LADY

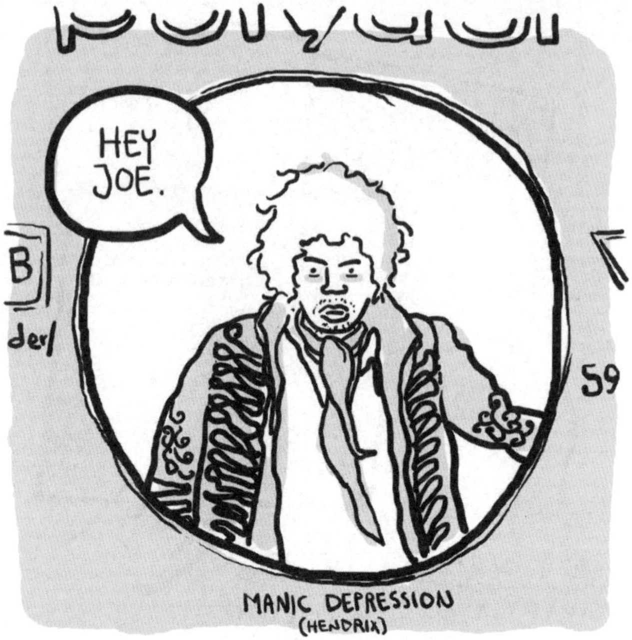
HEY JOE.
59
MANIC DEPRESSION
(HENDRIX)

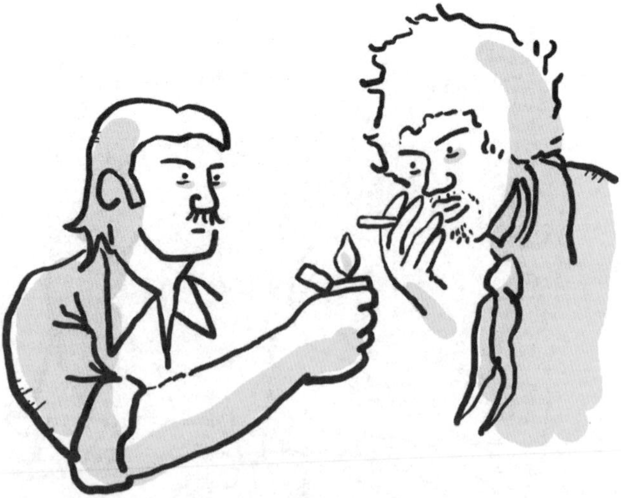

MY DAD DIDN'T SPEAK ENGLISH BUT HE UNDERSTOOD THAT JIMI WAS ASKING FOR A LIGHT.

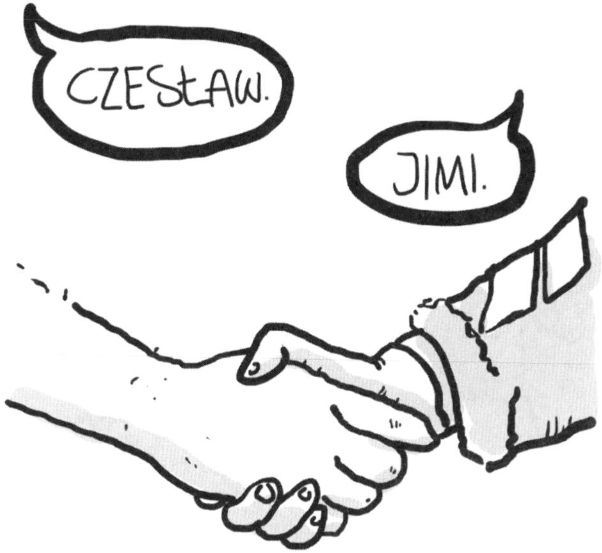
CZESłAW.
JIMI.

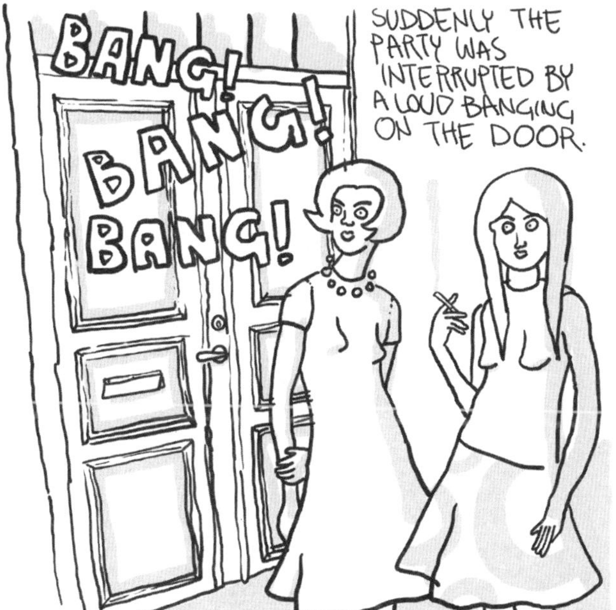
SUDDENLY THE PARTY WAS INTERRUPTED BY A LOUD BANGING ON THE DOOR.
BANG!
BANG!
BANG!

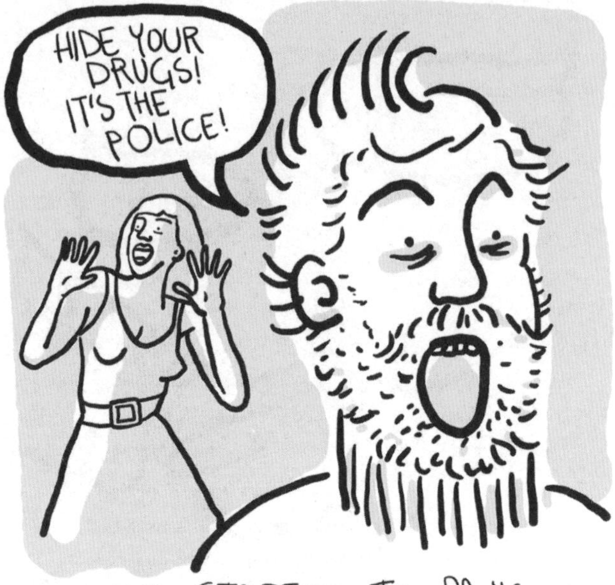
HIDE YOUR DRUGS! IT'S THE POLICE!

PEOPLE STARTED TO PANIC.

MY DAD TRIPPED AND FELL ON THE STEREO IN THE CONFUSION THAT FOLLOWED.

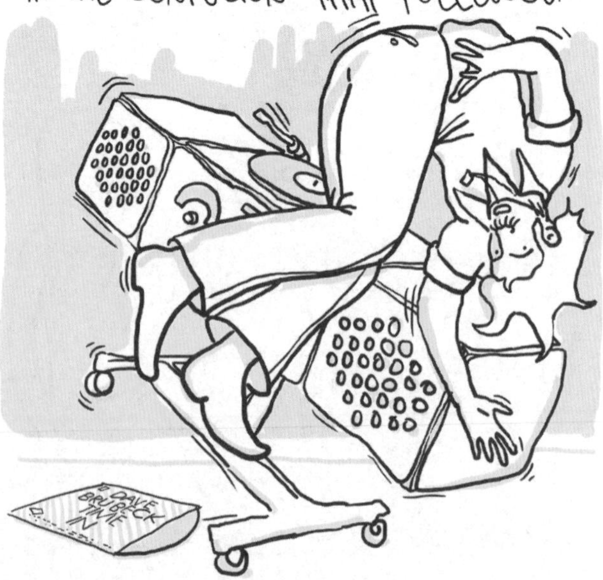
DAVE BRUBECK TIME IN

HE LANDED ON AN ORIGINAL
ALVAR AALTO VASE, SMASHING
IT TO PIECES.

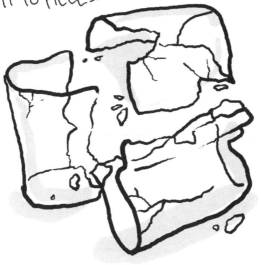

THE LAST THING HE HEARD BEFORE
SLIPPING INTO UNCONSCIOUSNESS WAS
JANNE'S HYSTERIC LAUGHTER AND JIMI
HUMMING
"LITTLE WING".

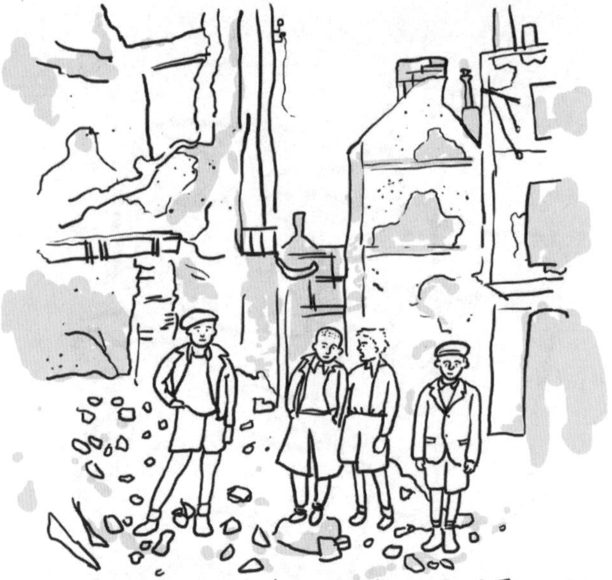

A LOST CHILDHOOD MEMORY RESURFACED IN HIS MIND.

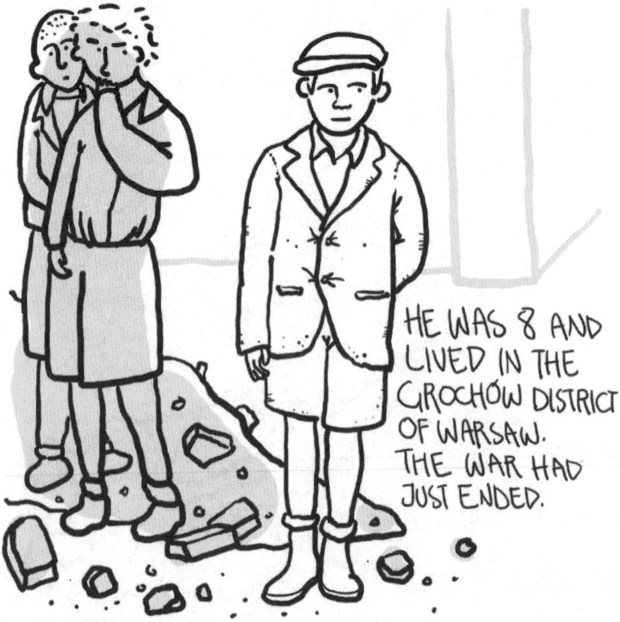
HE WAS 8 AND LIVED IN THE GROCHOW DISTRICT OF WARSAW. THE WAR HAD JUST ENDED.

HE PLAYED WITH HIS PEERS IN THE COURTYARDS OF BOMBED-OUT HOUSES. A DANGEROUS PLAYGROUND.

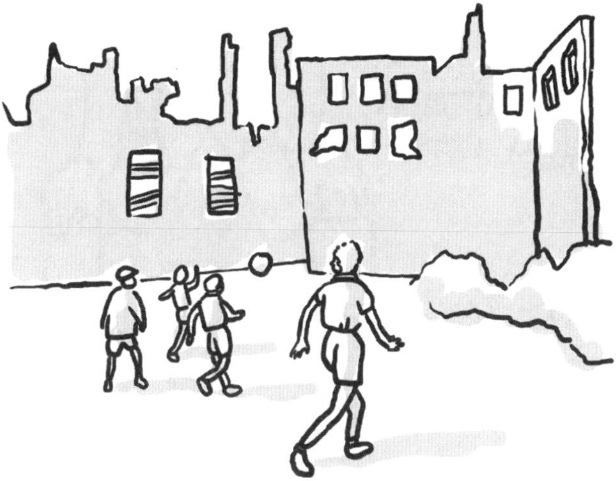

DUD BOMBS COULD BE FOUND ALMOST EVERYWHERE.

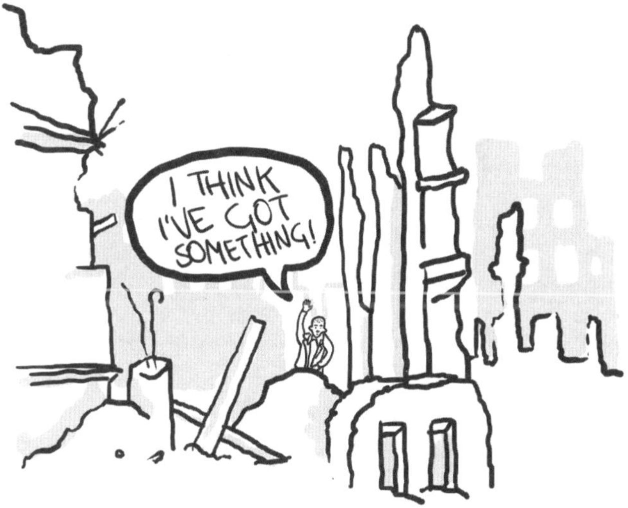
I THINK I'VE GOT SOMETHING!

CRAZY JASIO HAD A NOSE FOR FINDING THESE GEMS.

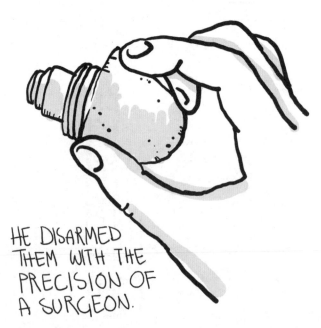

HE DISARMED THEM WITH THE PRECISION OF A SURGEON.

NEXT HE WOULD POUR
OUT THE BLACK POWDER.

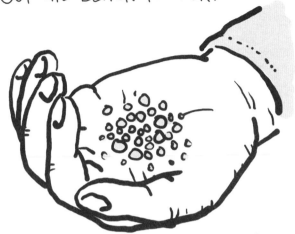

THIS WAS A TREASURE CRAVED
BY ALL THE BOYS.

ALTHOUGH THIS WAS VERY DANGEROUS
HE DIDN'T FEEL ANY FEAR. HENCE THE
NICKNAME — CRAZY JASIO. HE PRETENDED
TO BE A RUFFIAN AS HE HAD LOST BOTH HIS
PARENTS IN THE WAR.

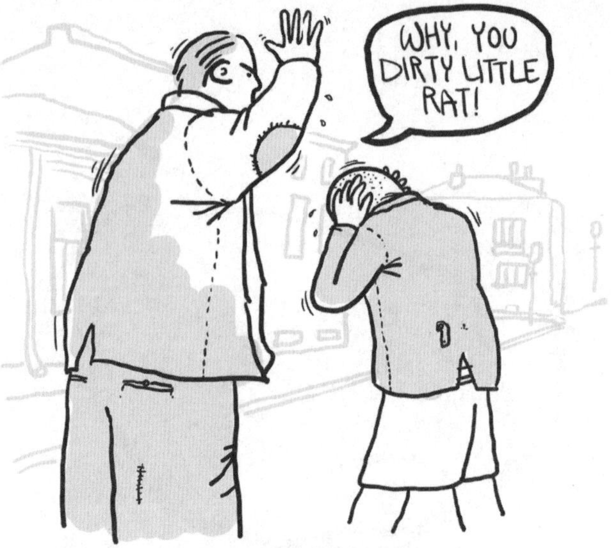
WHY, YOU DIRTY LITTLE RAT!

HE LIVED WITH HIS UNCLE IN A BASEMENT. WHEN HIS UNCLE WAS DRUNK (WHICH WASN'T UNCOMMON) HE WOULD BEAT JASIO UP FOR NO REASON.

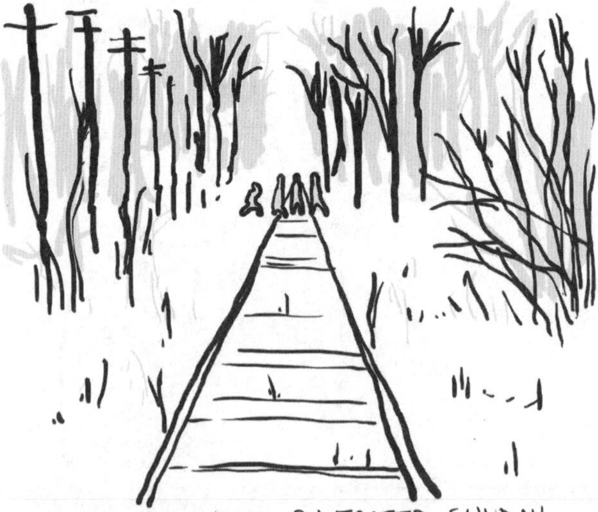

ONE EARLY MORNING, ON EASTER SUNDAY, MY DAD AND HIS PALS CROSSED THE RAILROAD TRACKS AND WENT INTO THE OLSZYNKA GROCHOWSKA FOREST.

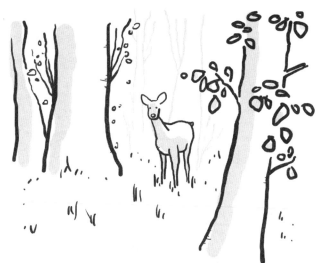

THE EASTER SUNDAY FIREWORKS HAD NOT YET STARTED. THE FOREST WAS QUIET AND PEACEFUL.

THEY HAD BROUGHT MATCHES WITH THEM AND AN ARTILLERY CARTRIDGE FILLED WITH BLACK POWDER.

ZÜNDHOLZ MONOPOL
IM
GENERALGOUVERNEMENT

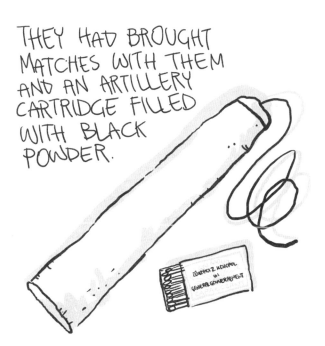

IN THE CHURCH ON SZEMBEK'S SQUARE,
NOT FAR AWAY, THE DEAN WAS ENDING THE MASS.

THE BOYS, HOWEVER, HAD THEIR
MINDS SET ON MORE IMPORTANT THINGS.

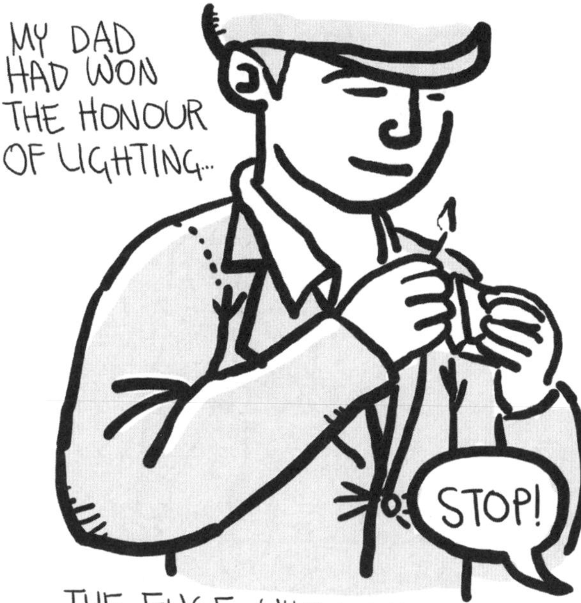
MY DAD HAD WON THE HONOUR OF LIGHTING...
STOP!

...THE FUSE WHEN SUDDENLY...

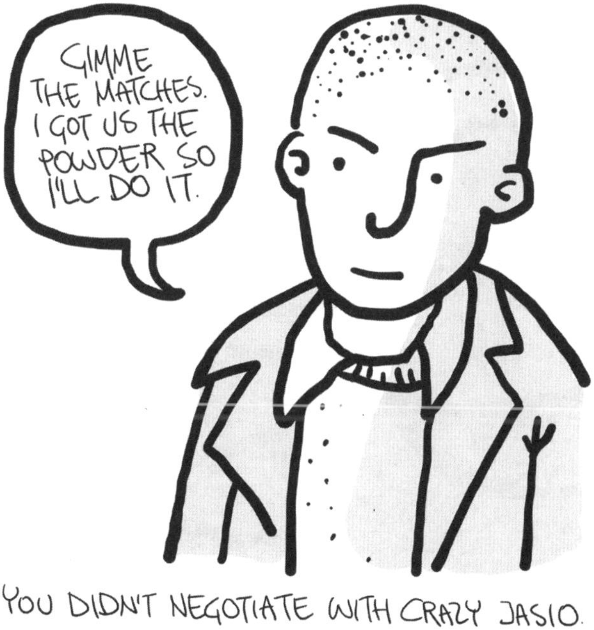
GIMME THE MATCHES. I GOT US THE POWDER SO I'LL DO IT.

YOU DIDN'T NEGOTIATE WITH CRAZY JASIO.

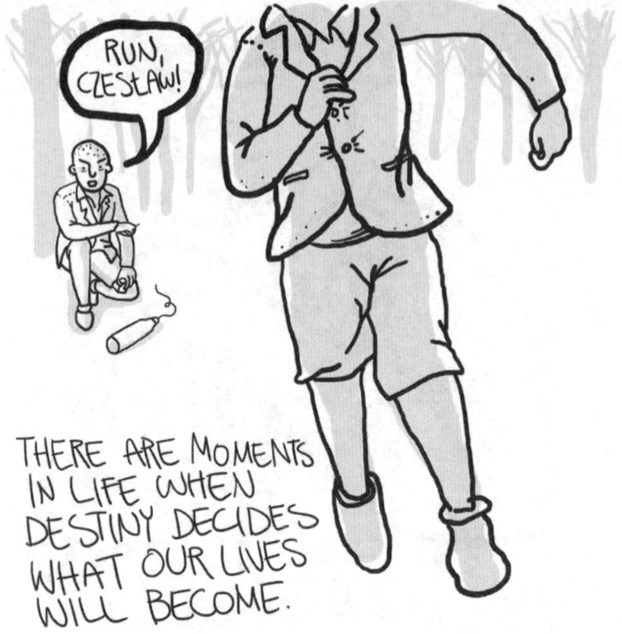
RUN, CZESŁAW!
THERE ARE MOMENTS IN LIFE WHEN DESTINY DECIDES WHAT OUR LIVES WILL BECOME.

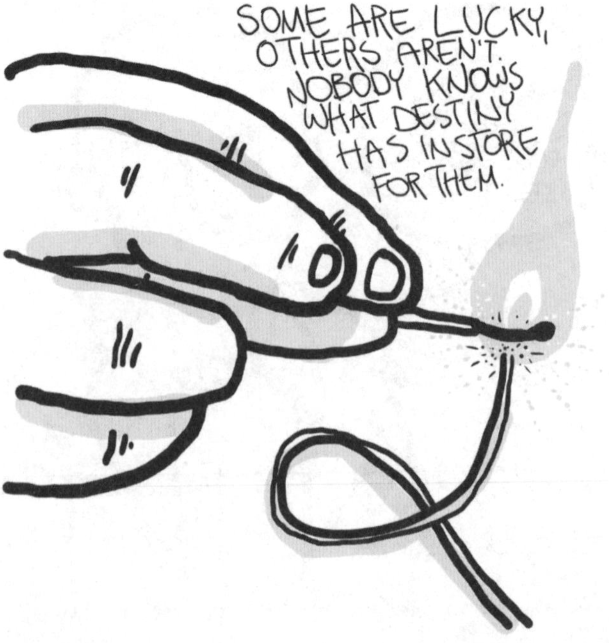
SOME ARE LUCKY, OTHERS AREN'T. NOBODY KNOWS WHAT DESTINY HAS IN STORE FOR THEM.

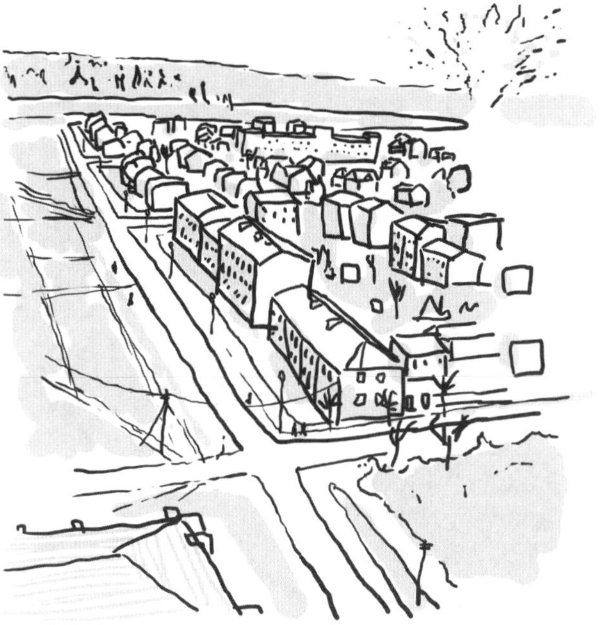

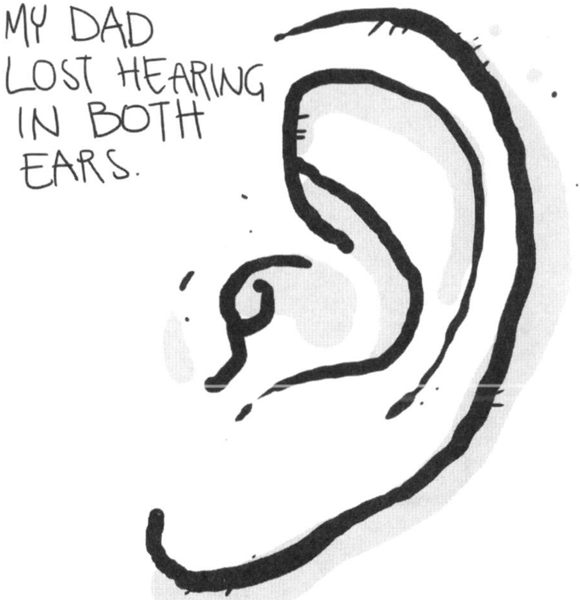
MY DAD LOST HEARING IN BOTH EARS.

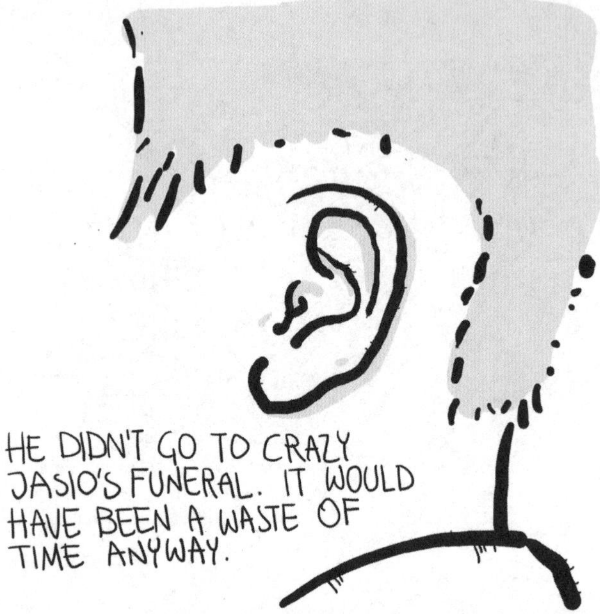
HE DIDN'T GO TO CRAZY JASIO'S FUNERAL. IT WOULD HAVE BEEN A WASTE OF TIME ANYWAY.

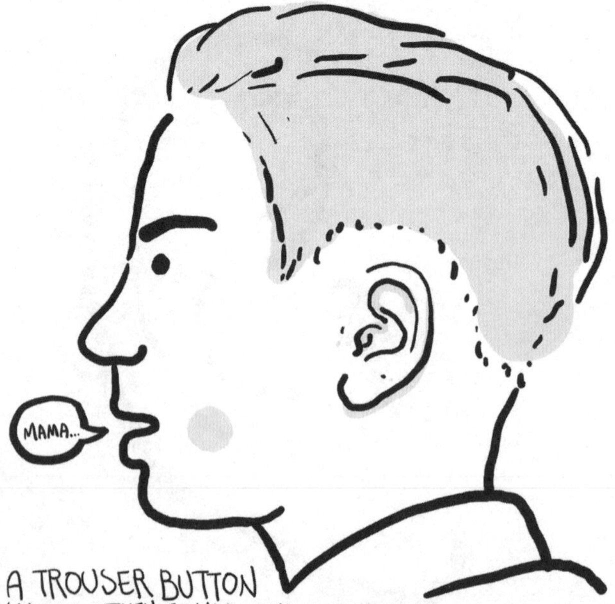
MAMA...
A TROUSER BUTTON WAS ALL THEY COULD FIND OF HIM.

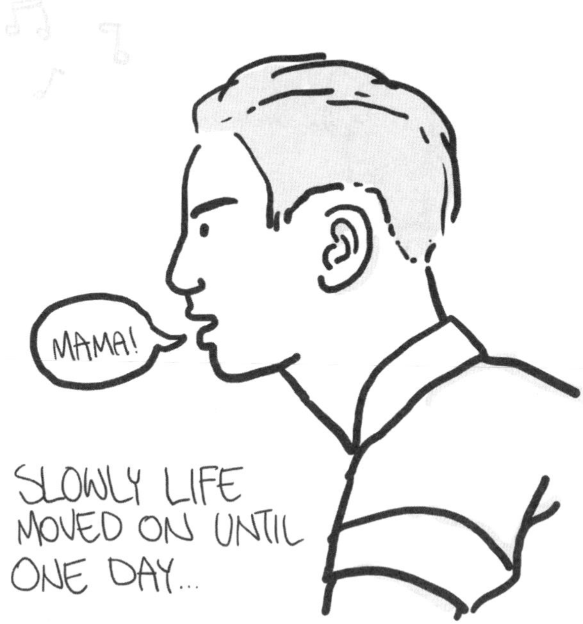
MAMA!
SLOWLY LIFE MOVED ON UNTIL ONE DAY...

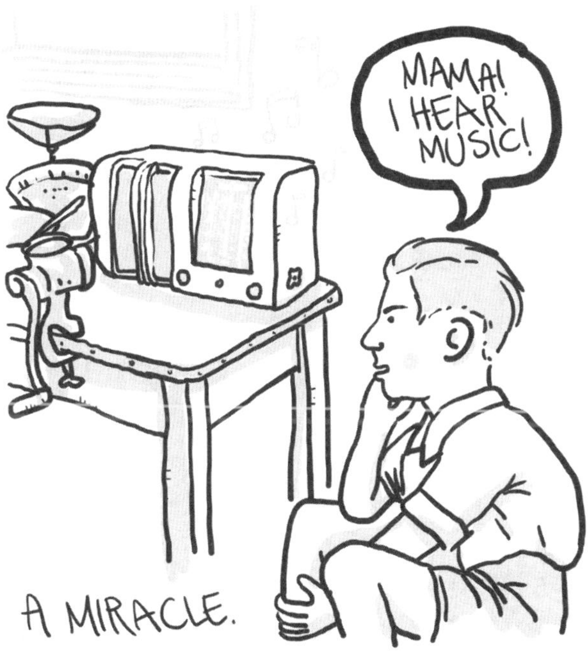
MAMA! I HEAR MUSIC!
A MIRACLE.

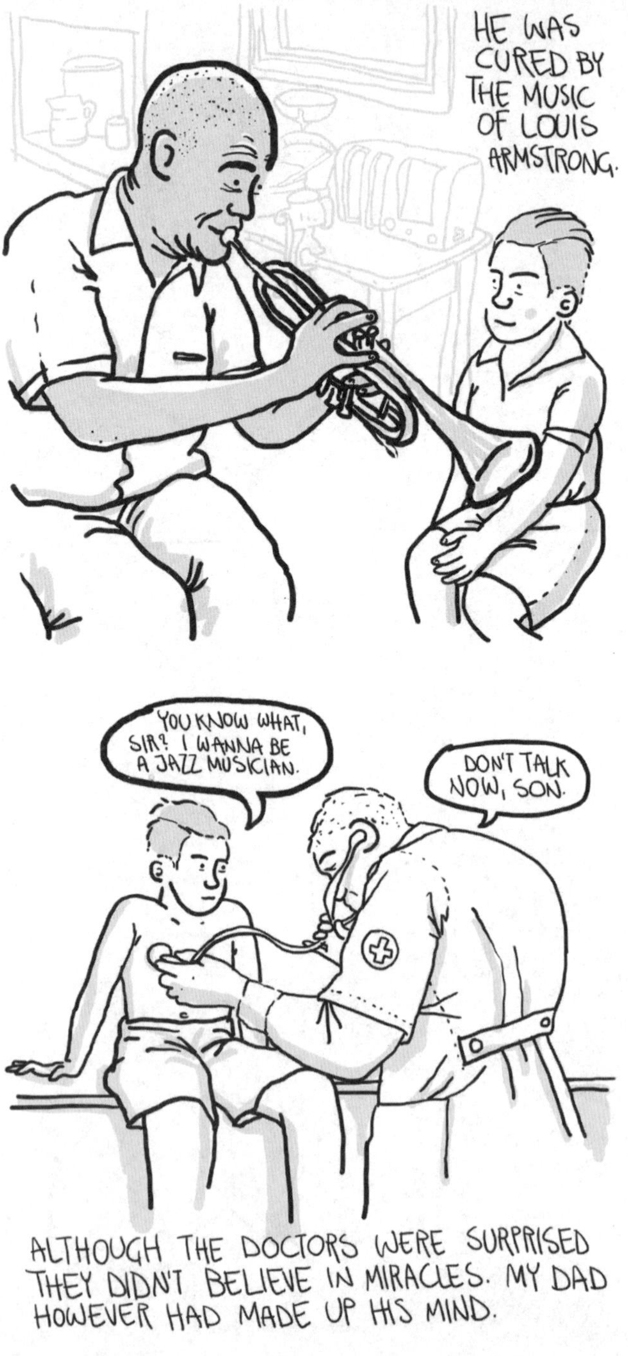
HE WAS CURED BY THE MUSIC OF LOUIS ARMSTRONG.
YOU KNOW WHAT, SIR? I WANNA BE A JAZZ MUSICIAN.
DON'T TALK NOW, SON.
ALTHOUGH THE DOCTORS WERE SURPRISED THEY DIDN'T BELIEVE IN MIRACLES. MY DAD HOWEVER HAD MADE UP HIS MIND.

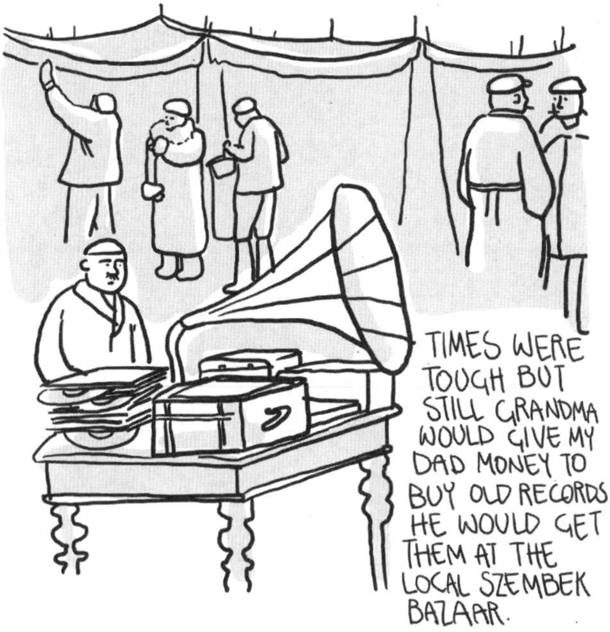
TIMES WERE TOUGH BUT STILL GRANDMA WOULD GIVE MY DAD MONEY TO BUY OLD RECORDS. HE WOULD GET THEM AT THE LOCAL SZEMBEK BAZAAR.

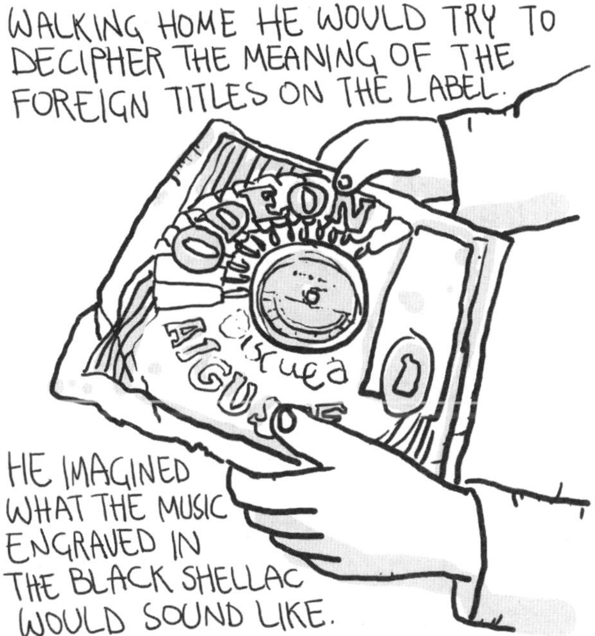
WALKING HOME HE WOULD TRY TO DECIPHER THE MEANING OF THE FOREIGN TITLES ON THE LABEL.
ODEON
HE IMAGINED WHAT THE MUSIC ENGRAVED IN THE BLACK SHELLAC WOULD SOUND LIKE.

IF IT WEREN'T FOR JADZIA, MY DAD'S OLDEST SISTER, HE'D STILL HAVE TO IMAGINE HIS MUSIC.
IN EXCHANGE FOR A LARGE AMOUNT OF CIGARETTES SHE GOT HIM A PORTABLE RECORD PLAYER.

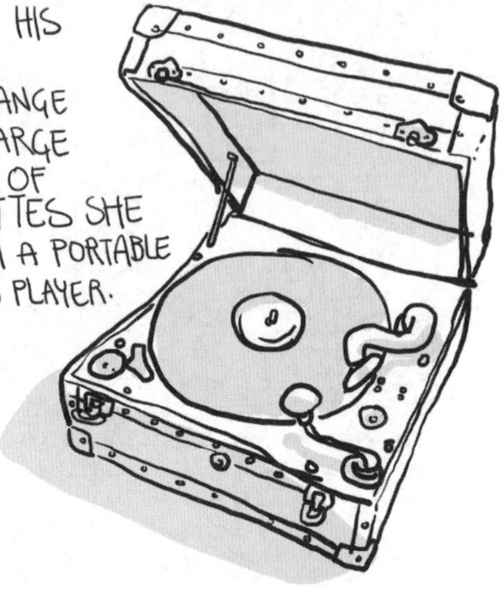

THANKS TO THE CIGARETTES THE FAMILY COULD BUY FOOD.

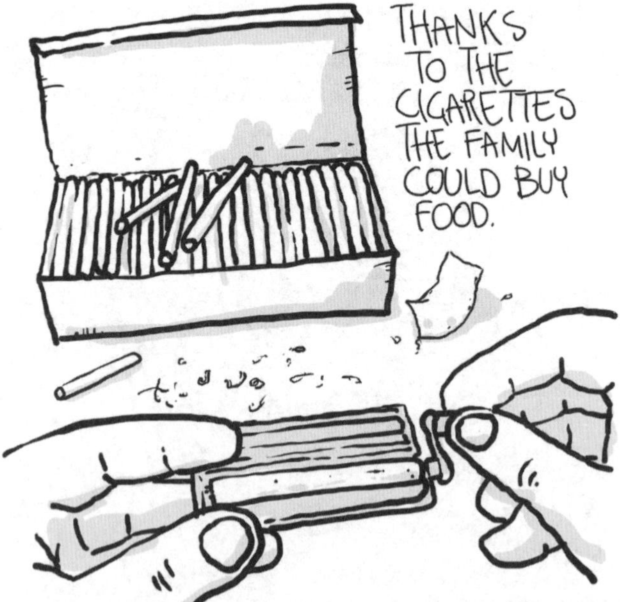

ALREADY DURING THE OCCUPATION.
MY DAD AND HIS SISTERS HAD HAD TO HELP
THEIR PARENTS IN THE HOME MANUFACTURING.

AUNT JADZIA GOT ADDICTED FROM TESTING THE QUALITY OF THE TOBACCO. SHE WAS ABOUT 10 YEARS OLD. THE OTHERS WERE MAKING FUN OF HER.

WILL YOU LEAVE ME ALONE!

MY DAD'S FAMILY MOVED IN TO AN ABANDONED HOUSE ON BYCZYŃSKA STREET 8. THEY DIDN'T HAVE ANYWHERE TO GO AND NUMBER 8 WAS IN GOOD CONDITION.

THEIR PREVIOUS HOME ON BYCZYŃSKA 24 WAS A RUIN.

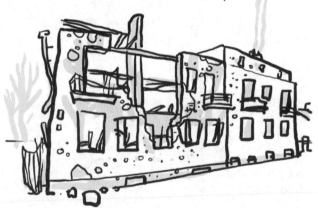

IT WAS THE ONLY HOUSE IN THE STREET THAT WAS COMPLETELY DESTROYED.

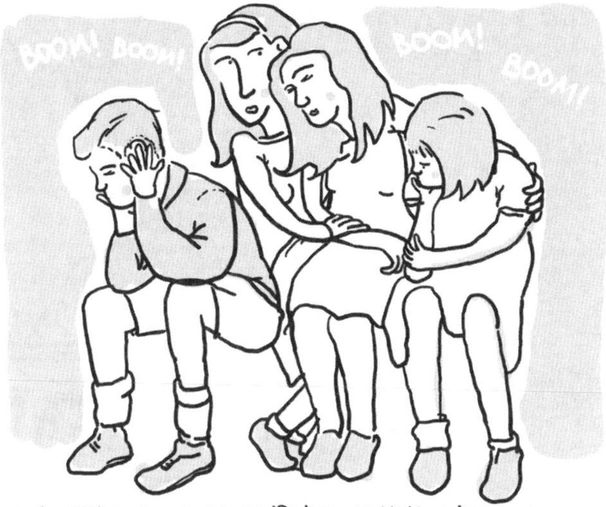
BOOM! BOOM!
BOOM!
BOOM!

ON THE DAY IT BURNED THEY WERE HIDING IN THE BASEMENT. OUTSIDE THERE WAS SHOOTING GOING ON BETWEEN THE ESCAPING GERMANS AND ATTACKING RUSSIANS.

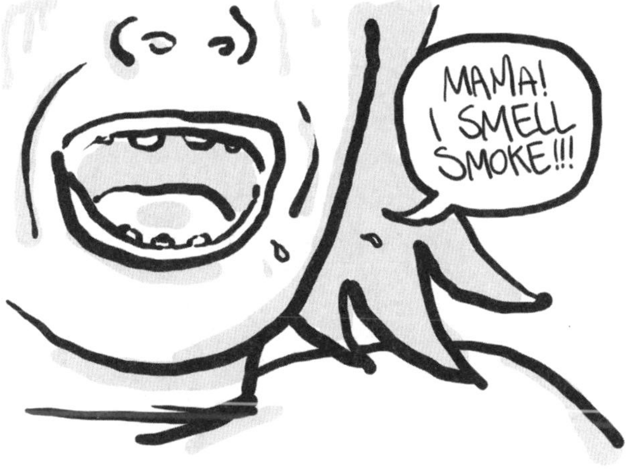
MAMA! I SMELL SMOKE!!!

THEN KRYSTYNA, THE YOUNGEST OF THE GIRLS, STARTED TO YELL.

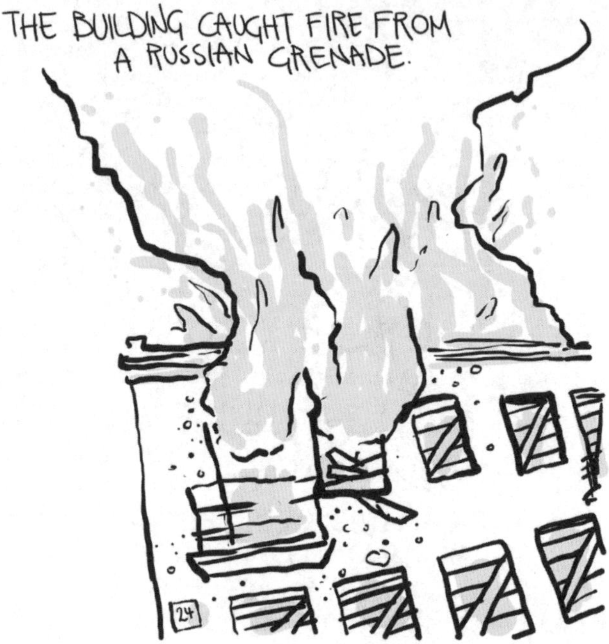
THE BUILDING CAUGHT FIRE FROM A RUSSIAN GRENADE.
24

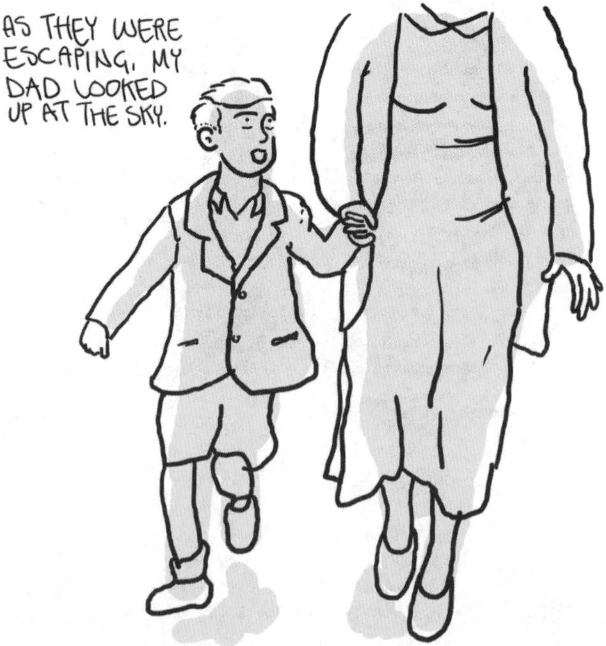
AS THEY WERE ESCAPING, MY DAD LOOKED UP AT THE SKY.

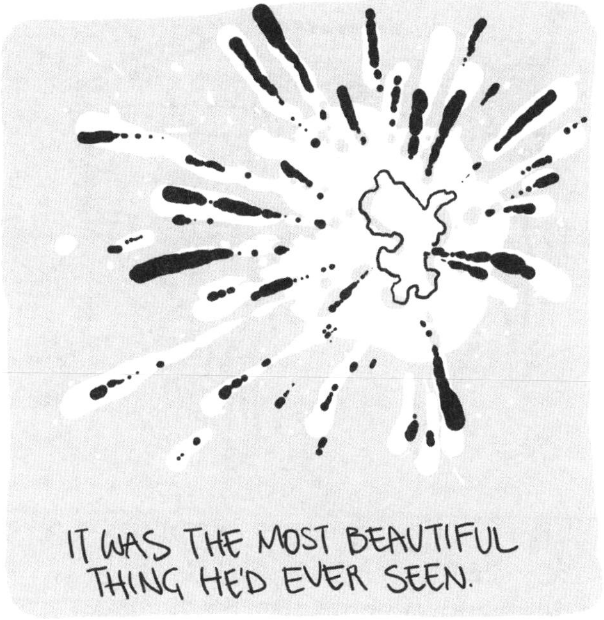
IT WAS THE MOST BEAUTIFUL THING HE'D EVER SEEN.

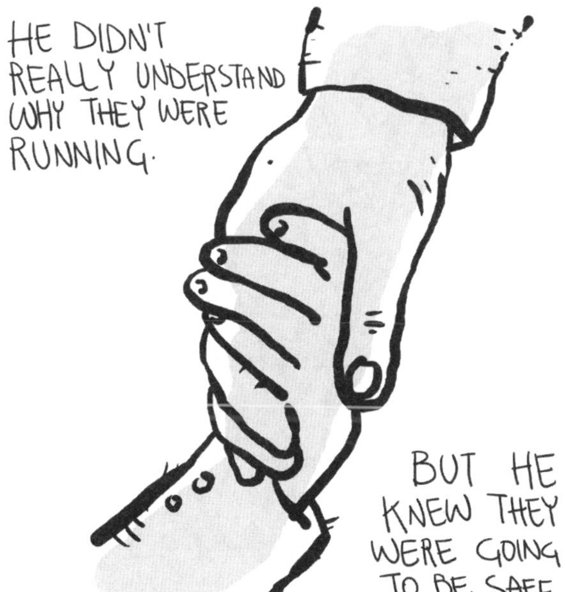
HE DIDN'T REALLY UNDERSTAND WHY THEY WERE RUNNING.
BUT HE KNEW THEY WERE GOING TO BE SAFE.

THEN SUDDENLY HE REMEMBERED
HIS DAD'S RABBITS, THEIR CAGES
LEANING AGAINST THE BACK WALL.

THEIR PINK NOSES GLIMMERED IN THE LIGHT OF
THE FIRE. HE NOTICED THEIR STRANGE CALMNESS.

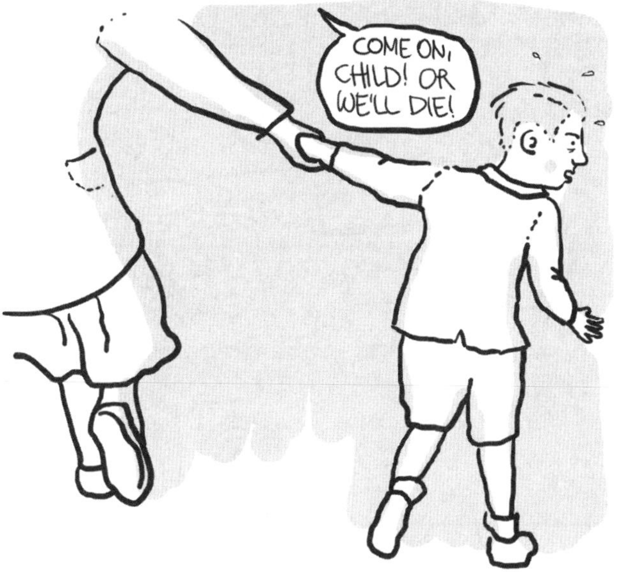
COME ON, CHILD! OR WE'LL DIE!

HE COULD DO NOTHING TO SAVE THEM.

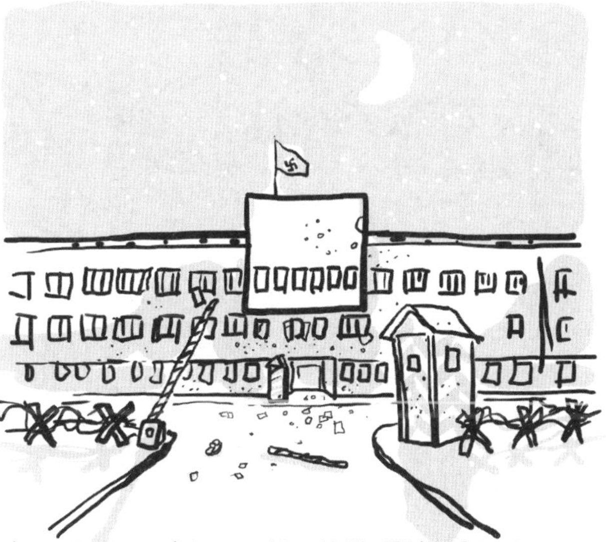

NEXT TO MY DAD'S HOUSE THE SS HAD ABANDONED THEIR QUARTERS ONLY A FEW HOURS EARLIER.

THAT'S WHERE THEY TOOK REFUGE AS THE
FIGHTING OUTSIDE CONTINUED UNTIL DAWN.

IN THE MORNING THE RED ARMY
SHOWED UP ON THE STREETS OF GROCHÓW.

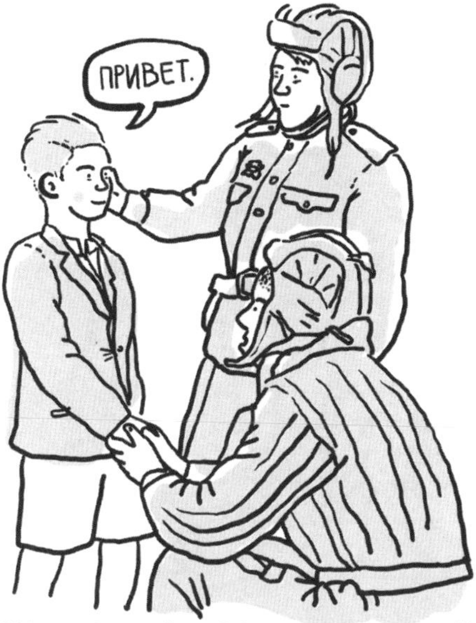
ПРИВЕТ.

THE RUSSIANS SET UP A BASE IN THE BUILDING WHERE MY DAD'S FAMILY WAS HIDING. THEY LET THEM AND THE REST OF THE REFUGEES STAY. THEY TOLD THEM THE WAR WAS OVER.

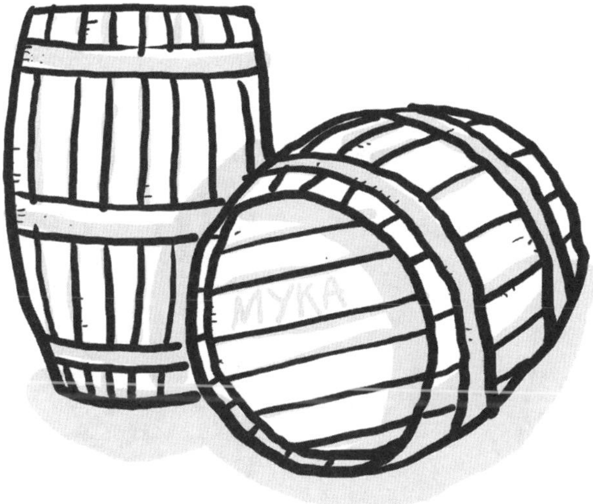
МУКА

THEY HAD BROUGHT TWO BARRELS WITH THEM. ONE WITH FLOUR AND THE OTHER WITH JAM.

MY GRANDMA HAD TO MAKE THEM PANCAKES FOR 24 HOURS IN A ROW. SHE WAS TOO FRIGHTENED TO PROTEST.

SHE NEVER TOUCHED A PANCAKE FOR THE REST OF HER DAYS. AT LEAST THE KIDS WEREN'T HUNGRY.

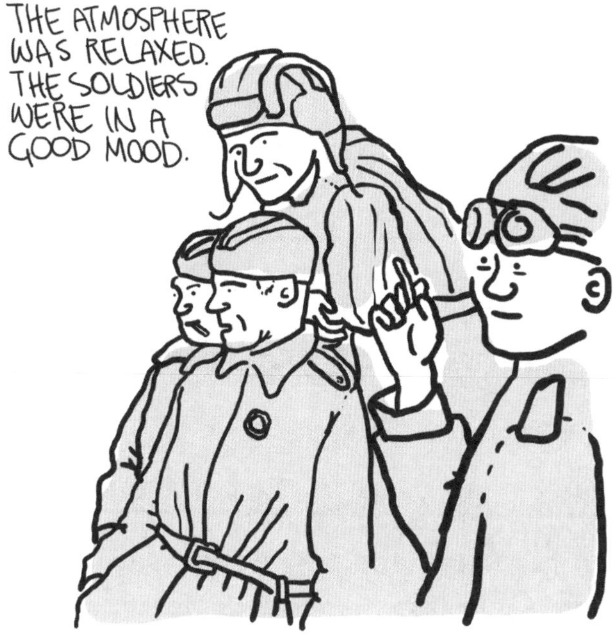
THE ATMOSPHERE WAS RELAXED. THE SOLDIERS WERE IN A GOOD MOOD.

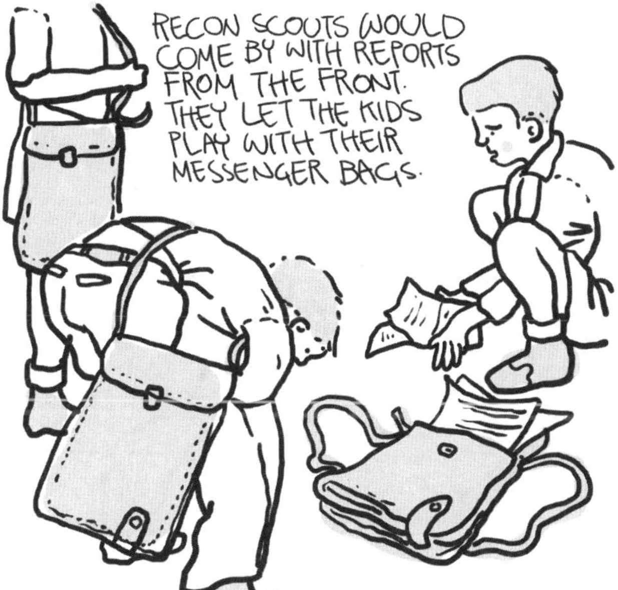
RECON SCOUTS WOULD COME BY WITH REPORTS FROM THE FRONT. THEY LET THE KIDS PLAY WITH THEIR MESSENGER BAGS.

THEY WOULD ALSO TALK ABOUT THE FIGHTING,* SEEN ON THE LEFT SIDE OF THE RIVER, BETWEEN THE POLES AND THE GERMANS. (* THE WARSAW UPRISING IN 1944)

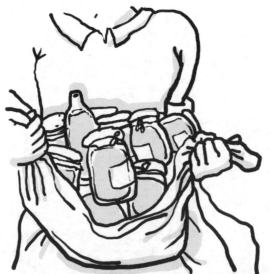

ONCE IN A WHILE GRANDMA WOULD GO TO THE OLD HOUSE TO LOOK FOR FOOD IN THE BASEMENT.

ONE DAY SHE ASKED
JADZIA TO LOOK AFTER
HER YOUNGER SIBLINGS
WHILE SHE WENT OFF TO
GET FOOD. HOWEVER JADZIA
HAD A BETTER IDEA HOW TO SPEND
HER FREE TIME.

THEY APPROACHED HER IN THE STAIRWAY.
THEIR BREATH REEKED OF VODKA.

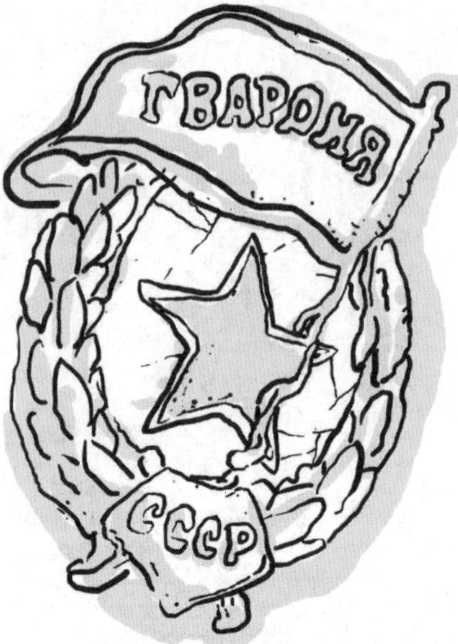
ГВАРДИЯ
СССР

SHE WAS AFRAID TO LOOK THEM IN THE EYES.

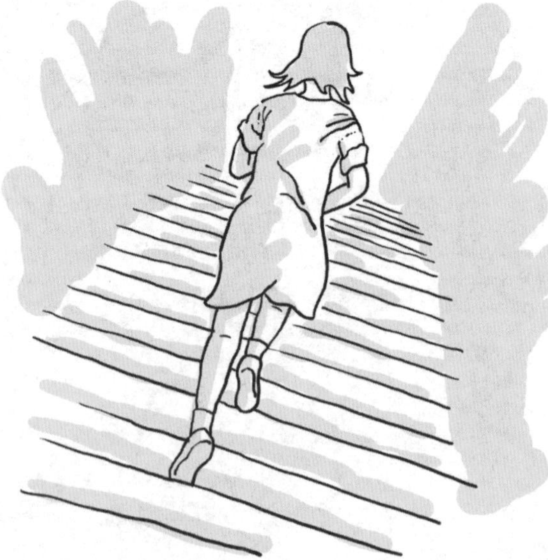

...OR SAY ANYTHING.

SHE YEARNED
FOR THE WAR
TO FINALLY END.

SHE COULD
FEEL IT CLOSER
THAN EVER.

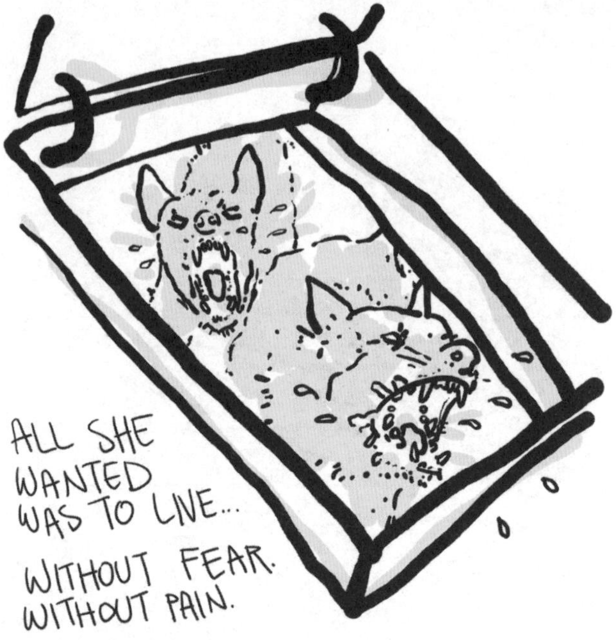
ALL SHE WANTED WAS TO LIVE...
WITHOUT FEAR.
WITHOUT PAIN.

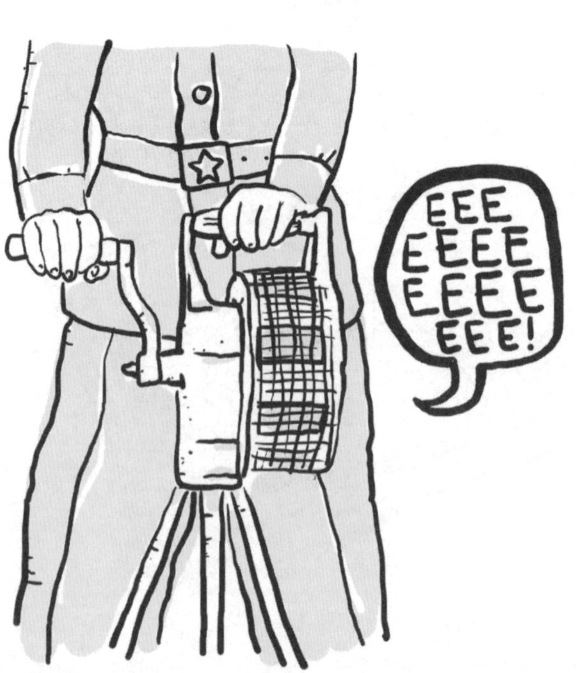
EEE EEEE EEEE EEE!

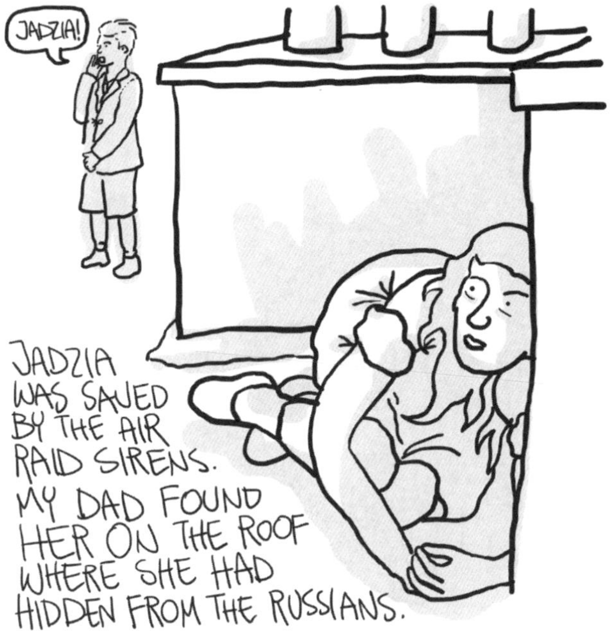
JADZIA!
JADZIA WAS SAVED BY THE AIR RAID SIRENS.
MY DAD FOUND HER ON THE ROOF WHERE SHE HAD HIDDEN FROM THE RUSSIANS.

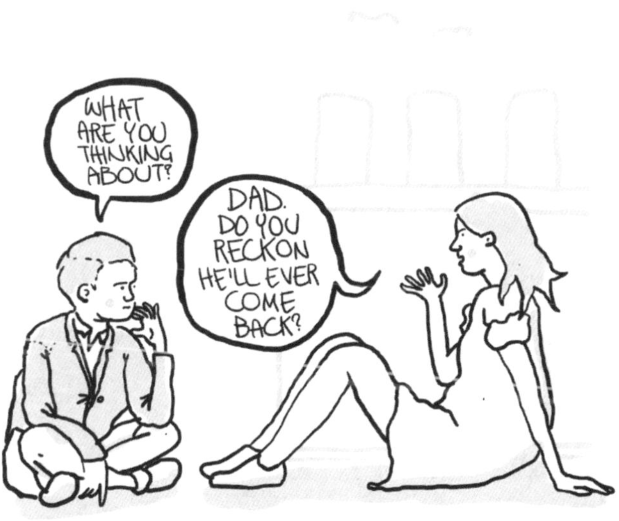
WHAT ARE YOU THINKING ABOUT?
DAD. DO YOU RECKON HE'LL EVER COME BACK?

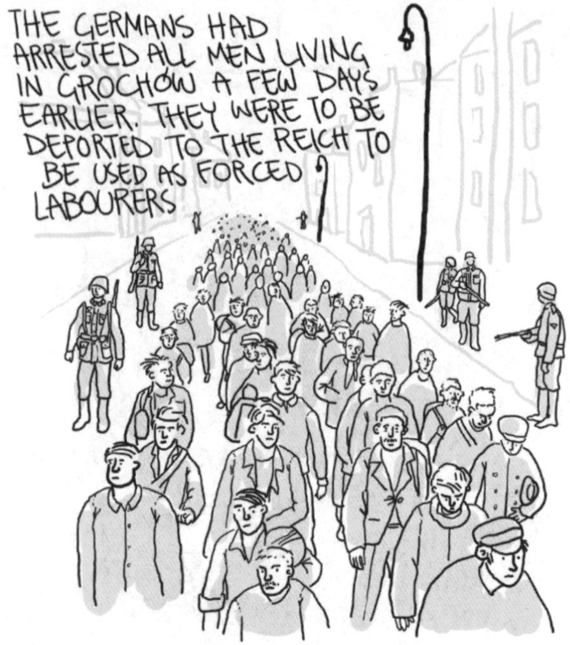
THE GERMANS HAD ARRESTED ALL MEN LIVING IN GROCHÓW A FEW DAYS EARLIER. THEY WERE TO BE DEPORTED TO THE REICH TO BE USED AS FORCED LABOURERS

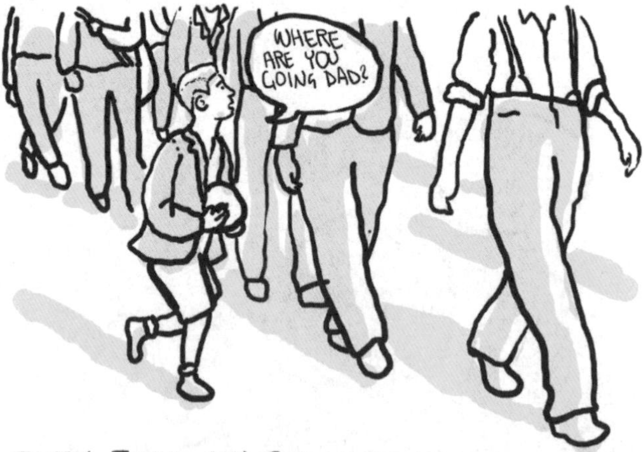
WHERE ARE YOU GOING DAD?

THEY TOOK MY GRANDPA TOO. GRANDMA TOLD MY DAD TO CATCH UP WITH HIS FATHER. HE RAN FOR ALMOST 5 KM BEFORE HE FOUND HIM AMONGST THE OTHER PRISONERS.

THEY WERE JUST PASSING THE WEDEL CANDY
FACTORY. A SWEET SMELL OF CHOCOLATE
MIXED WITH SWEAT HUNG IN THE AIR.

GRANDMA WAS NOT EVEN ALLOWED
TO SAY GOODBYE.

SHE HAD PACKED HIM A LOAF OF
BREAD AND SAUSAGES FOR THE
ROAD. MY DAD WAS TO GIVE IT TO HIM.

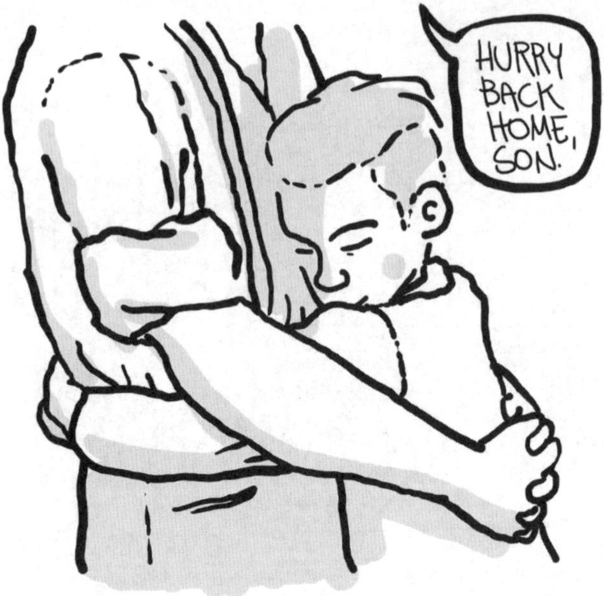
HURRY BACK HOME, SON.

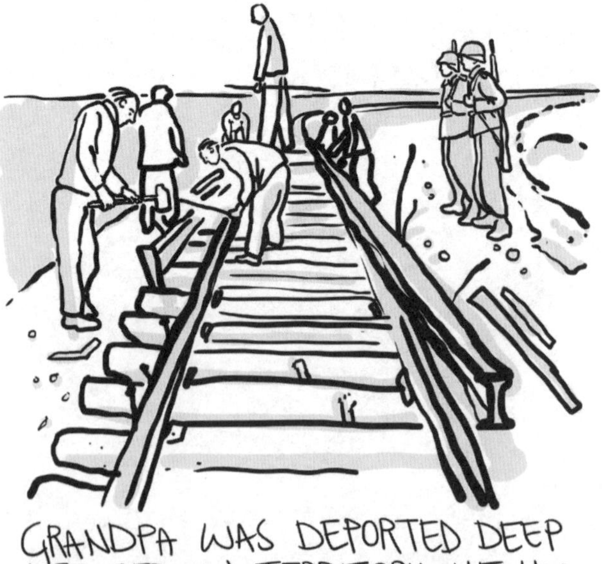

GRANDPA WAS DEPORTED DEEP INTO GERMAN TERRITORY. HE HAD TO REPAIR RAILROAD TRACKS.

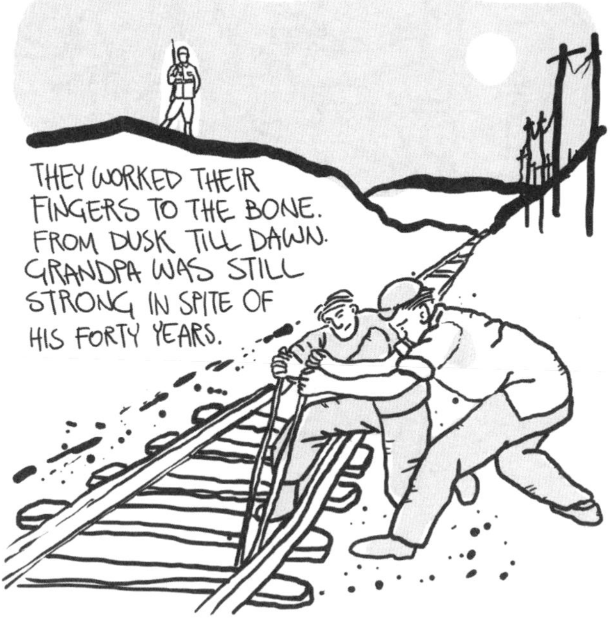
THEY WORKED THEIR FINGERS TO THE BONE. FROM DUSK TILL DAWN. GRANDPA WAS STILL STRONG IN SPITE OF HIS FORTY YEARS.

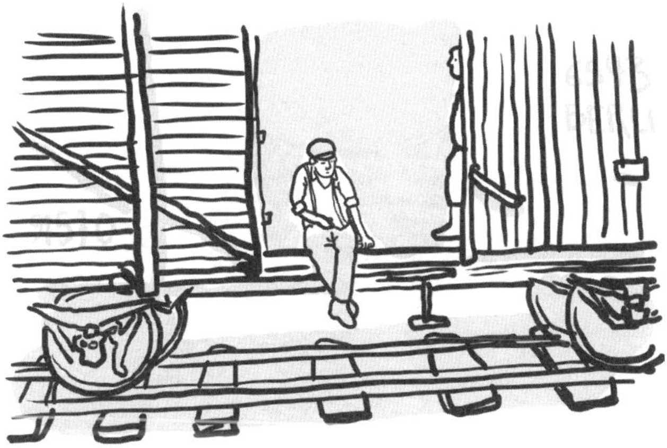

THEY SLEPT IN FREIGHT CARS THAT WERE KEPT LOCKED IN THE NIGHT.

GRANDPA HAD BEEN TAKEN ALONG WITH HIS BROTHER-IN-LAW AND ONE OF HIS NEIGHBOURS. THE THREE OF THEM STAYED TOGETHER.

THEY WERE STARVING AND COLD BUT WHAT THEY FEARED MOST WERE THE ALLIES' BOMBERS.

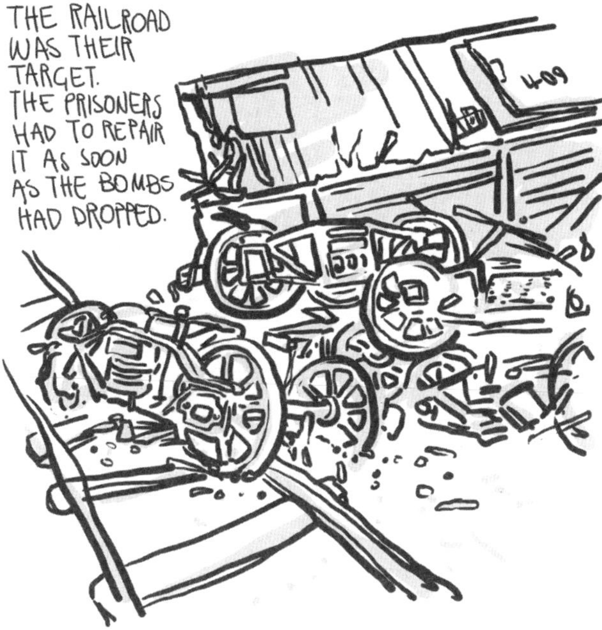
THE RAILROAD WAS THEIR TARGET.
THE PRISONERS HAD TO REPAIR IT AS SOON AS THE BOMBS HAD DROPPED.

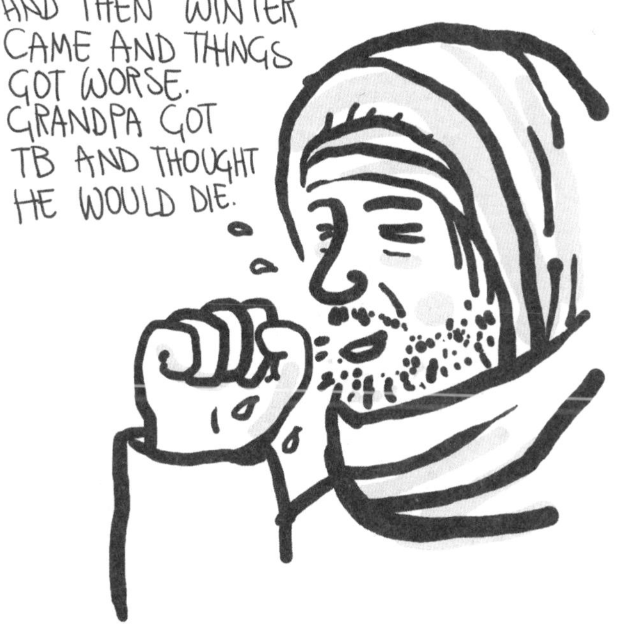
AND THEN WINTER CAME AND THINGS GOT WORSE.
GRANDPA GOT TB AND THOUGHT HE WOULD DIE.

AT LAST, SPRING CAME.

ONE DAY THEY
HAD TO TAKE
A BREAK TO LET
AN IMPORTANT
TRAIN
PASS.

ALL THE PRISONERS HAD TO TURN THEIR BACKS TO THE TRACKS. THEY WERE TOLD NOT TO LOOK AT THE TRAIN. GRANDPA DIDN'T OBEY.

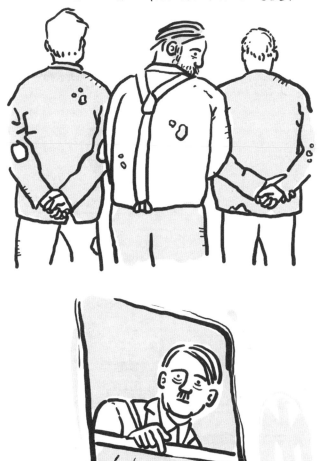

HIS EYES MET THE EYES OF A MAN WITH A SAD AND WEARY FACE.

GRANDPA FELT AS IF HE'D LOOKED STRAIGHT INTO THE EYES OF DEATH. HE SHIVERED...

THE NEXT DAY NOBODY CAME TO LET THEM OUT FOR WORK.

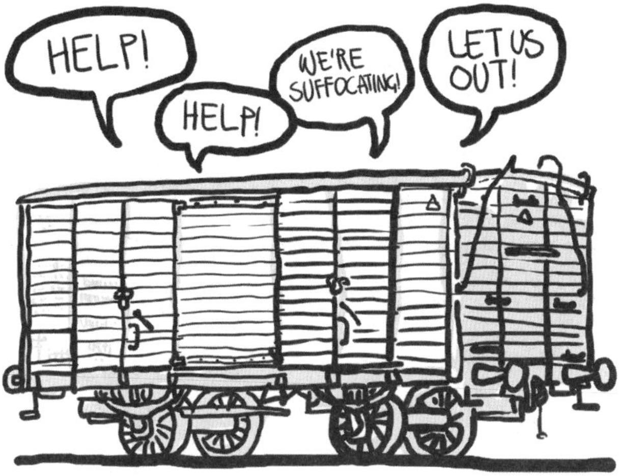
HELP!
HELP!
WE'RE SUFFOCATING!
LET US OUT!

THEY WERE LOCKED UP IN THE CARS FOR MANY DAYS WITHOUT FOOD AND WATER.

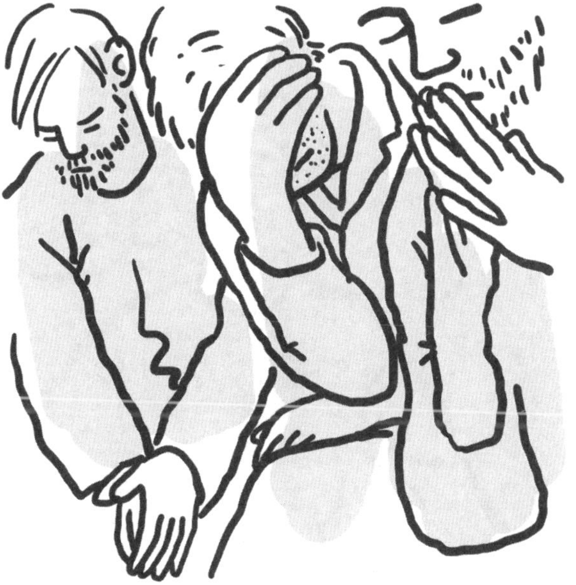

THERE WAS NO HOPE FOR THEM.

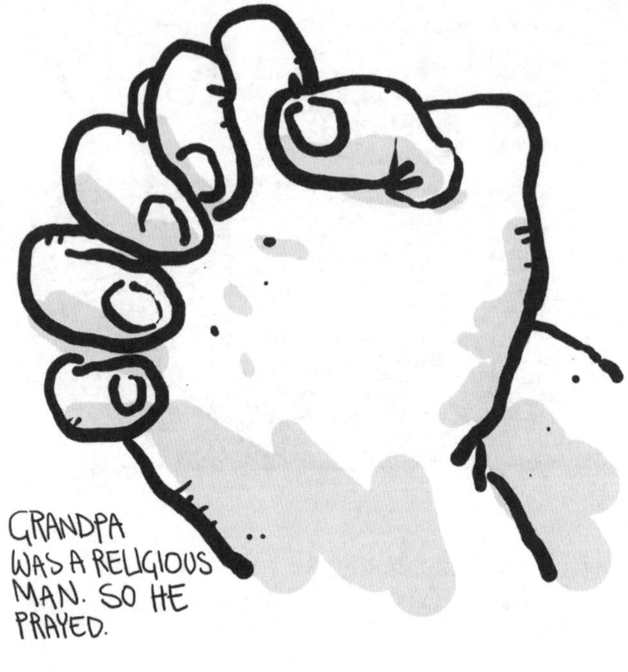
GRANDPA WAS A RELIGIOUS MAN. SO HE PRAYED.

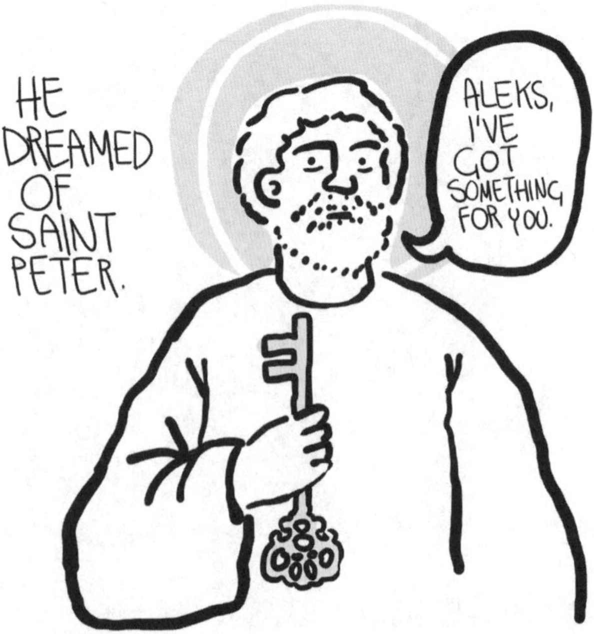
HE DREAMED OF SAINT PETER.
ALEKS, I'VE GOT SOMETHING FOR YOU.

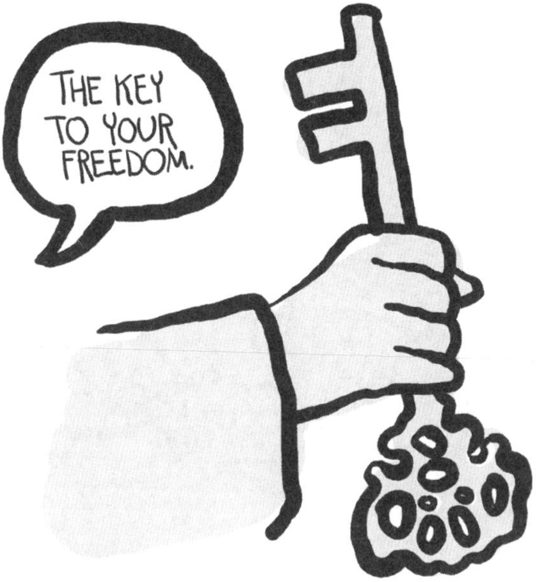
THE KEY
TO YOUR
FREEDOM.

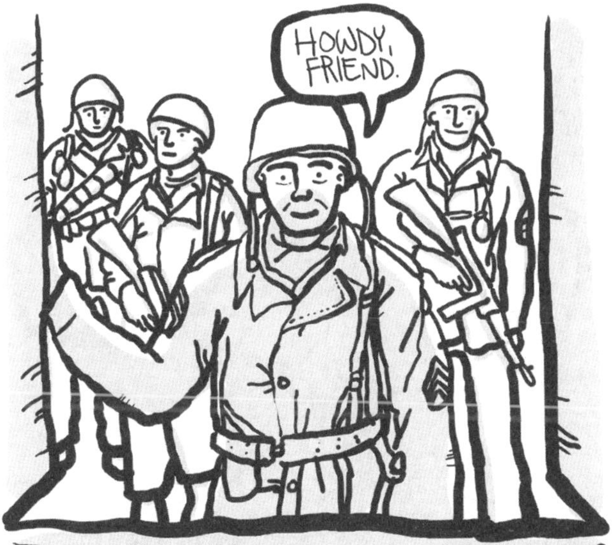
HOWDY,
FRIEND.

THE NEXT DAY AT DAWN.

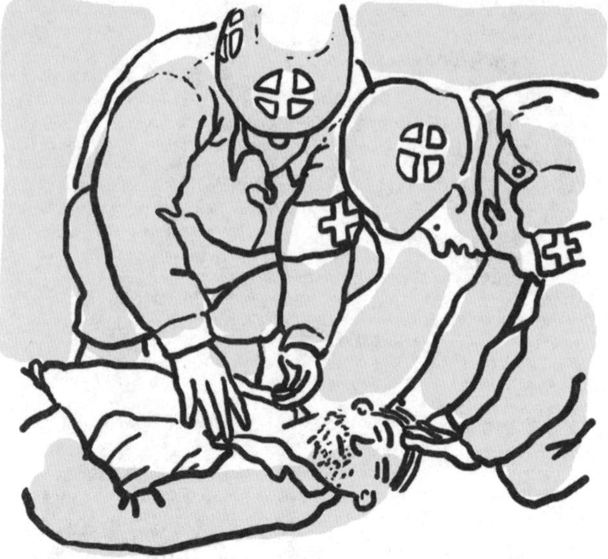

THEY WERE SAVED BY THE AMERICANS THOUGH IT WAS TOO LATE FOR SOME OF THEM.

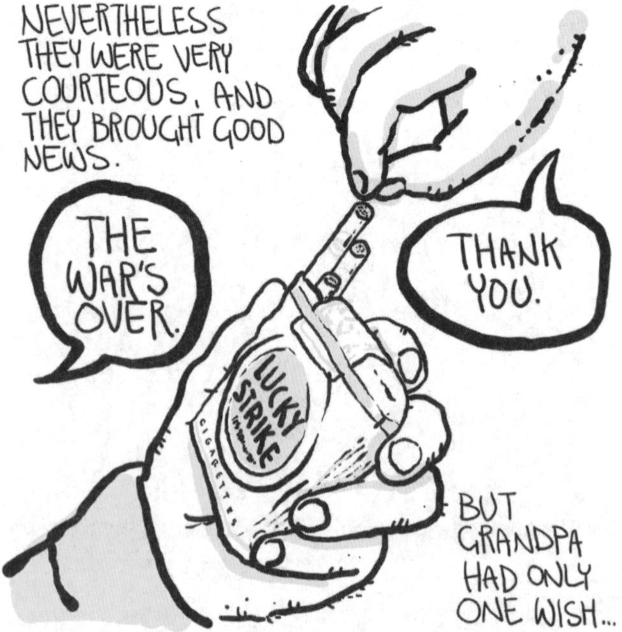
NEVERTHELESS THEY WERE VERY COURTEOUS, AND THEY BROUGHT GOOD NEWS.
THE WAR'S OVER.
THANK YOU.
LUCKY STRIKE
CIGARETTES
BUT GRANDPA HAD ONLY ONE WISH...

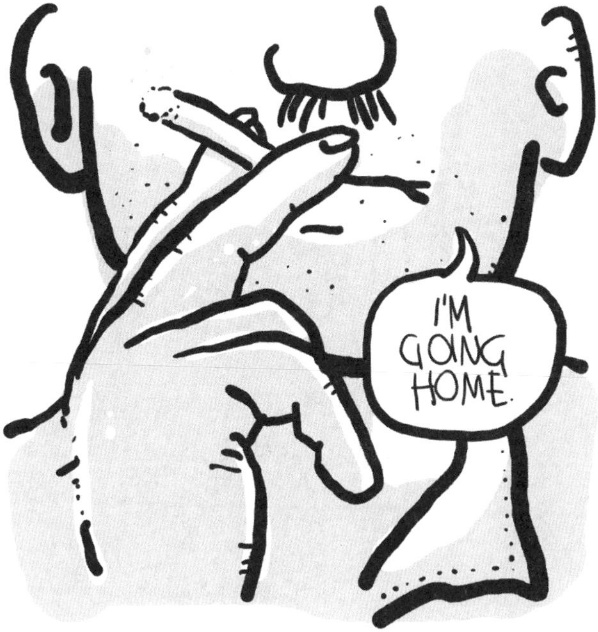
I'M GOING HOME.

HE SAID GOODBYE TO HIS FRIENDS.

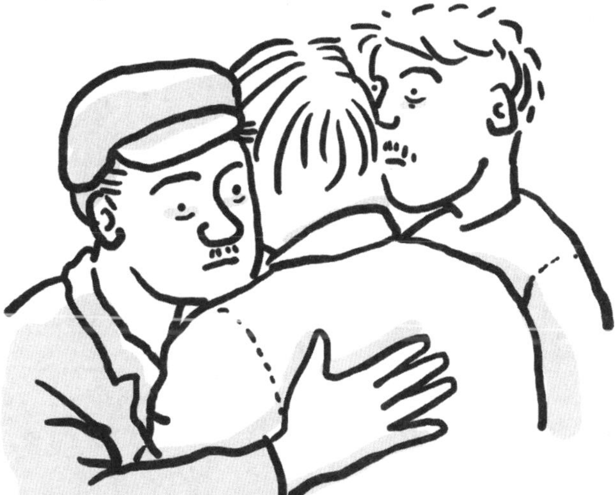

FIGHTING HAD NOT YET
COMPLETELY DIED
OUT AND TRAVELLING
WAS UNSAFE.
HE WAS STILL FAR
FROM HOME.

HE FOUND
POVERTY AND
MISERY EVERYWHERE.

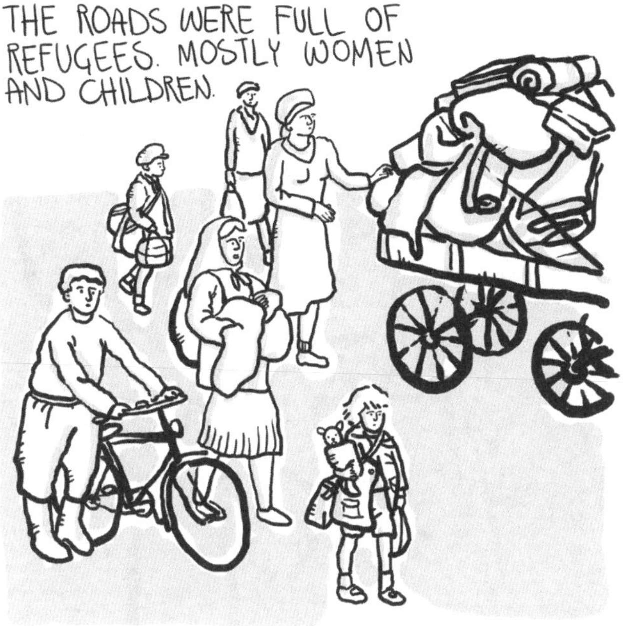
THE ROADS WERE FULL OF REFUGEES. MOSTLY WOMEN AND CHILDREN.

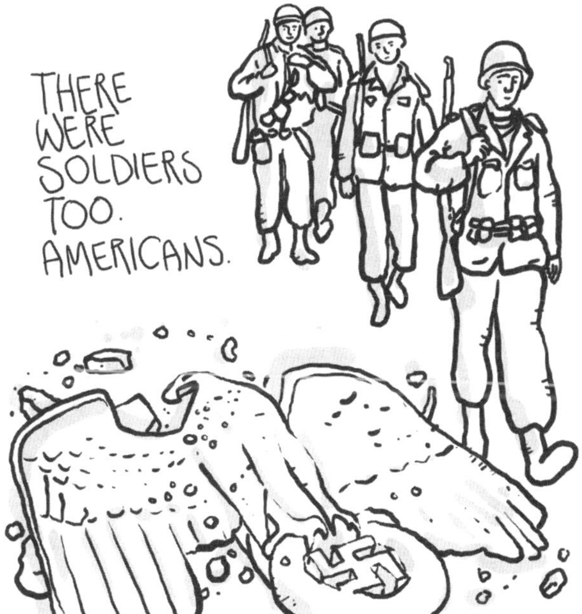
THERE WERE SOLDIERS TOO. AMERICANS.

SOMETIMES HE ASKED FOR DIRECTIONS.

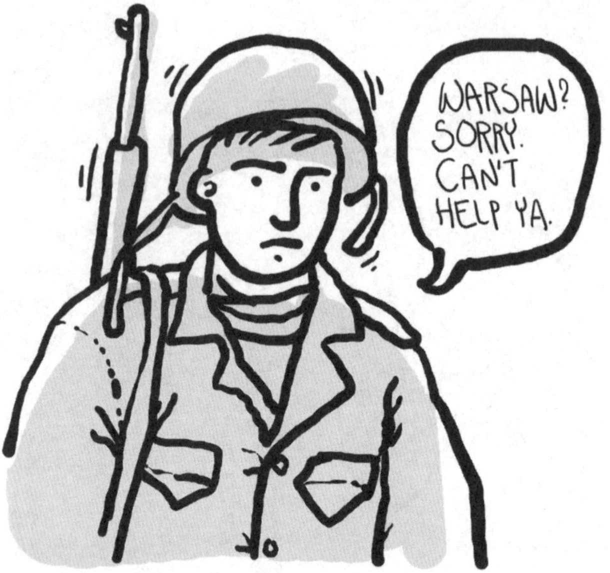
WARSAW? SORRY. CAN'T HELP YA.

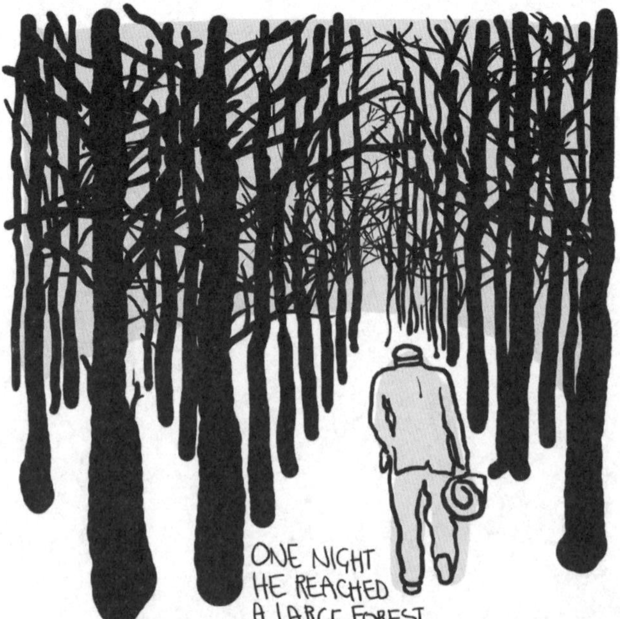
ONE NIGHT HE REACHED A LARGE FOREST.

HE HADN'T HAD ANYTHING
TO EAT FOR A LONG TIME.

FOOD WAS ALL HE COULD THINK OF.

WHEN HE FINALLY
REACHED THE END
OF THE FOREST HE
FOUND HIMSELF BY
A MEADOW.

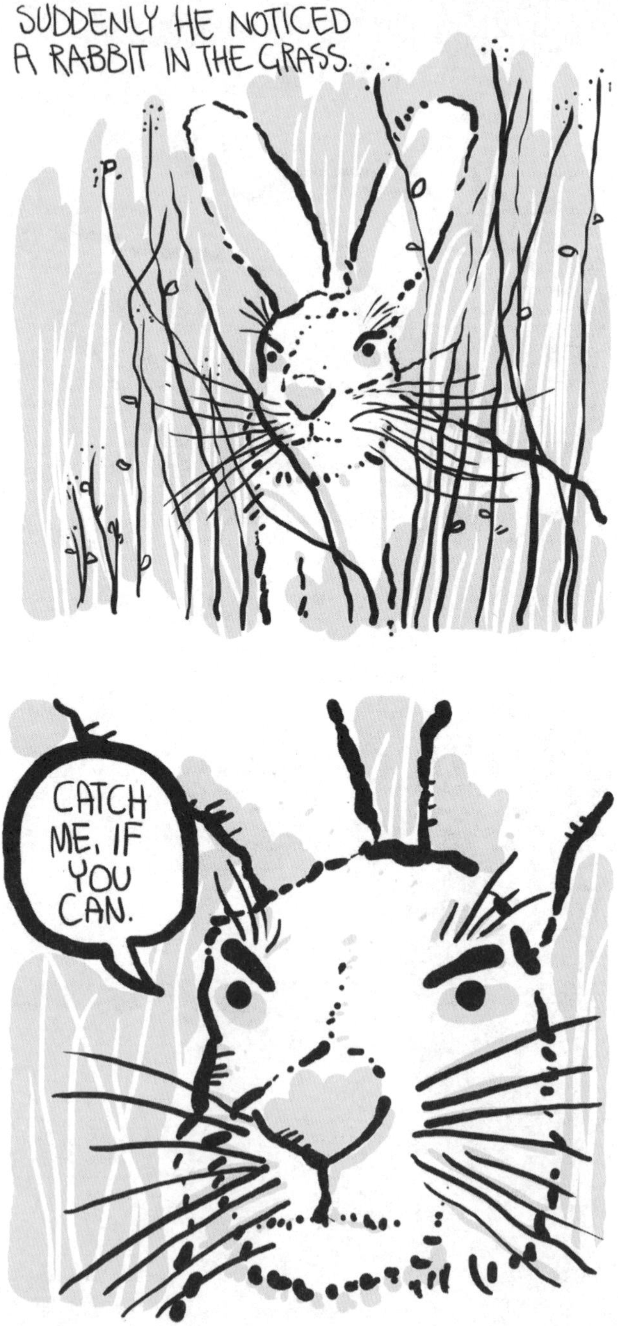
SUDDENLY HE NOTICED A RABBIT IN THE GRASS.
CATCH ME, IF YOU CAN.

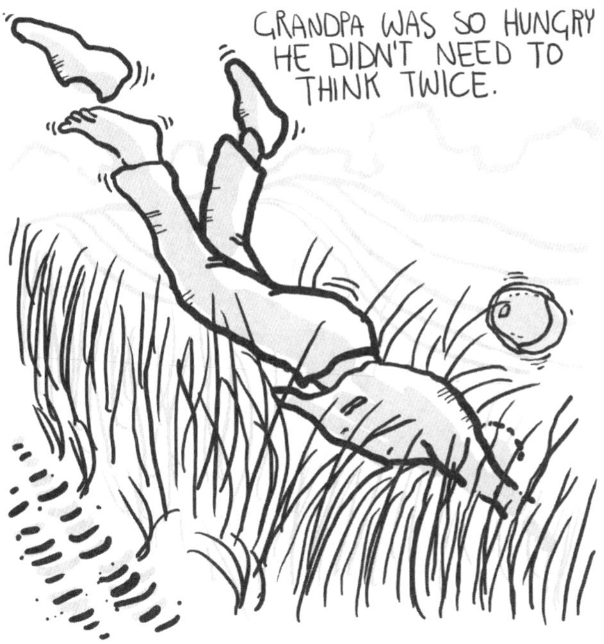
GRANDPA WAS SO HUNGRY HE DIDN'T NEED TO THINK TWICE.

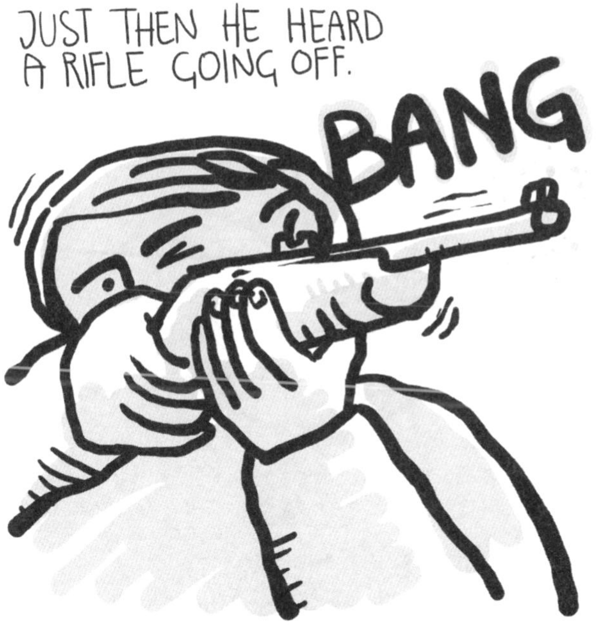
JUST THEN HE HEARD A RIFLE GOING OFF.
BANG

THE BULLET ONLY GRAZED HIM. HE HAD
NO IDEA WHO HAD FIRED THE SHOT AT
HIM BUT TO BE ON THE SAFE SIDE, HE WAITED
IN THE HIGH GRASS UNTIL DAWN.

WHAT ABOUT THE RABBIT?
IT DISAPPEARED AS QUICK AS IT CAME.

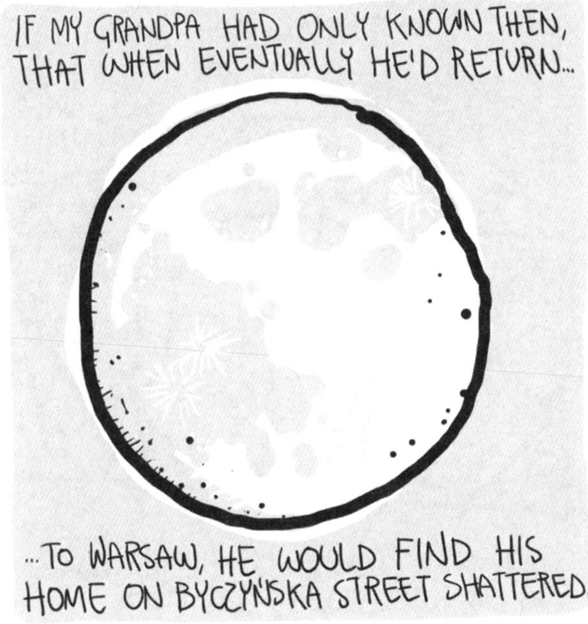
IF MY GRANDPA HAD ONLY KNOWN THEN, THAT WHEN EVENTUALLY HE'D RETURN...
...TO WARSAW, HE WOULD FIND HIS HOME ON BYCZYŃSKA STREET SHATTERED.

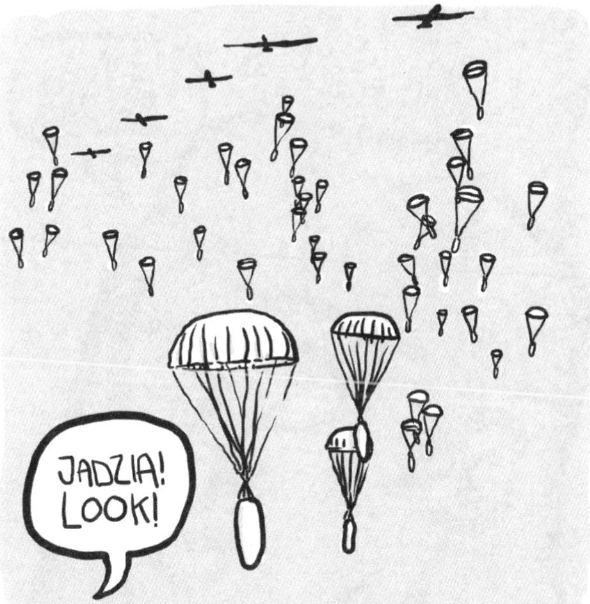
JADZIA! LOOK!

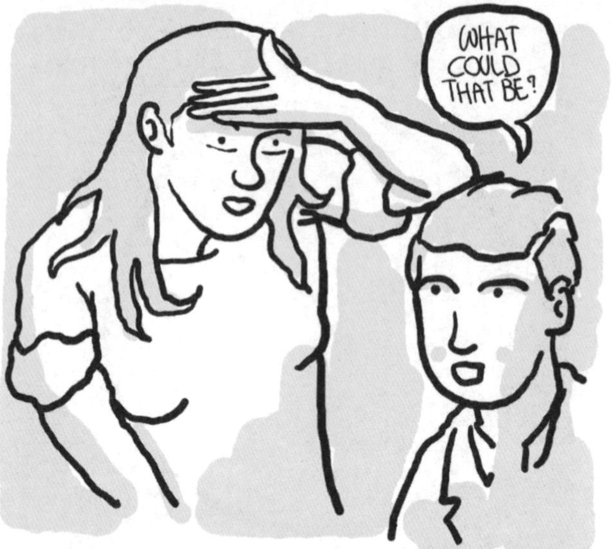
WHAT COULD THAT BE?

MY DAD WAS LUCKY HIS FAMILY LIVED ON THE RIGHT SIDE OF THE RIVER.

PEOPLE ON THE LEFT SIDE WERE DYING LIKE FLIES.

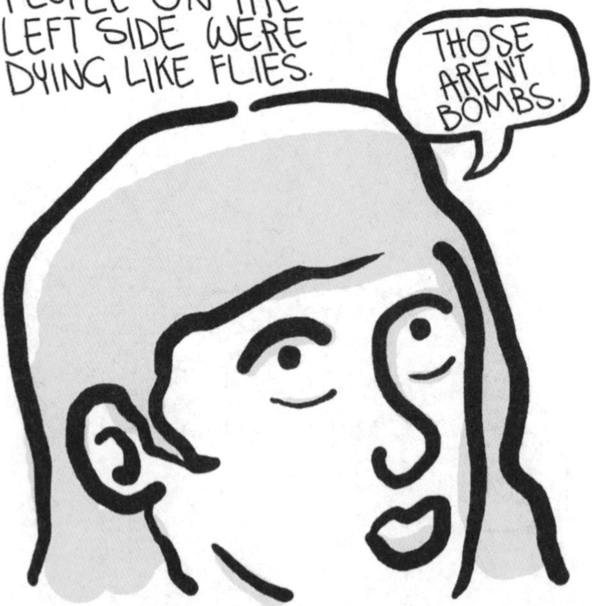
THOSE AREN'T BOMBS.

MOST OF THEM WEREN'T HEROES. THEY WERE ORDINARY FOLK. THEY JUST WANTED THEIR WIVES, HUSBANDS AND KIDS TO SURVIVE.

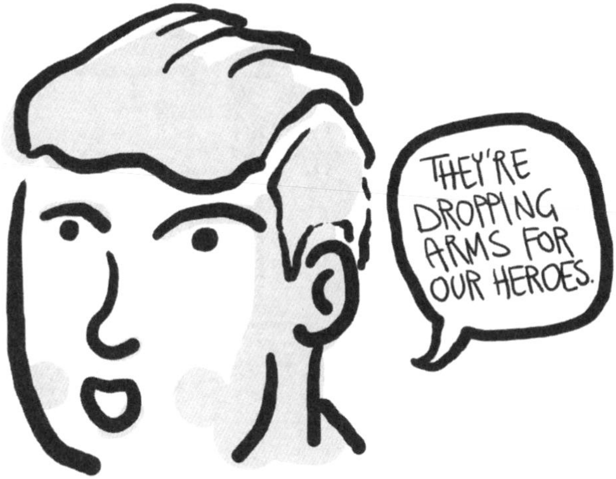
THEY'RE DROPPING ARMS FOR OUR HEROES.

JUST ORDINARY FOLK...

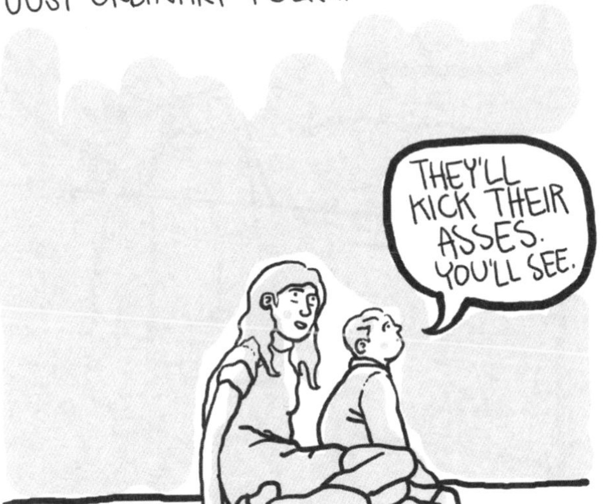
THEY'LL KICK THEIR ASSES. YOU'LL SEE.

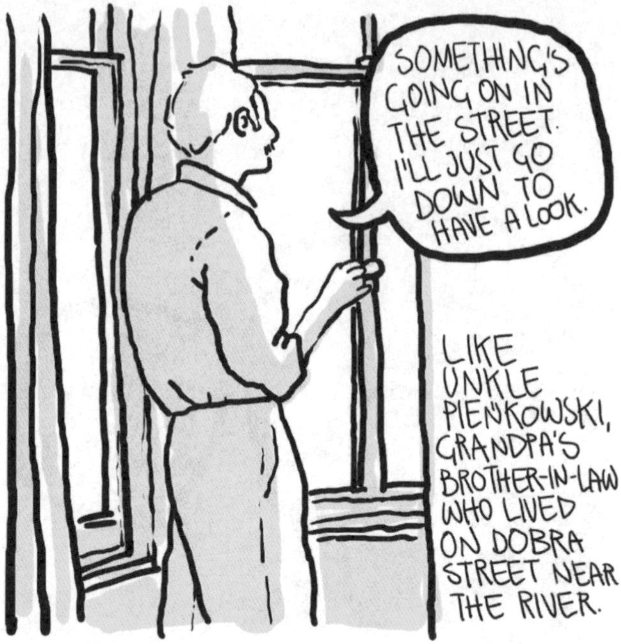
SOMETHING'S GOING ON IN THE STREET. I'LL JUST GO DOWN TO HAVE A LOOK.
LIKE UNKLE PIEŃKOWSKI, GRANDPA'S BROTHER-IN-LAW WHO LIVED ON DOBRA STREET NEAR THE RIVER.

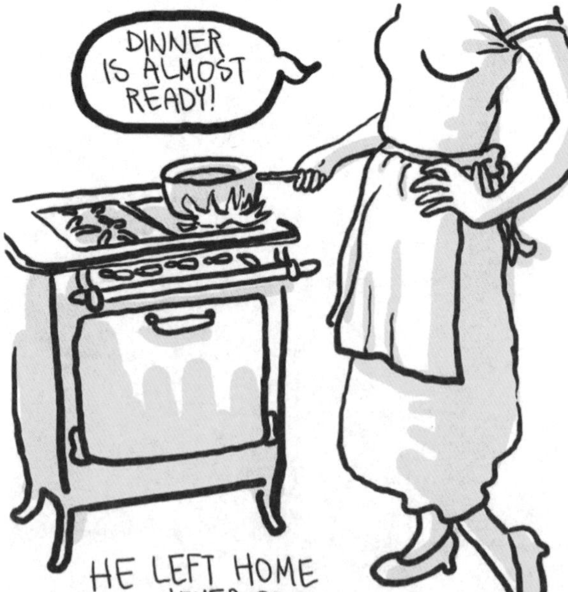
DINNER IS ALMOST READY!
HE LEFT HOME AND NEVER CAME BACK.

MARIA, HIS WIFE, NEVER FOUND OUT WHAT ACTUALLY HAPPENED TO HIM.

SOME SAID HE WAS CAUGHT IN A STREET ROUNDUP. OTHERS, THAT HE WAS SHOT.

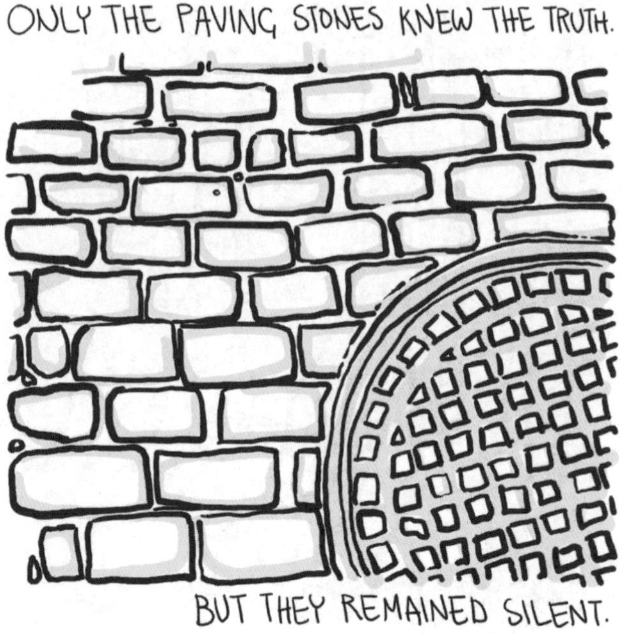
ONLY THE PAVING STONES KNEW THE TRUTH.
BUT THEY REMAINED SILENT.

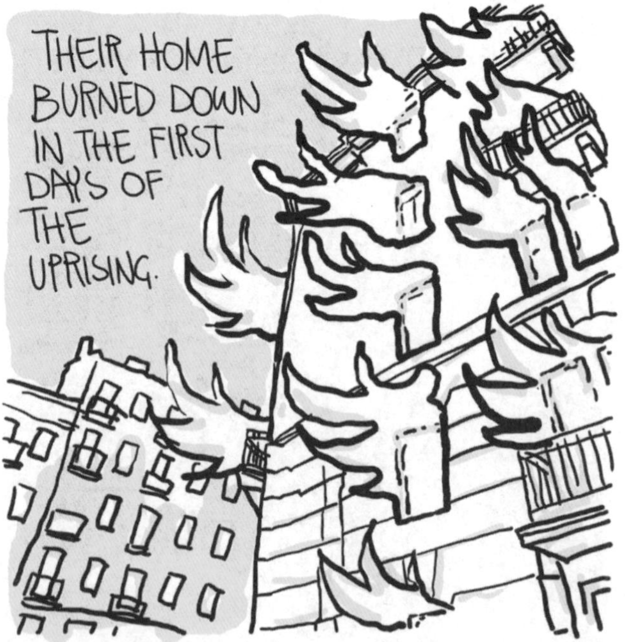
THEIR HOME BURNED DOWN IN THE FIRST DAYS OF THE UPRISING.

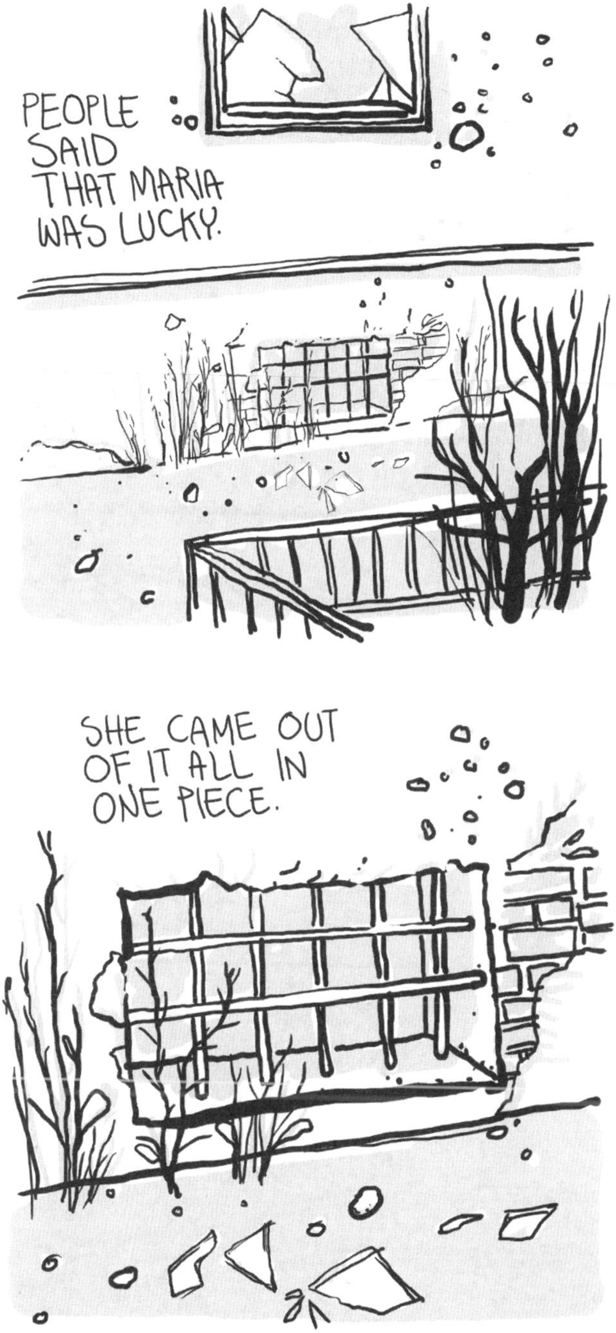
PEOPLE SAID THAT MARIA WAS LUCKY.
SHE CAME OUT OF IT ALL IN ONE PIECE.

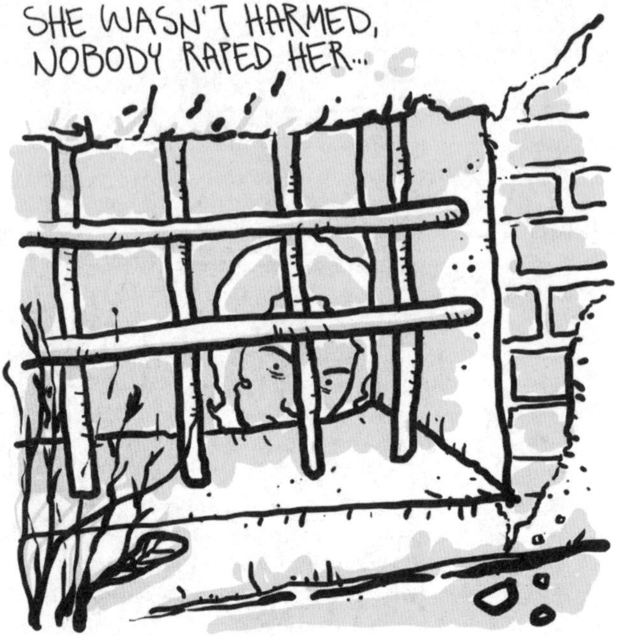
SHE WASN'T HARMED, NOBODY RAPED HER...

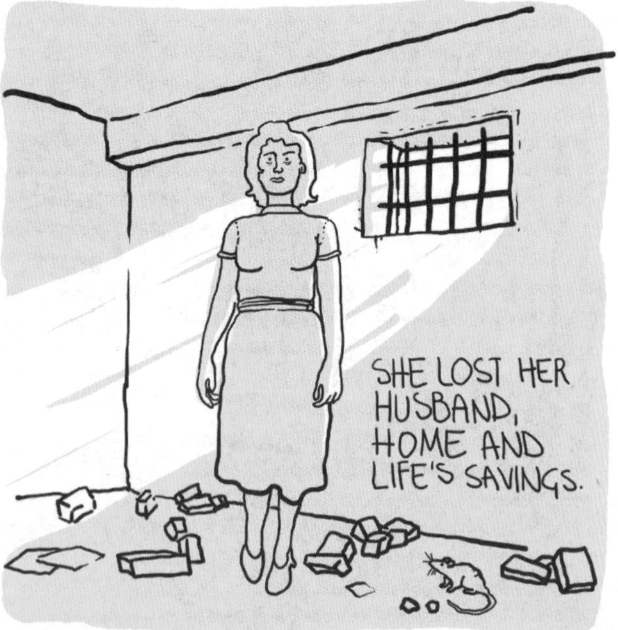
SHE LOST HER HUSBAND, HOME AND LIFE'S SAVINGS.

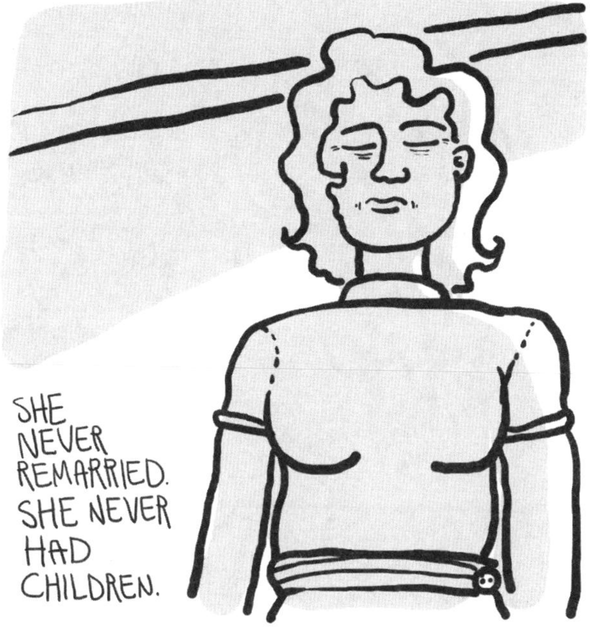
SHE NEVER REMARRIED. SHE NEVER HAD CHILDREN.

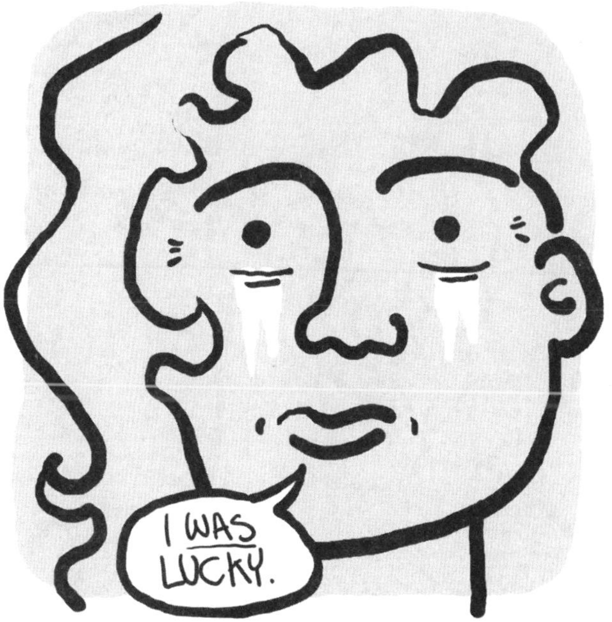
I WAS LUCKY.

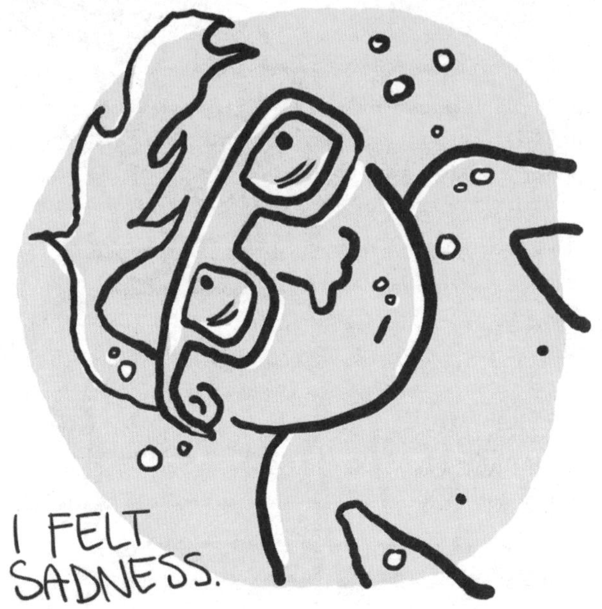
I FELT SADNESS.

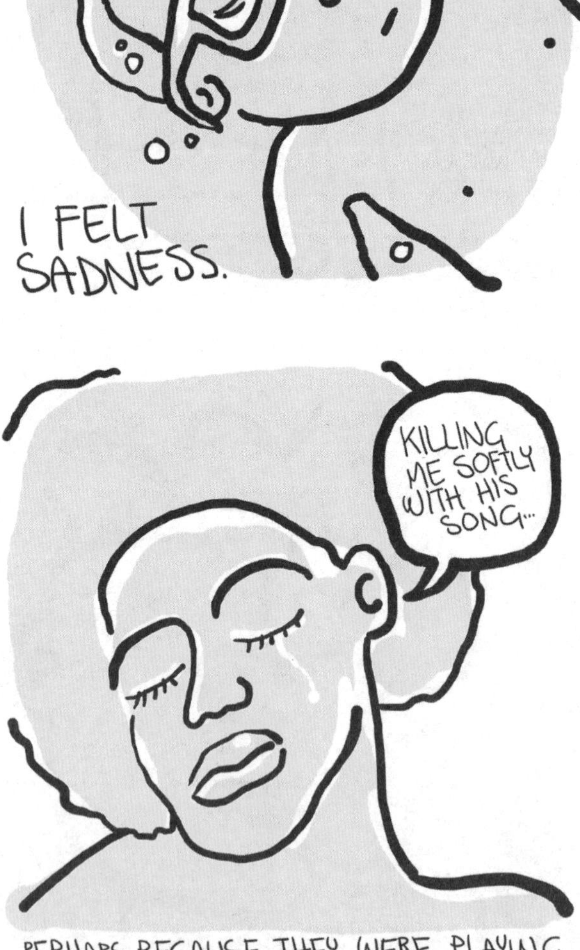
KILLING ME SOFTLY WITH HIS SONG...
PERHAPS BECAUSE THEY WERE PLAYING ROBERTA FLACK ON THE RADIO.

MY MUM WOULD ALWAYS LISTEN TO
THE RADIO WHEN SHE WAS DRIVING.

AND SHE ONLY DROVE WHEN SHE
WAS SAD. OR ANGRY.

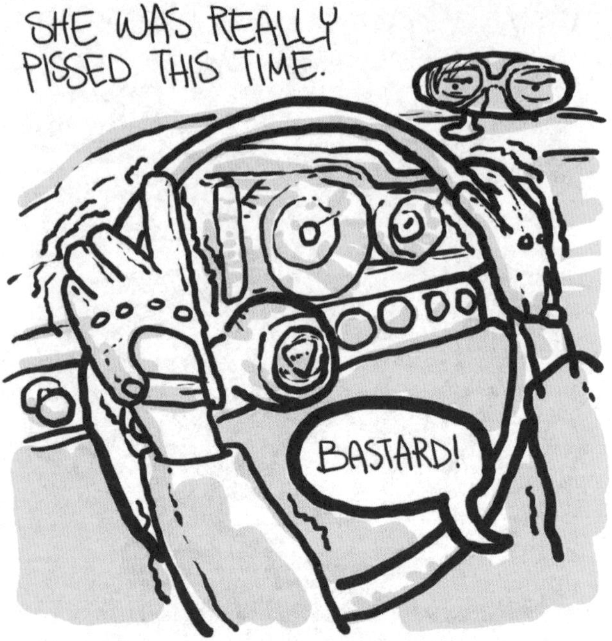
SHE WAS REALLY PISSED THIS TIME.
BASTARD!

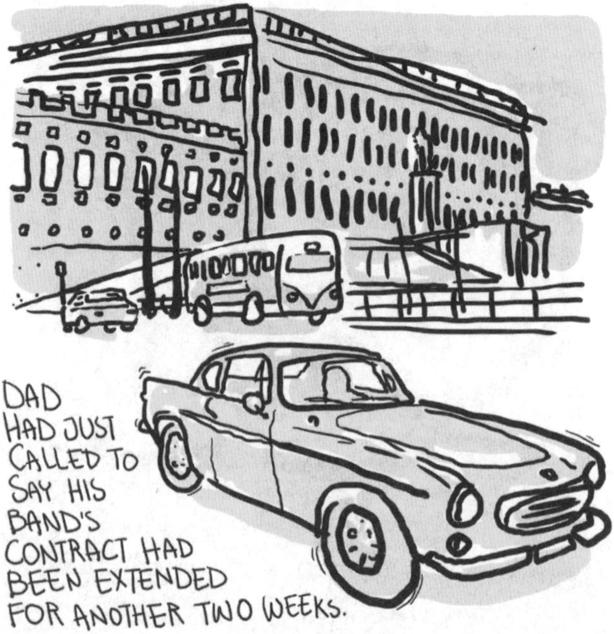
DAD HAD JUST CALLED TO SAY HIS BAND'S CONTRACT HAD BEEN EXTENDED FOR ANOTHER TWO WEEKS.

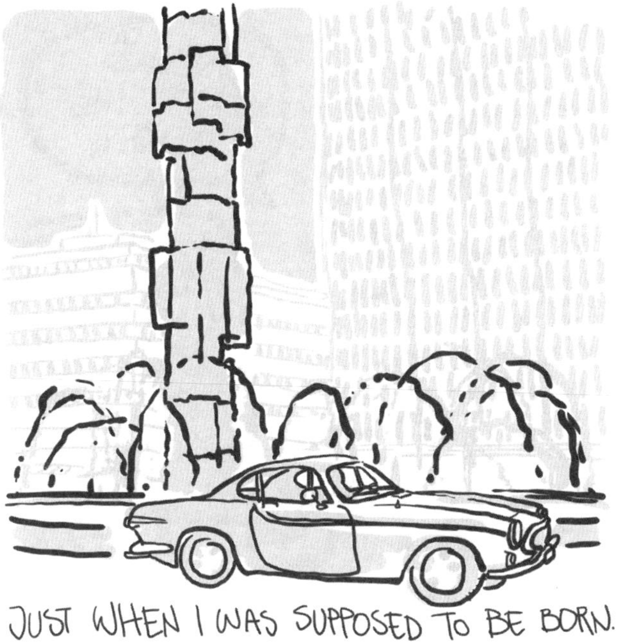
JUST WHEN I WAS SUPPOSED TO BE BORN.

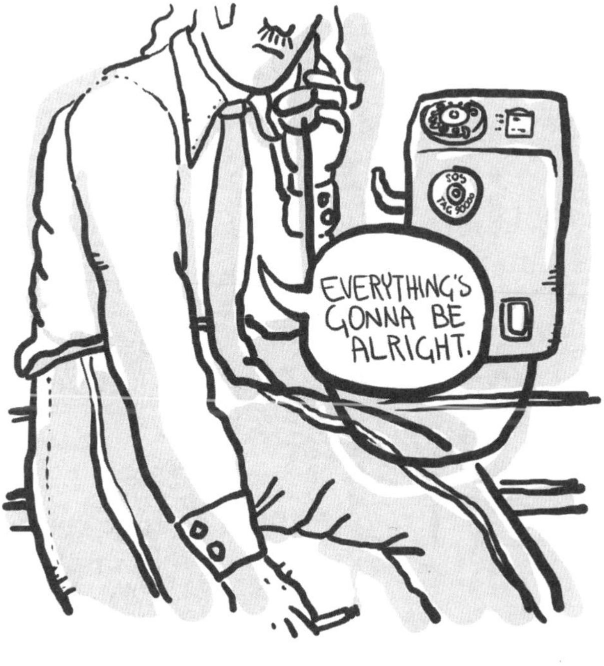
EVERYTHING'S GONNA BE ALRIGHT.

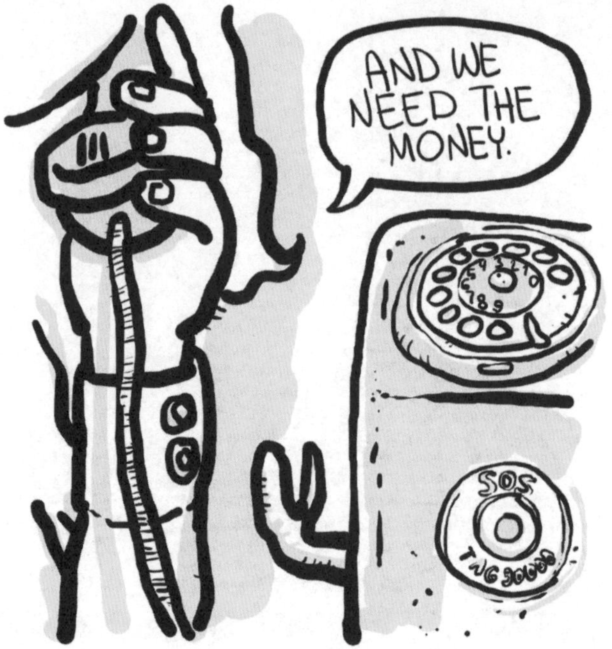
AND WE NEED THE MONEY.
SOS

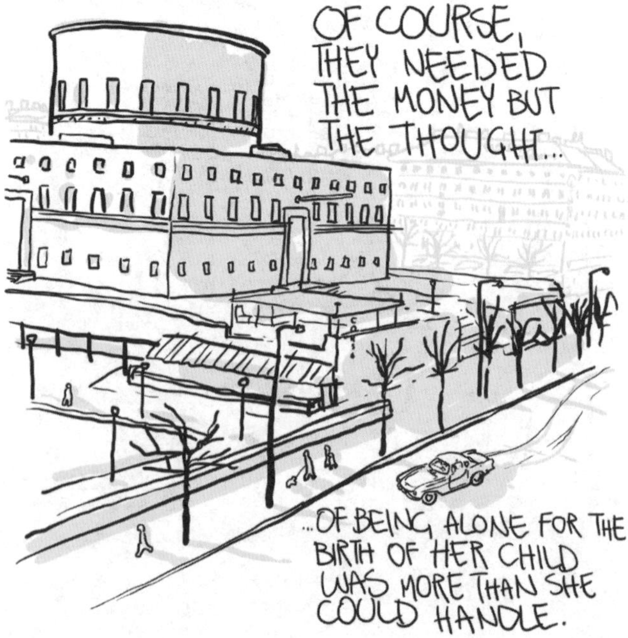
OF COURSE, THEY NEEDED THE MONEY BUT THE THOUGHT...
...OF BEING ALONE FOR THE BIRTH OF HER CHILD WAS MORE THAN SHE COULD HANDLE.

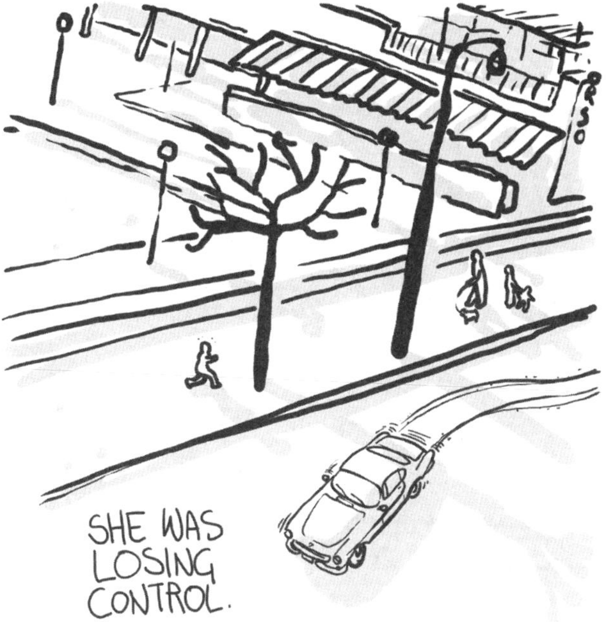
SHE WAS LOSING CONTROL.

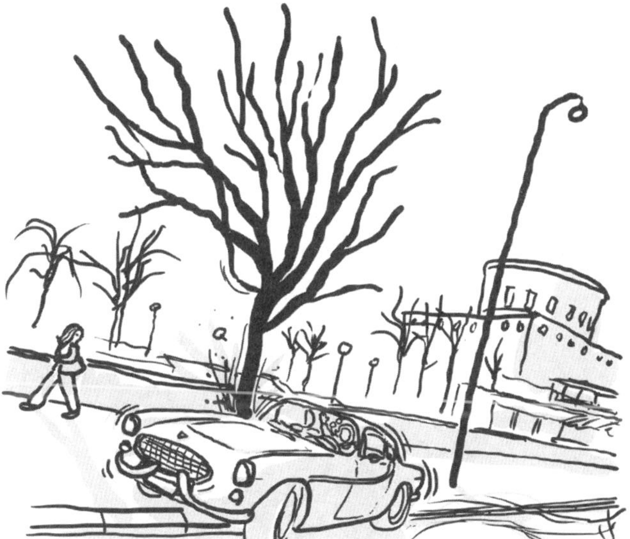
COMPLETELY...

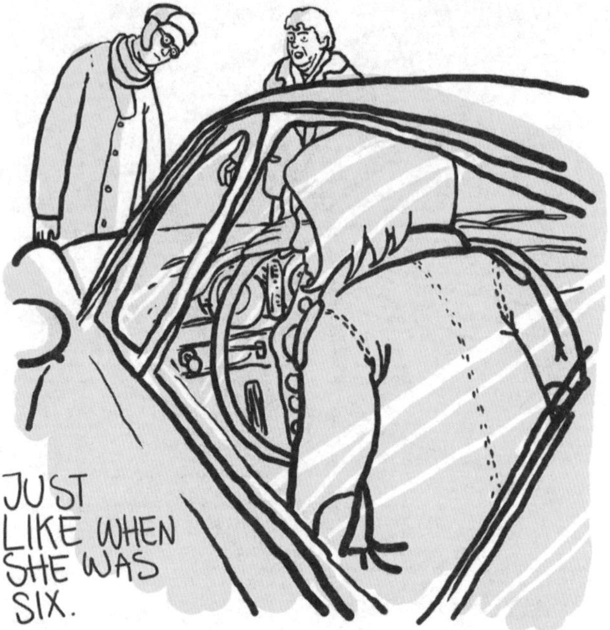
JUST LIKE WHEN SHE WAS SIX.

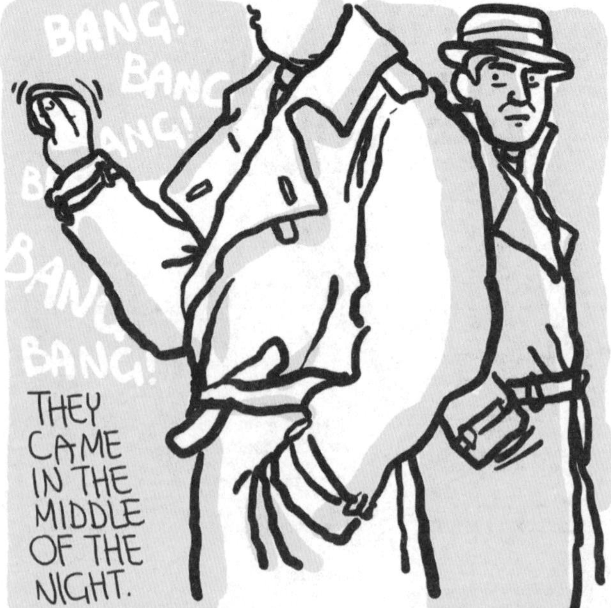
BANG!
BANG
BANG!
BANG!
BANG!
THEY CAME IN THE MIDDLE OF THE NIGHT.

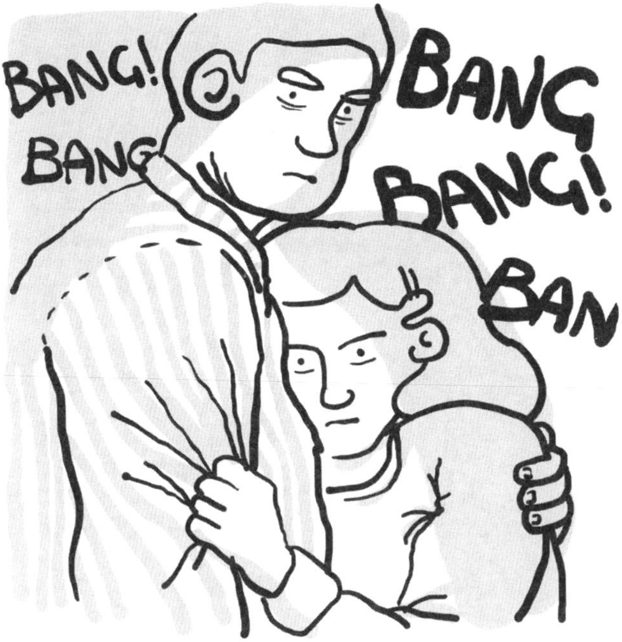
BANG!
BANG
BANG
BANG!
BAN

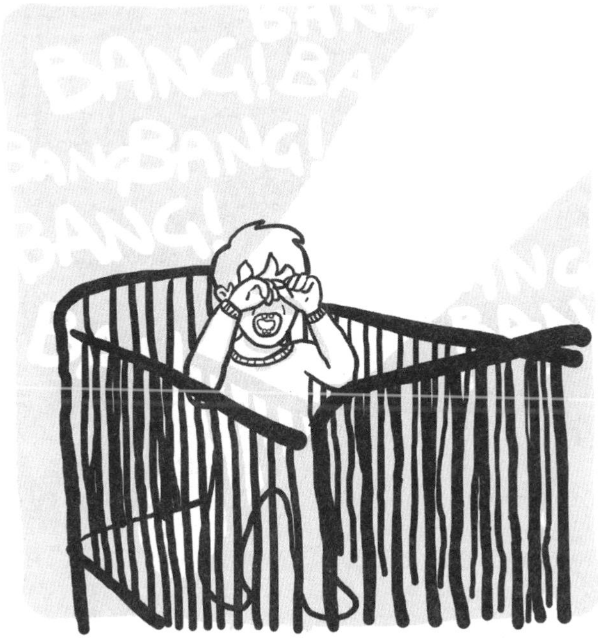

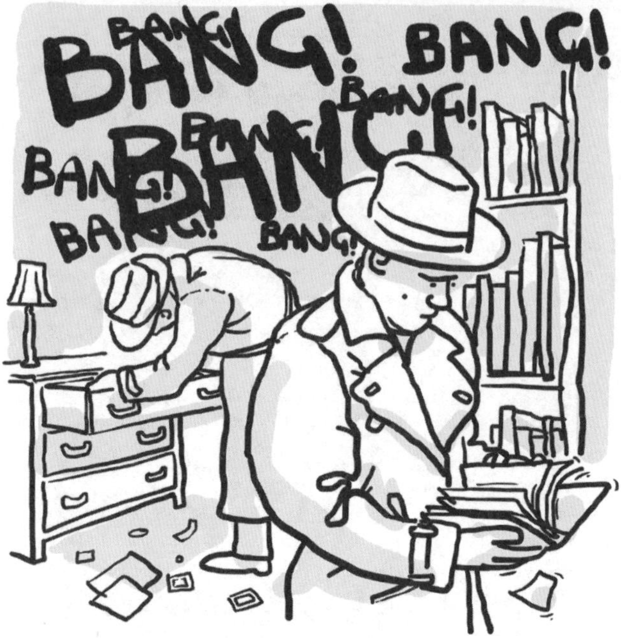
BANG!
BANG!
BANG!
BANG!
BANG!
BANG!

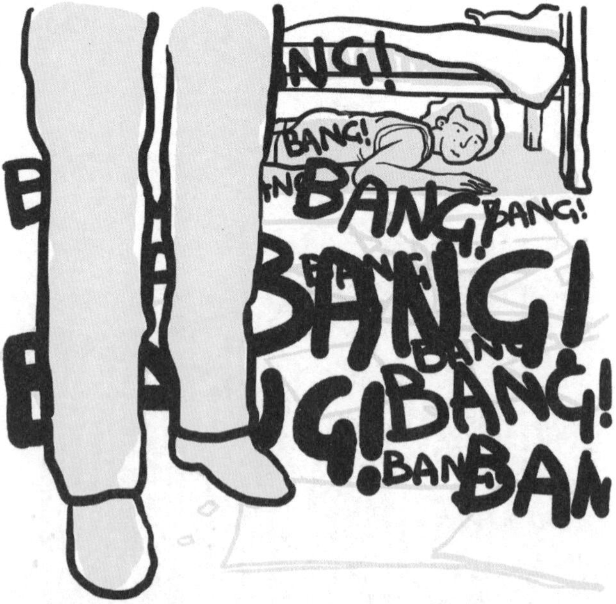
BANG!
BANG!
BANG!
BANG!
BANG!

BANG!
BANG!
BAN
BANG!
BANG!
BANG
BANG
BANG!
BANG!
BANG
BANG!
BANG!

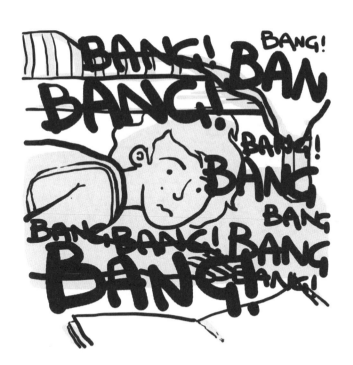

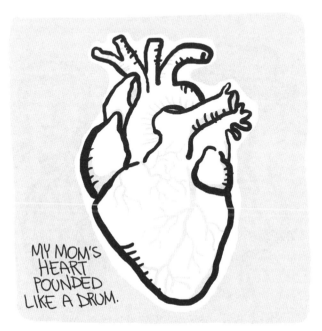

MY MOM'S HEART POUNDED LIKE A DRUM.

THAT NIGHT HER WORLD SHATTERED.

FOR THE FIRST TIME IN HER LIFE SHE WAS AFRAID.

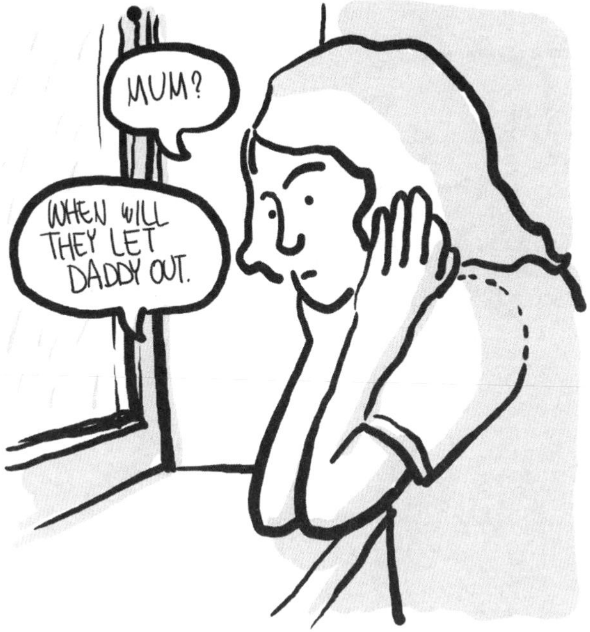
MUM?
WHEN WILL THEY LET DADDY OUT.

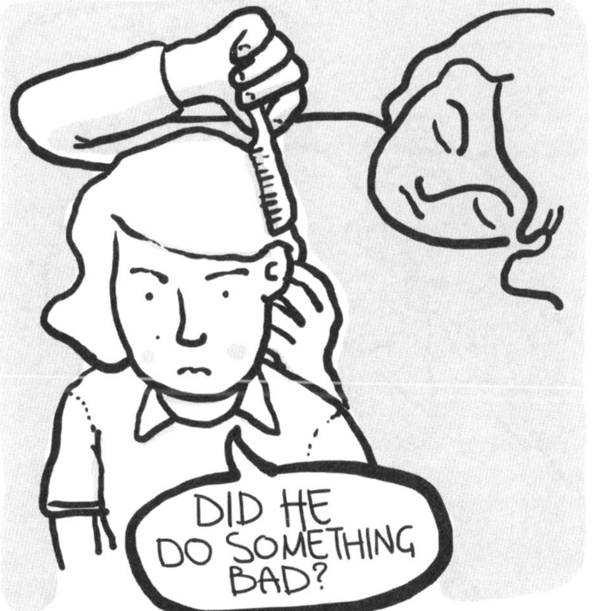
DID HE DO SOMETHING BAD?

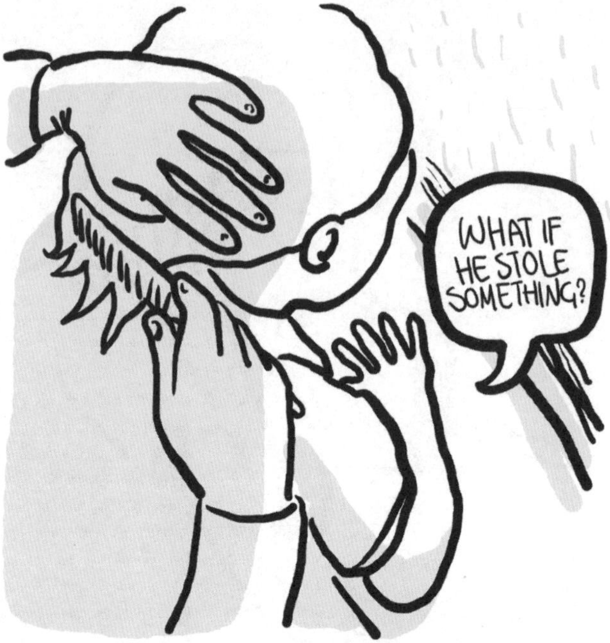
WHAT IF HE STOLE SOMETHING?

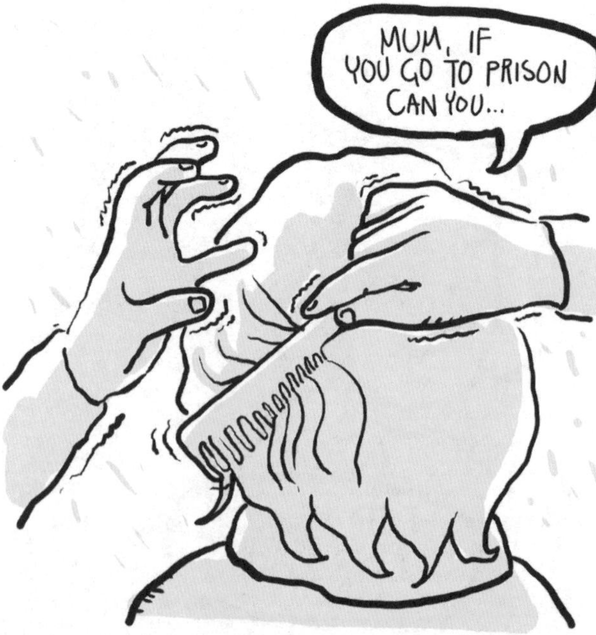
MUM, IF YOU GO TO PRISON CAN YOU...

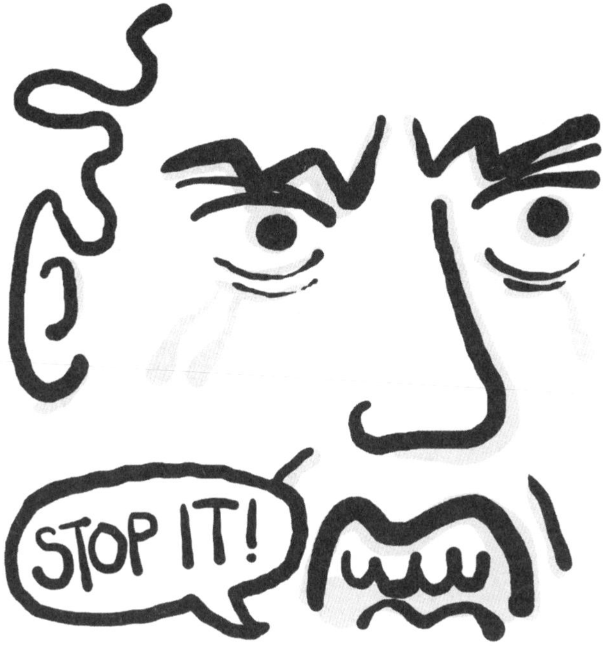
STOP IT!

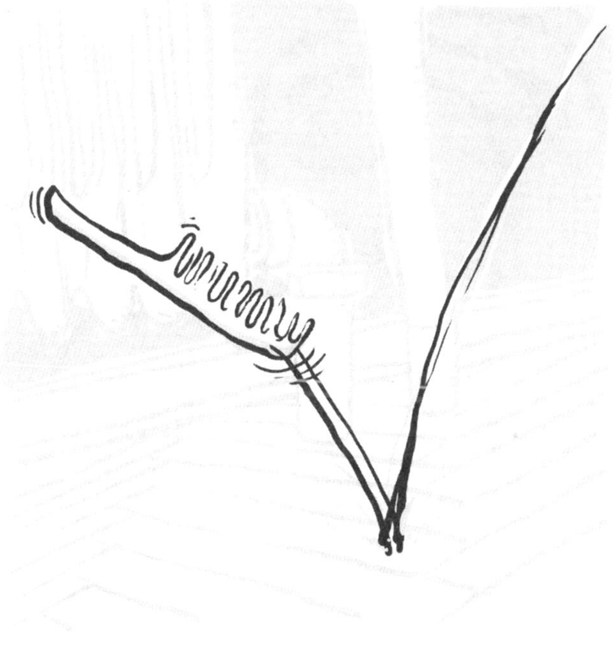

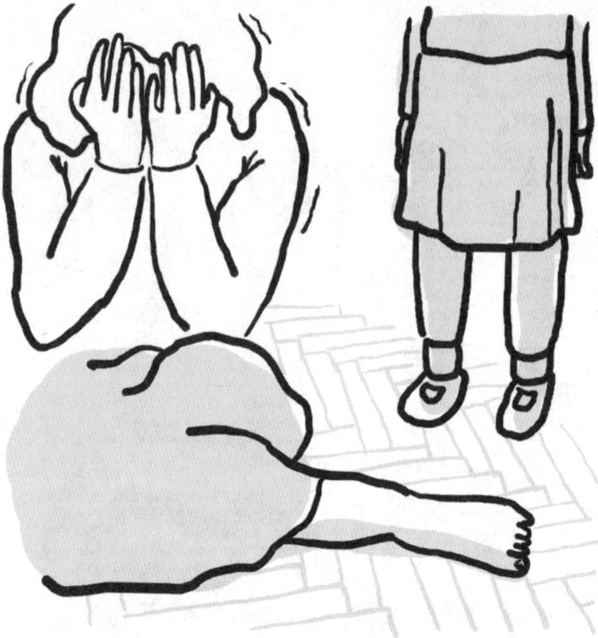

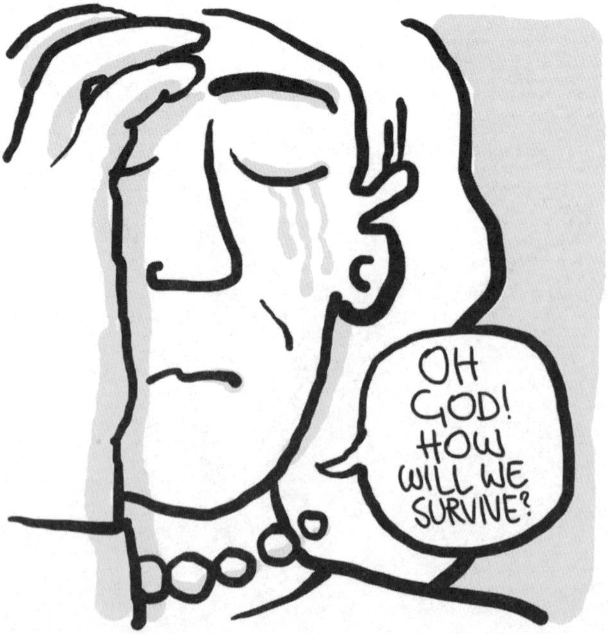
OH GOD! HOW WILL WE SURVIVE?

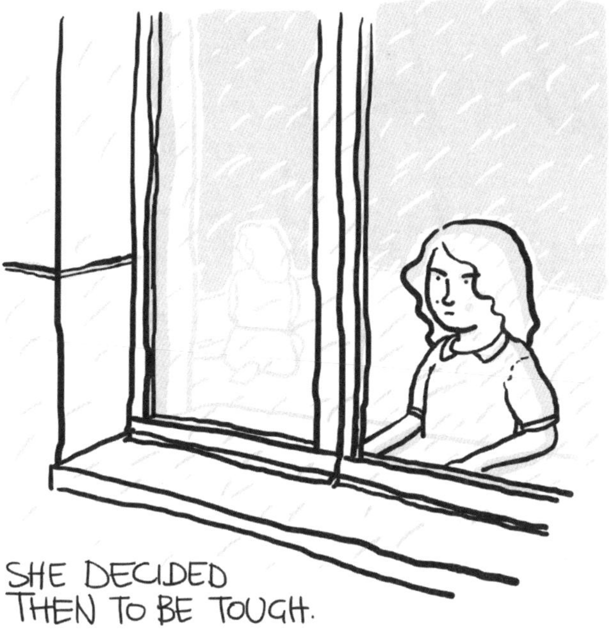
SHE DECIDED THEN TO BE TOUGH.

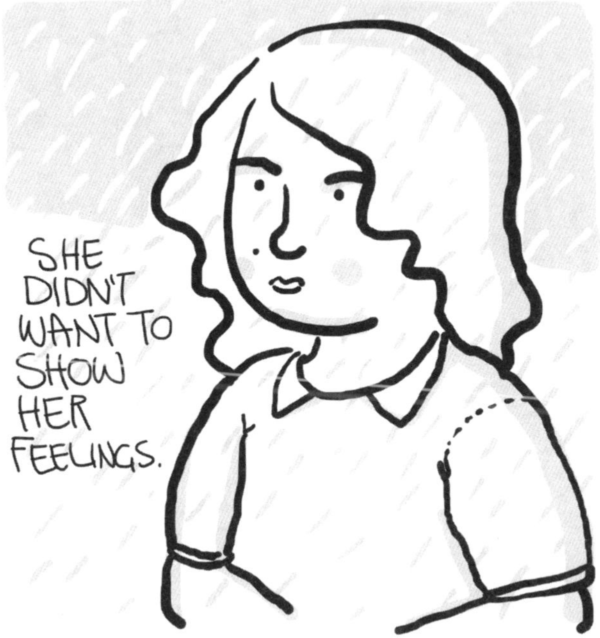
SHE DIDN'T WANT TO SHOW HER FEELINGS.

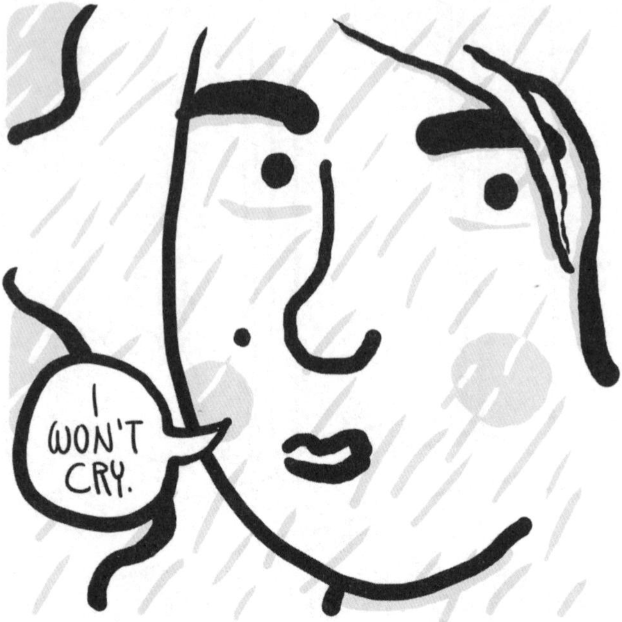
I WON'T CRY.

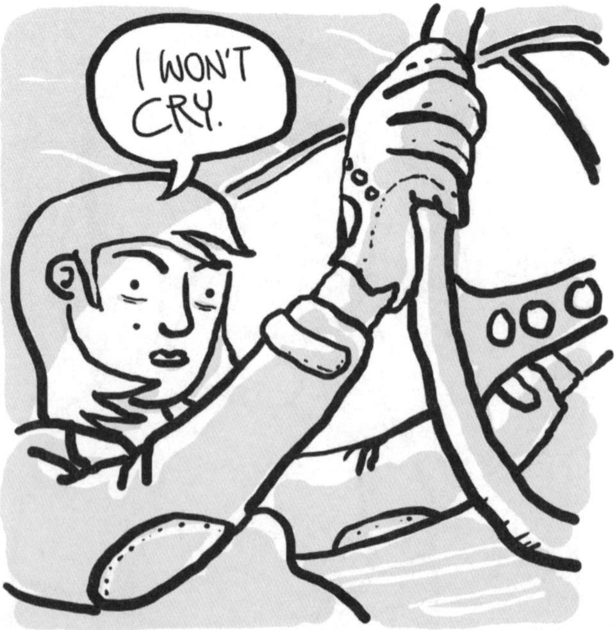
I WON'T CRY.

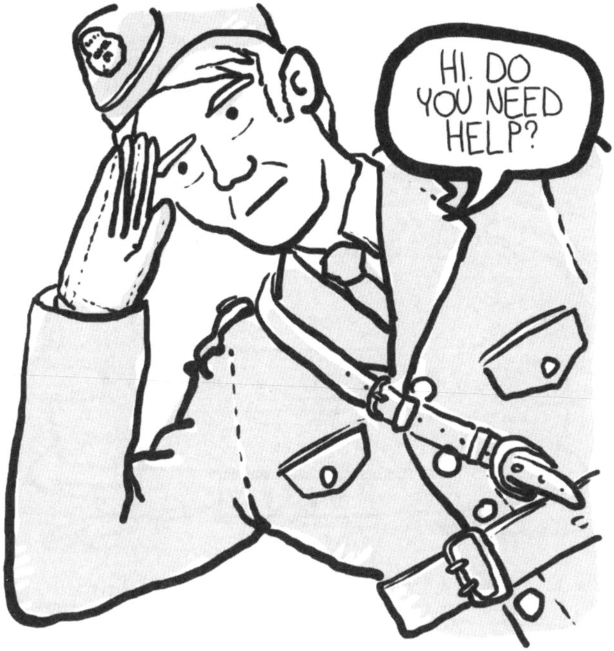
HI. DO YOU NEED HELP?

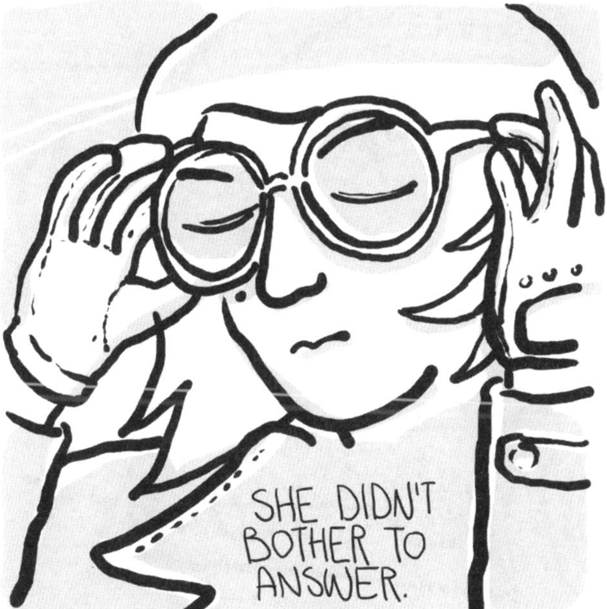
SHE DIDN'T BOTHER TO ANSWER.

SHE JUST STEPPED ON THE GAS
AND KEPT GOING.

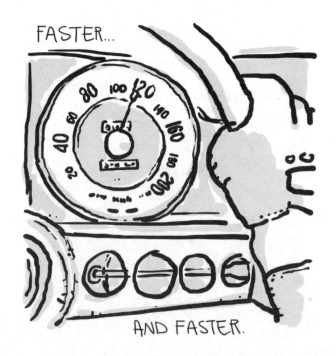

FASTER...

AND FASTER.

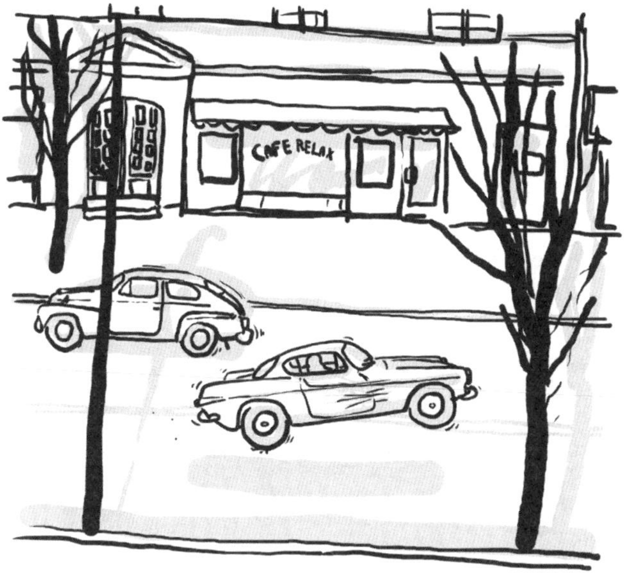
CAFE RELAX

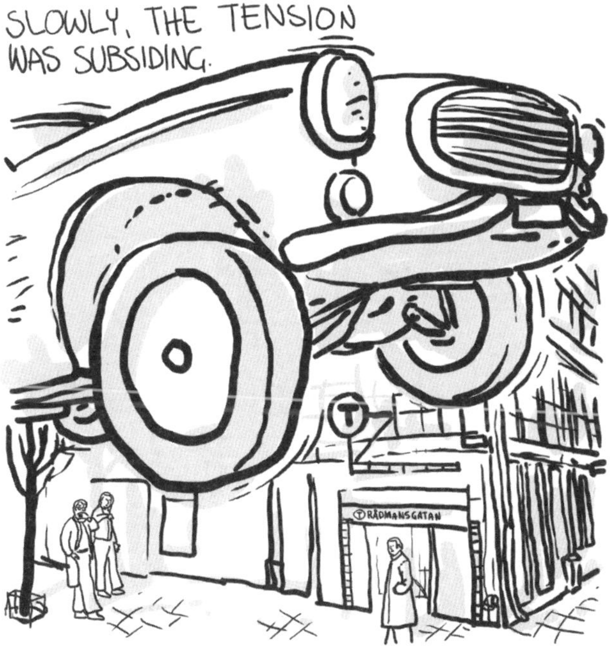
SLOWLY, THE TENSION WAS SUBSIDING.
RÅDMANSGATAN

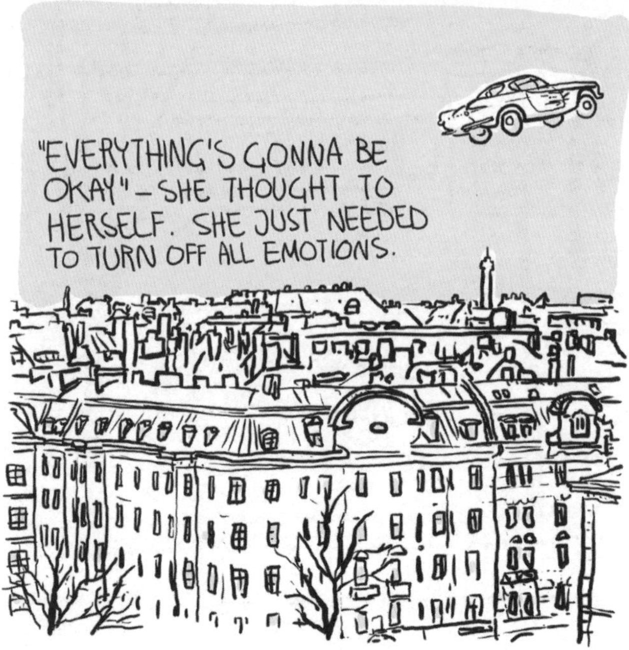
"EVERYTHING'S GONNA BE OKAY" – SHE THOUGHT TO HERSELF. SHE JUST NEEDED TO TURN OFF ALL EMOTIONS.

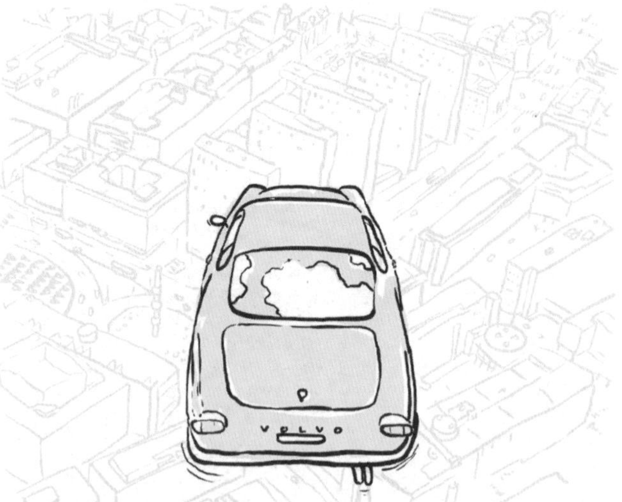
VOLVO

ZERO OUT HER FEELINGS.

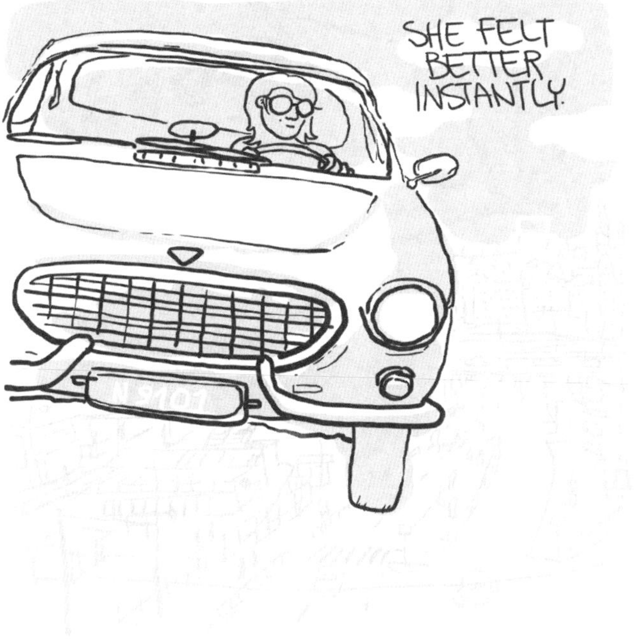
SHE FELT BETTER INSTANTLY.

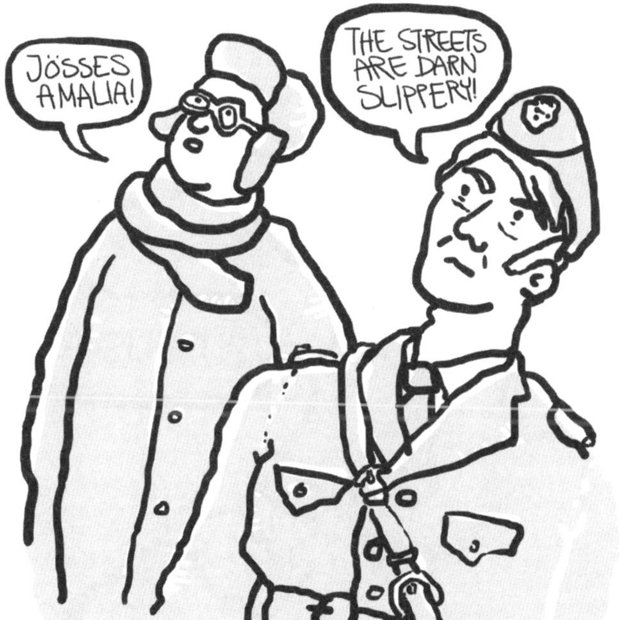
JÖSSES AMALIA!
THE STREETS ARE DARN SLIPPERY!

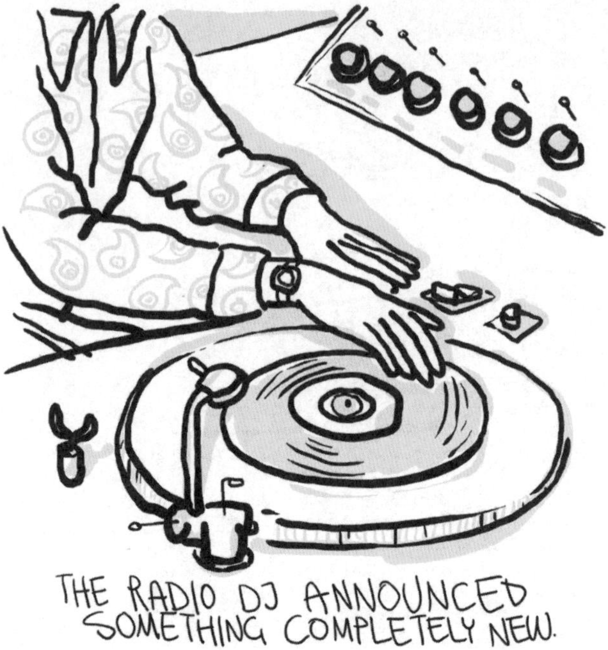
THE RADIO DJ ANNOUNCED SOMETHING COMPLETELY NEW.

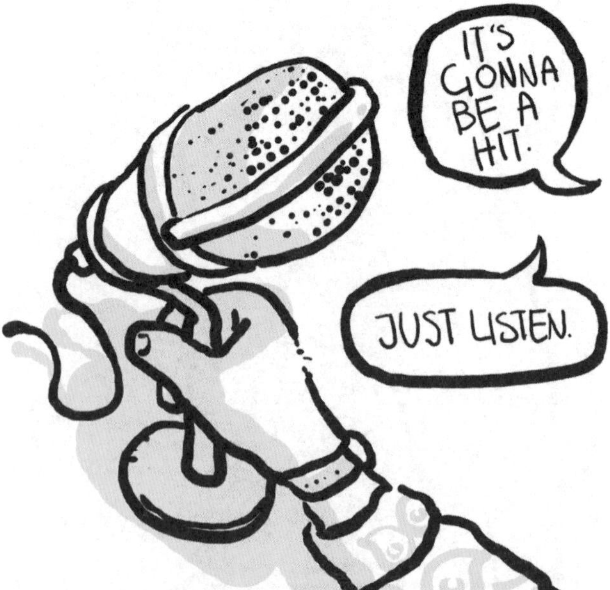
IT'S GONNA BE A HIT.
JUST LISTEN.

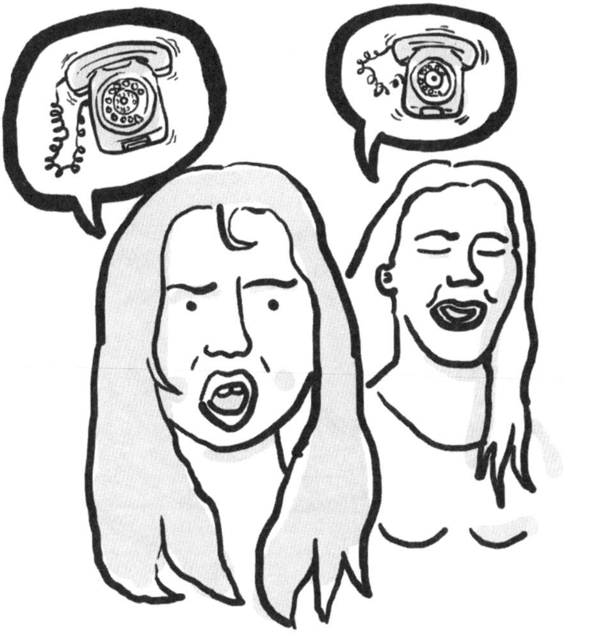

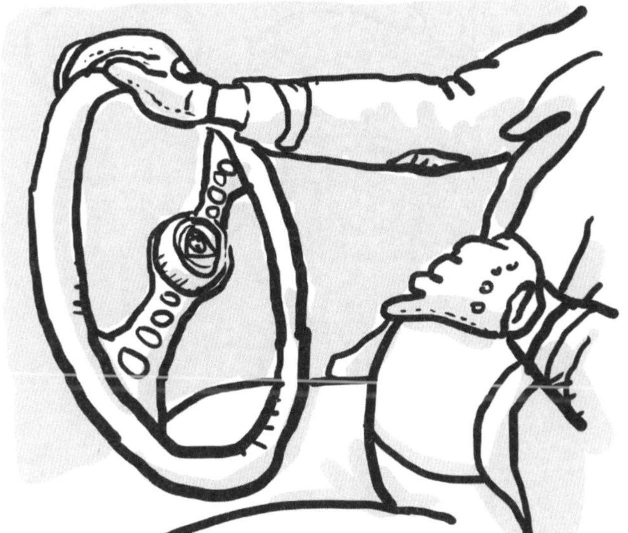
I STARTED TO KICK LIKE CRAZY.

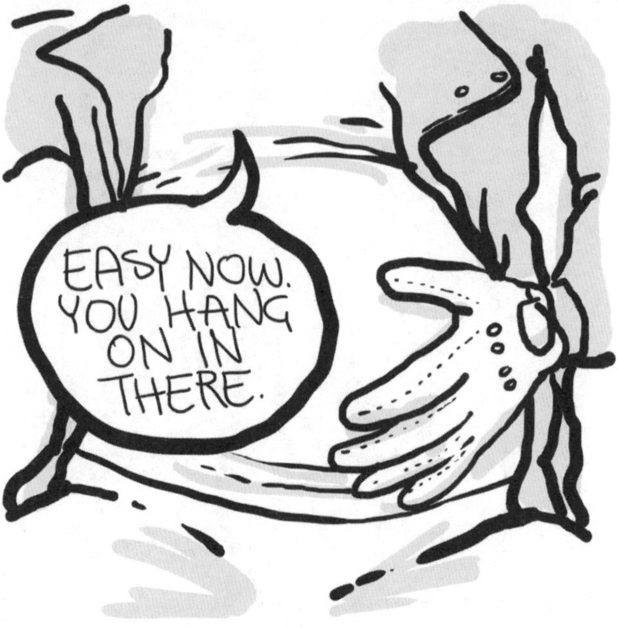
EASY NOW. YOU HANG ON IN THERE.

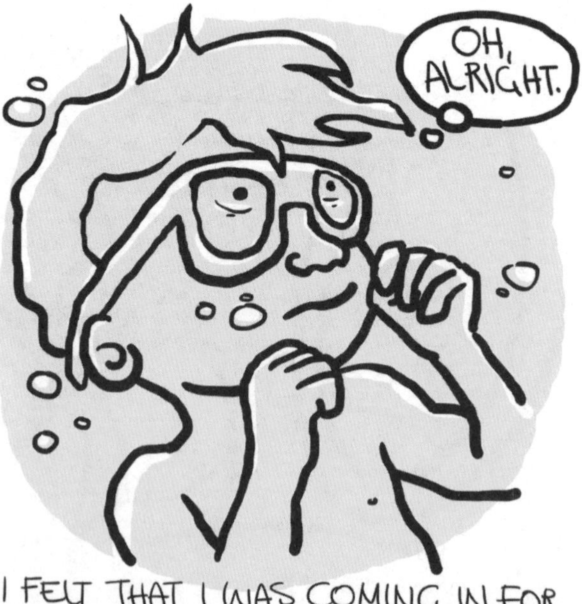
OH, ALRIGHT.

I FELT THAT I WAS COMING IN FOR LANDING. BUT I PROMISED TO WAIT.

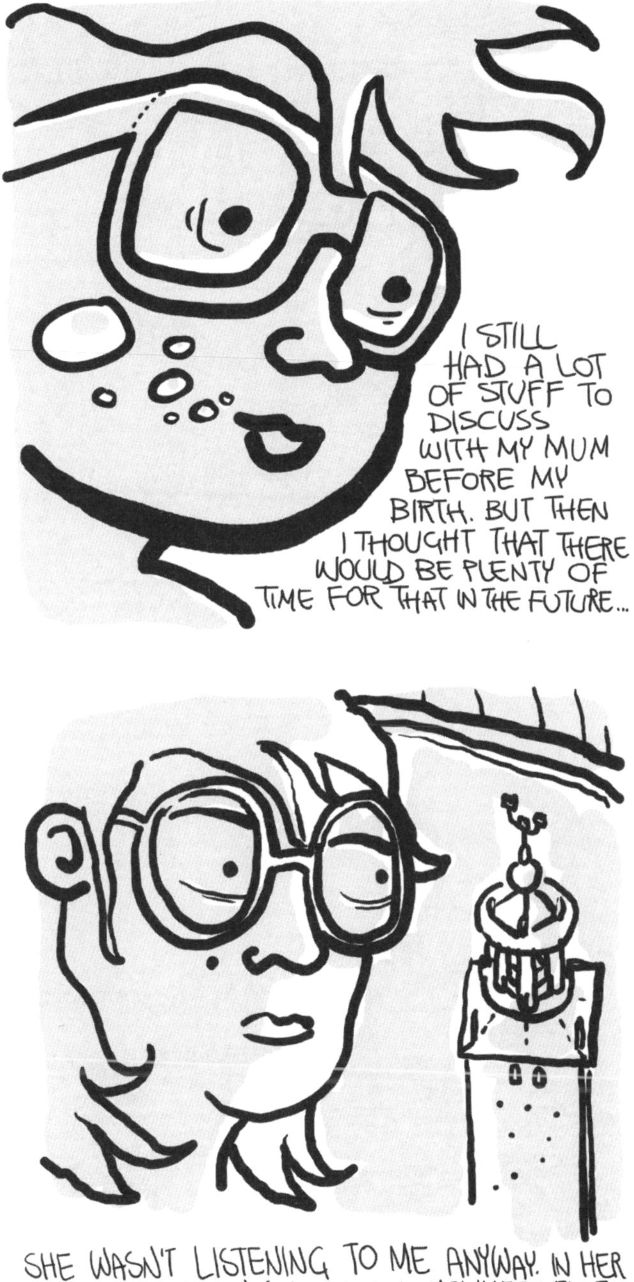
I STILL HAD A LOT OF STUFF TO DISCUSS WITH MY MUM BEFORE MY BIRTH. BUT THEN I THOUGHT THAT THERE WOULD BE PLENTY OF TIME FOR THAT IN THE FUTURE...
SHE WASN'T LISTENING TO ME ANYWAY. IN HER THOUGHTS SHE WAS ALREADY SOMEWHERE ELSE.

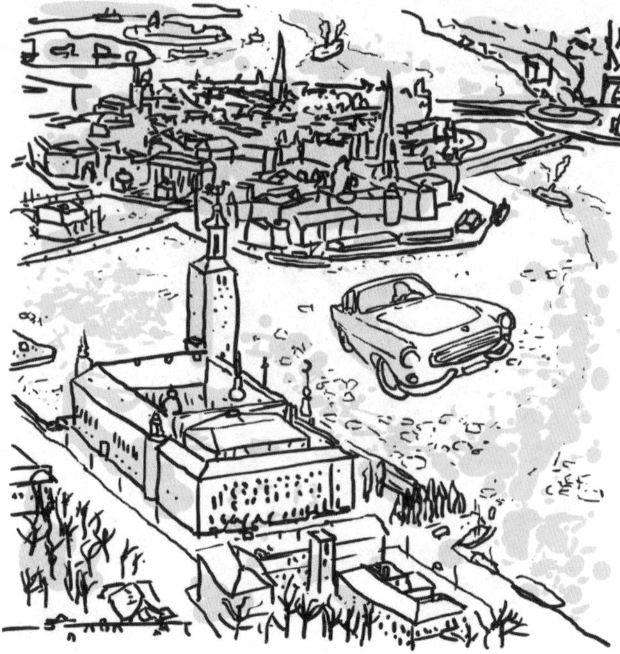

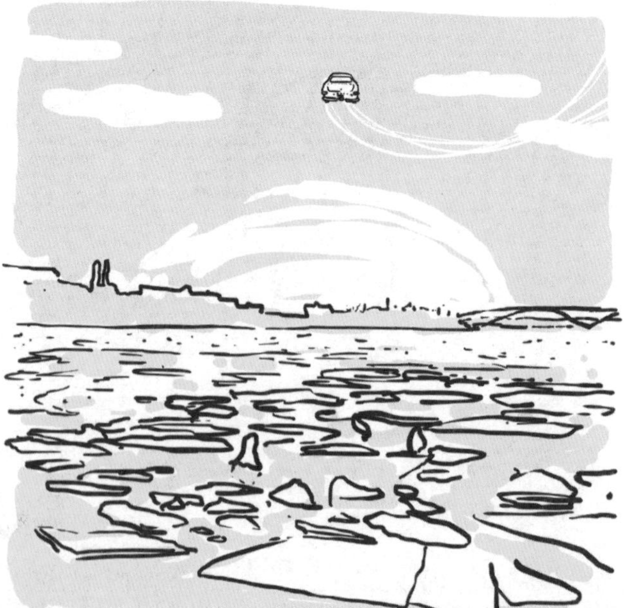

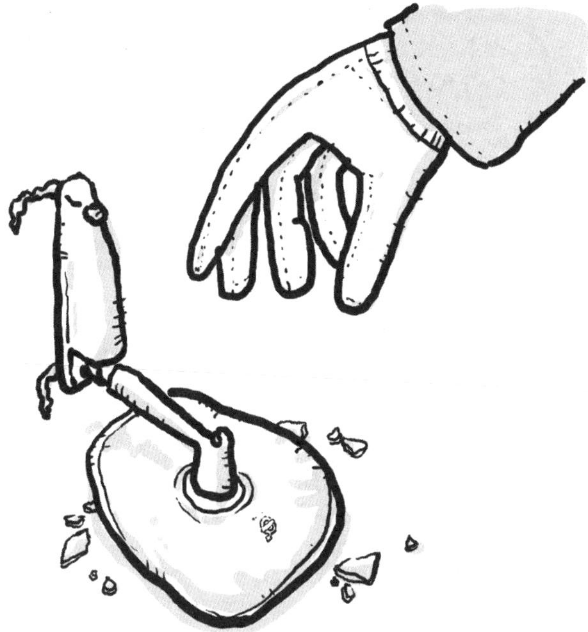

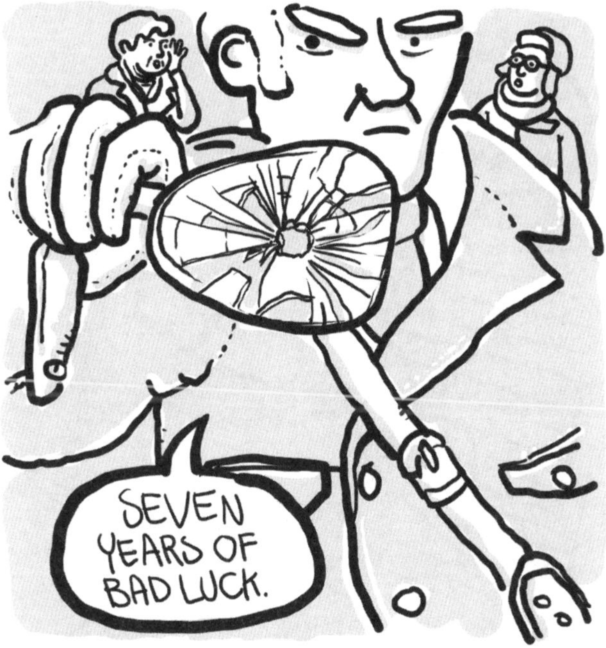
SEVEN YEARS OF BAD LUCK.

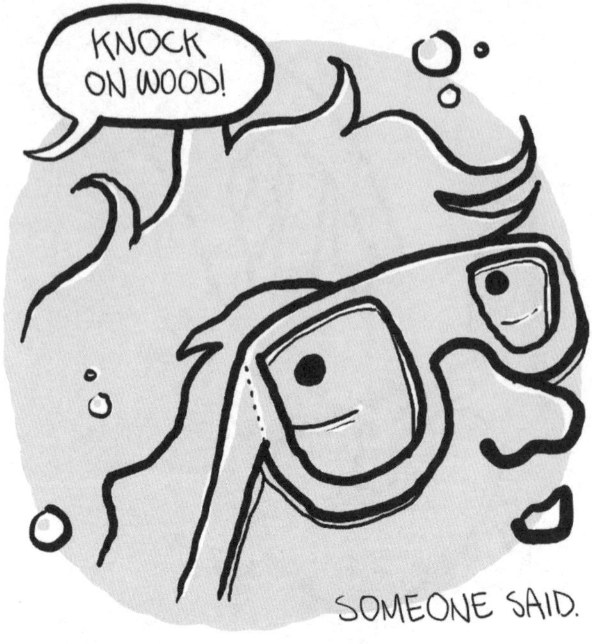
KNOCK ON WOOD!
SOMEONE SAID.

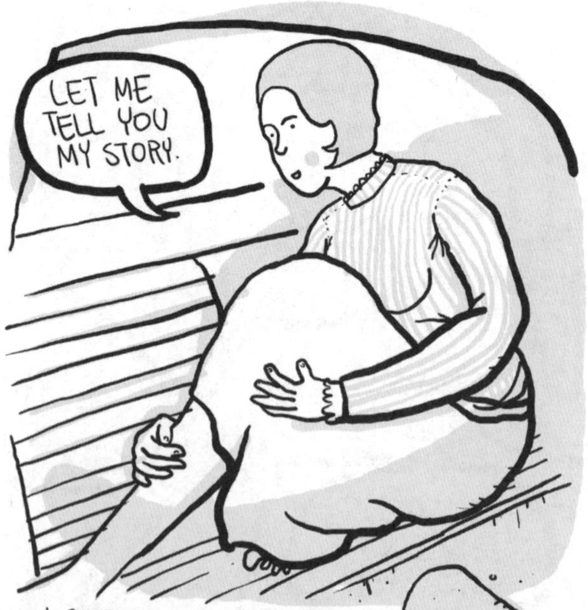
LET ME TELL YOU MY STORY.
MY GREAT-GRANDMOTHER.

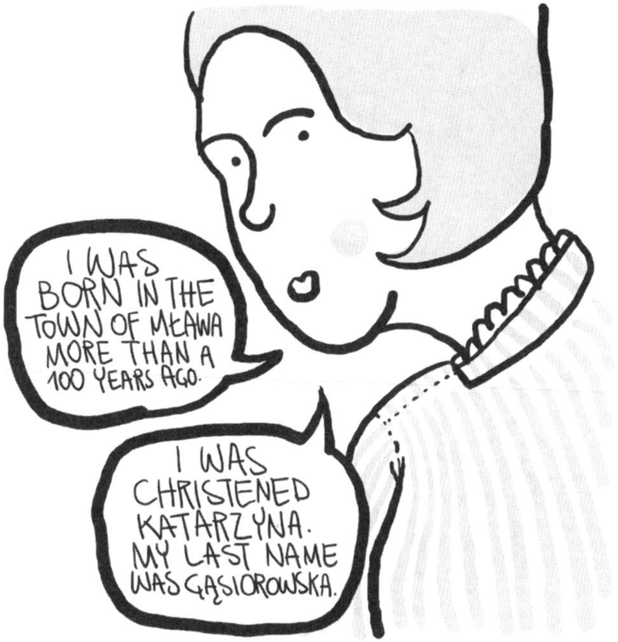
I WAS BORN IN THE TOWN OF MŁAWA MORE THAN A 100 YEARS AGO.
I WAS CHRISTENED KATARZYNA. MY LAST NAME WAS GĄSIOROWSKA.

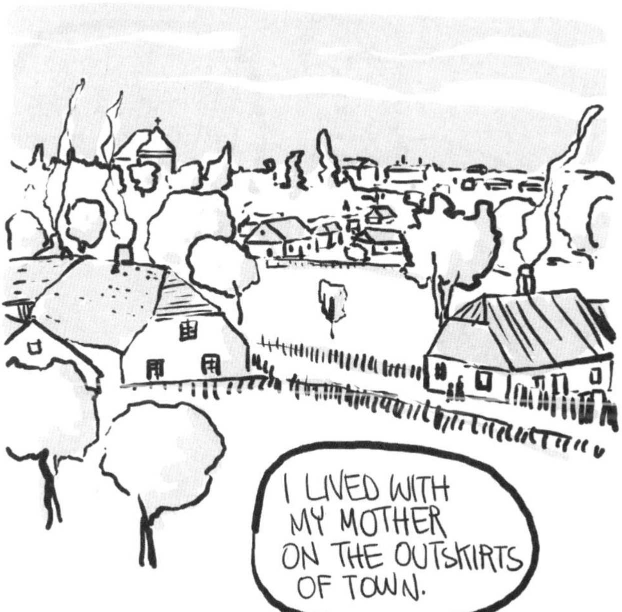
I LIVED WITH MY MOTHER ON THE OUTSKIRTS OF TOWN.

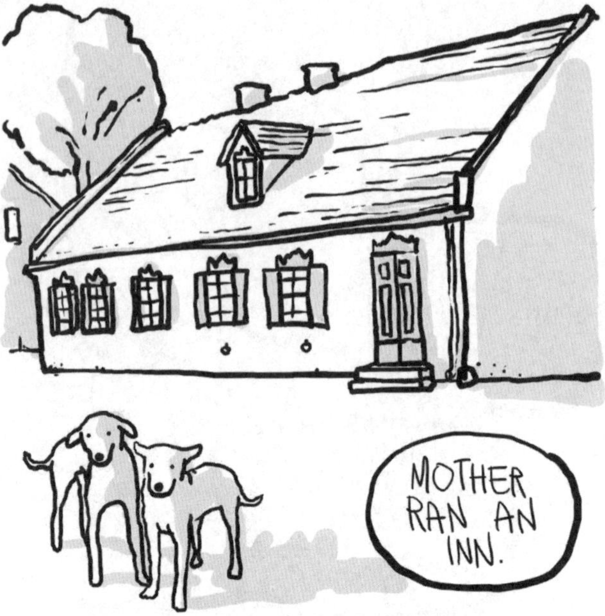
MOTHER RAN AN INN.

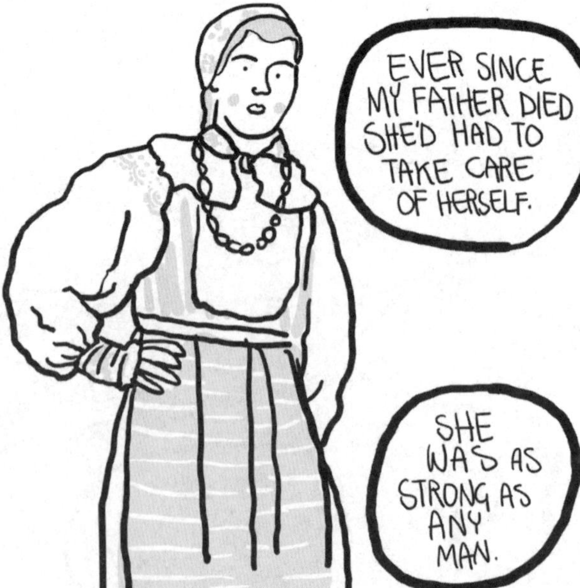
EVER SINCE MY FATHER DIED SHE'D HAD TO TAKE CARE OF HERSELF.
SHE WAS AS STRONG AS ANY MAN.

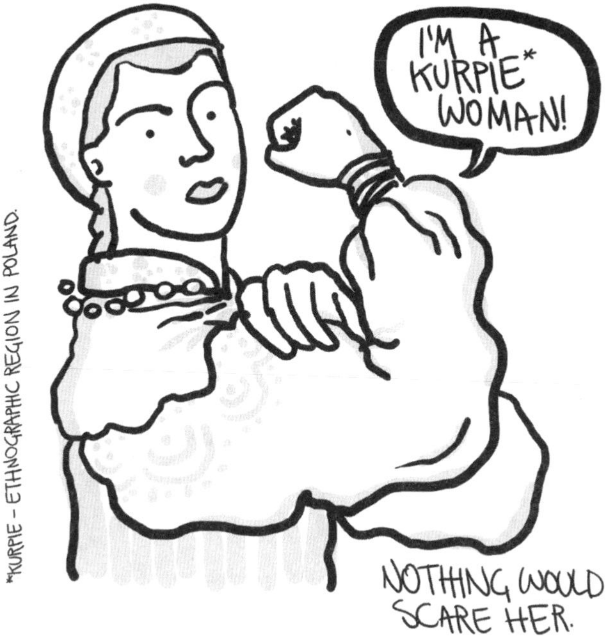
I'M A KURPIE* WOMAN!
NOTHING WOULD SCARE HER.
*KURPIE – ETHNOGRAPHIC REGION IN POLAND.

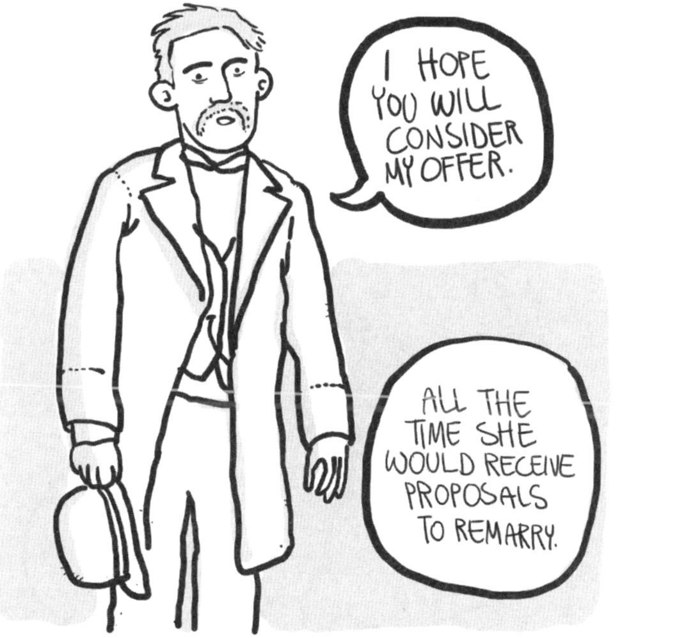
I HOPE YOU WILL CONSIDER MY OFFER.
ALL THE TIME SHE WOULD RECEIVE PROPOSALS TO REMARRY.

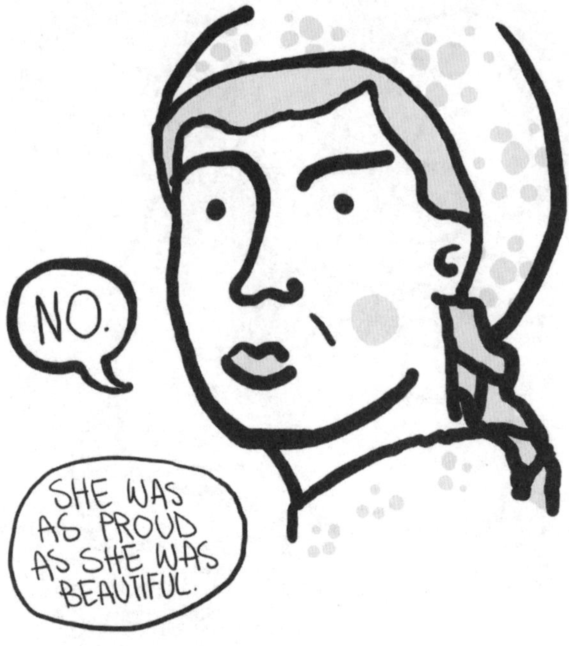
NO.
SHE WAS AS PROUD AS SHE WAS BEAUTIFUL.

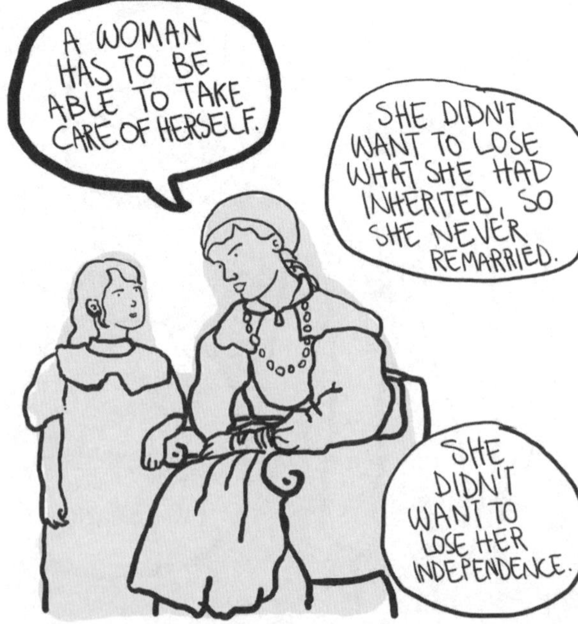
A WOMAN HAS TO BE ABLE TO TAKE CARE OF HERSELF.
SHE DIDN'T WANT TO LOSE WHAT SHE HAD INHERITED, SO SHE NEVER REMARRIED.
SHE DIDN'T WANT TO LOSE HER INDEPENDENCE.

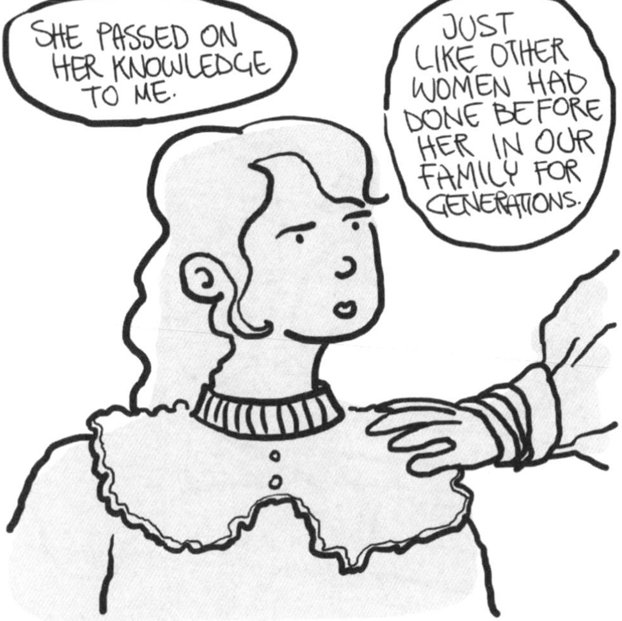
SHE PASSED ON HER KNOWLEDGE TO ME.
JUST LIKE OTHER WOMEN HAD DONE BEFORE HER IN OUR FAMILY FOR GENERATIONS.

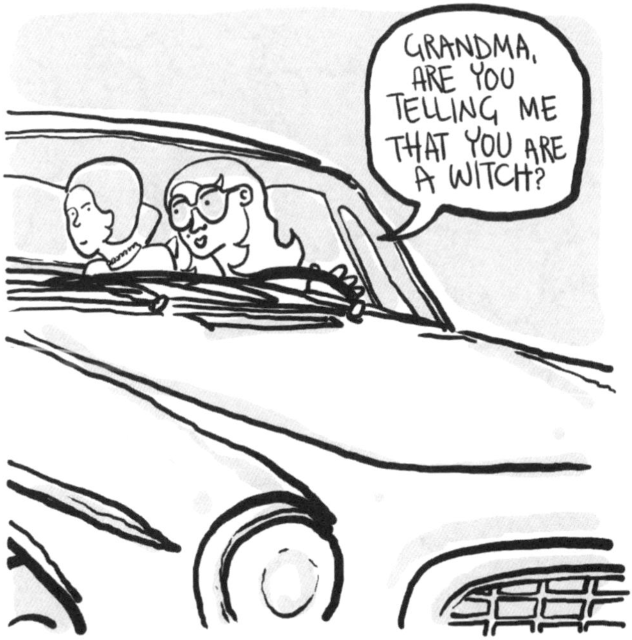
GRANDMA, ARE YOU TELLING ME THAT YOU ARE A WITCH?

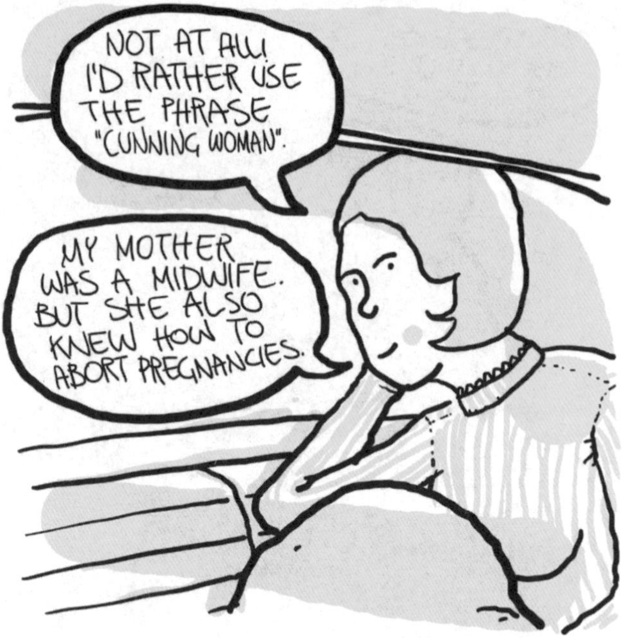
NOT AT ALL! I'D RATHER USE THE PHRASE "CUNNING WOMAN".
MY MOTHER WAS A MIDWIFE. BUT SHE ALSO KNEW HOW TO ABORT PREGNANCIES.

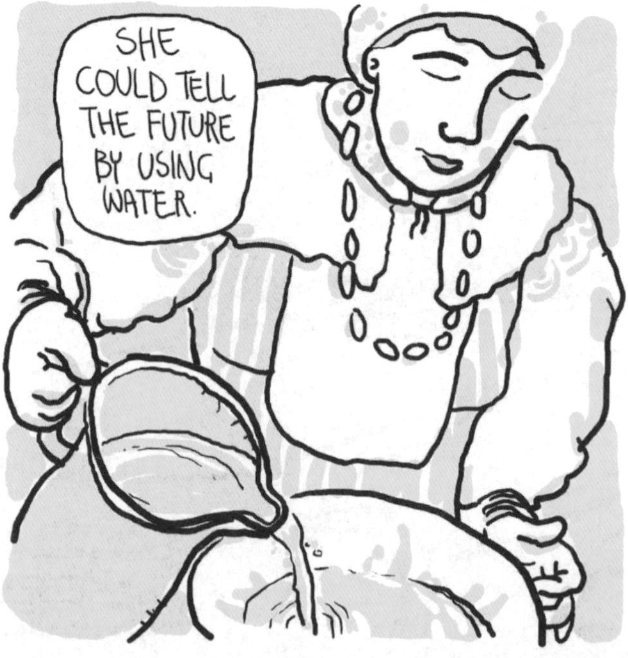
SHE COULD TELL THE FUTURE BY USING WATER.

AT NIGHT SHE WOULD GO OUT IN THE FOREST TO LISTEN TO THE DEAD TALKING.

SHE SHOWED ME ALL OF THIS TO TEACH ME.

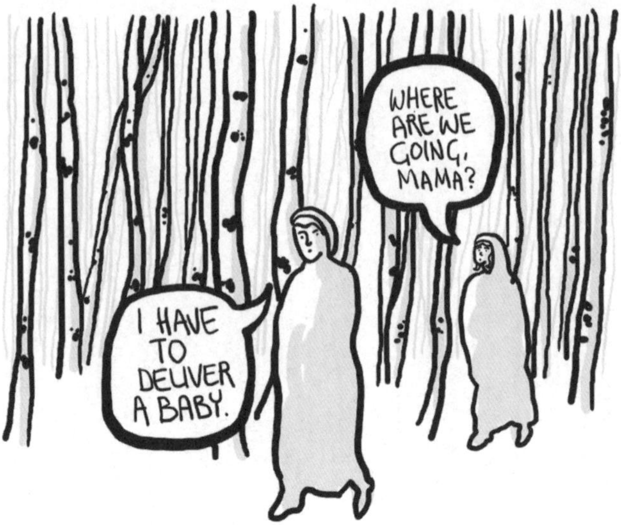
WHERE ARE WE GOING, MAMA?
I HAVE TO DELIVER A BABY.

SO THAT I COULD BECOME LIKE HER.

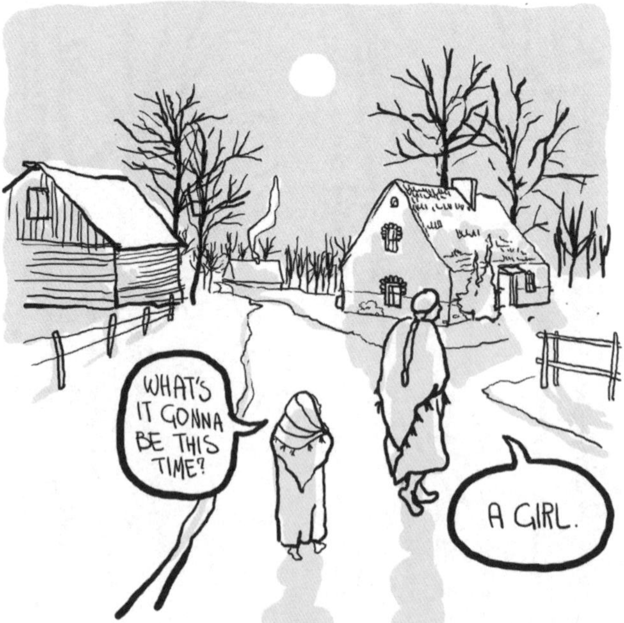
WHAT'S IT GONNA BE THIS TIME?
A GIRL.

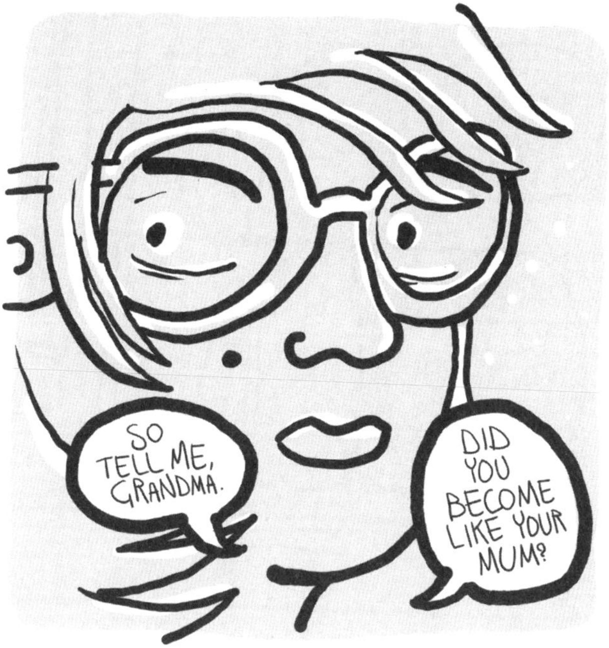
SO TELL ME, GRANDMA.
DID YOU BECOME LIKE YOUR MUM?

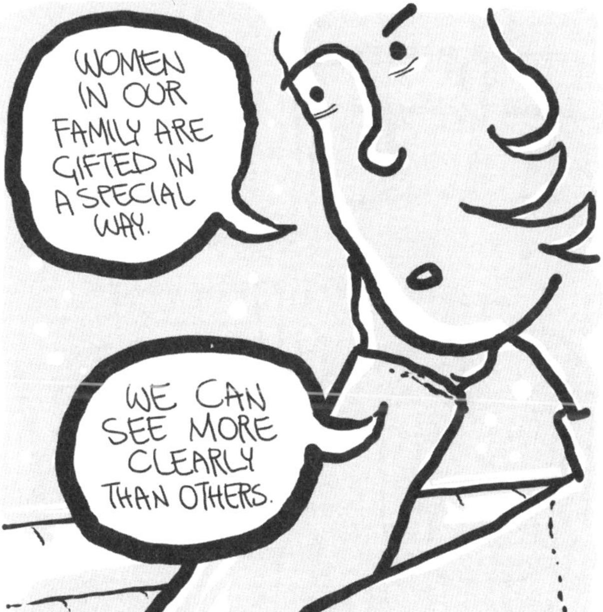
WOMEN IN OUR FAMILY ARE GIFTED IN A SPECIAL WAY.
WE CAN SEE MORE CLEARLY THAN OTHERS.

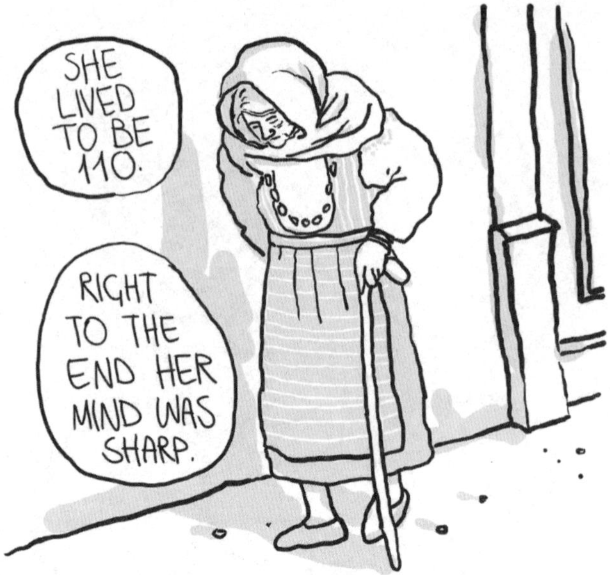
SHE LIVED TO BE 110.
RIGHT TO THE END HER MIND WAS SHARP.

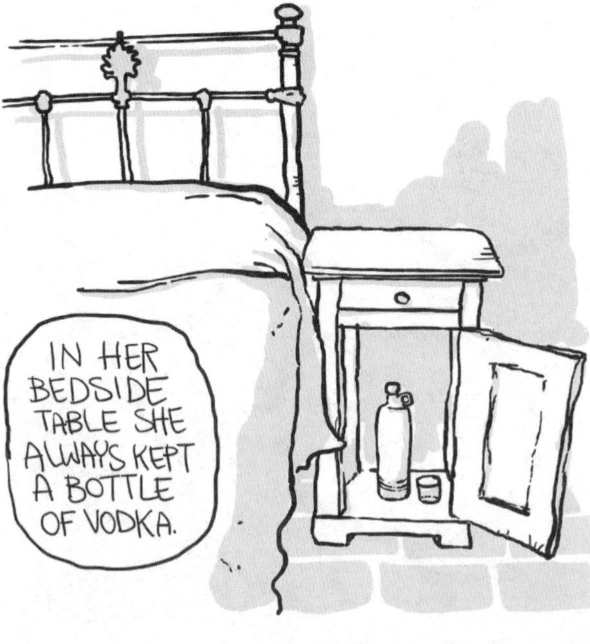
IN HER BEDSIDE TABLE SHE ALWAYS KEPT A BOTTLE OF VODKA.

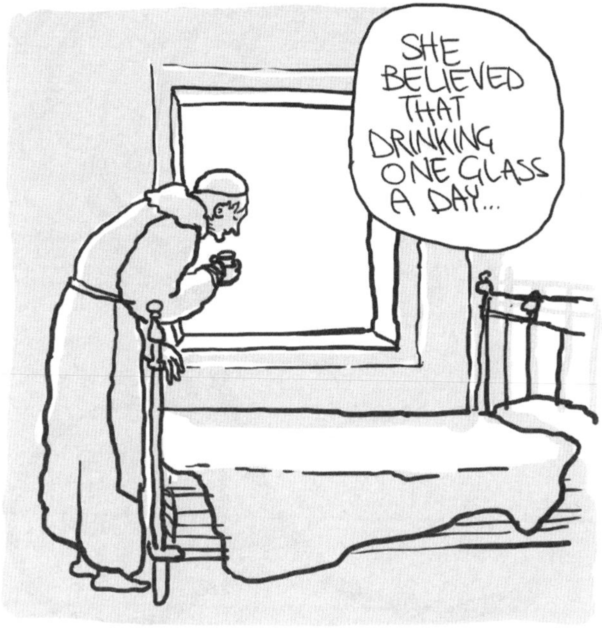
SHE BELIEVED THAT DRINKING ONE GLASS A DAY...

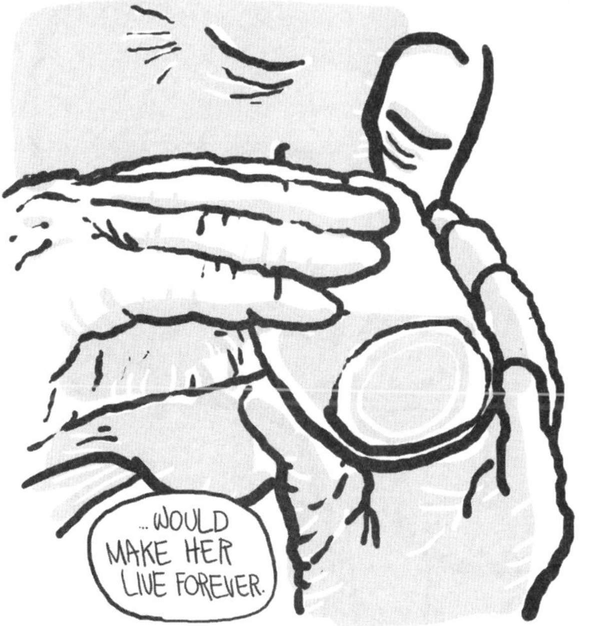
...WOULD MAKE HER LIVE FOREVER.

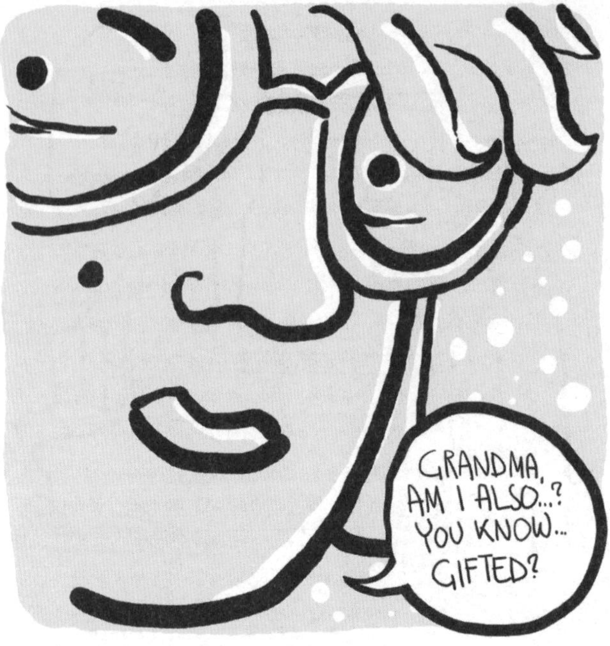
GRANDMA, AM I ALSO...? YOU KNOW... GIFTED?

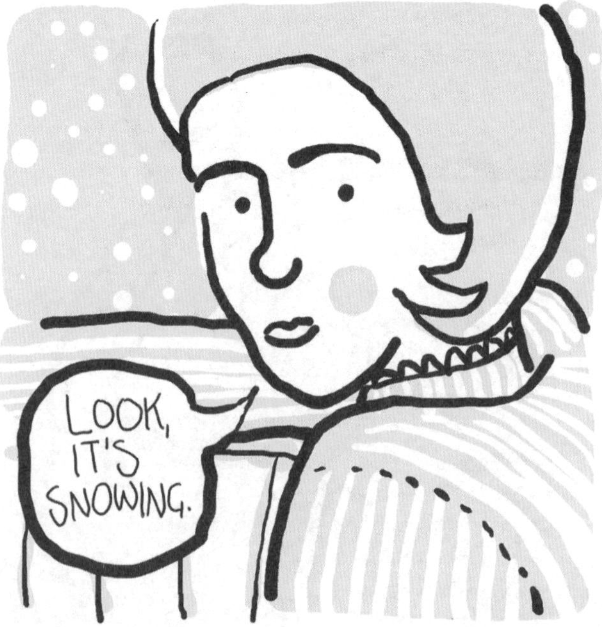
LOOK, IT'S SNOWING.

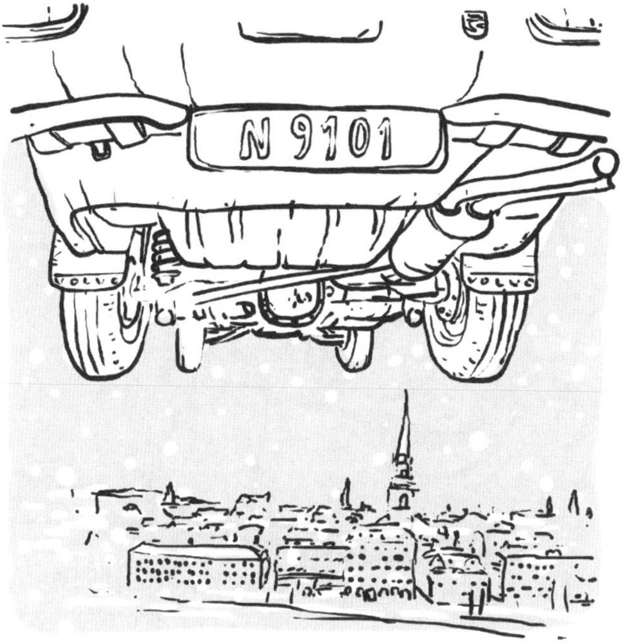
N 9101

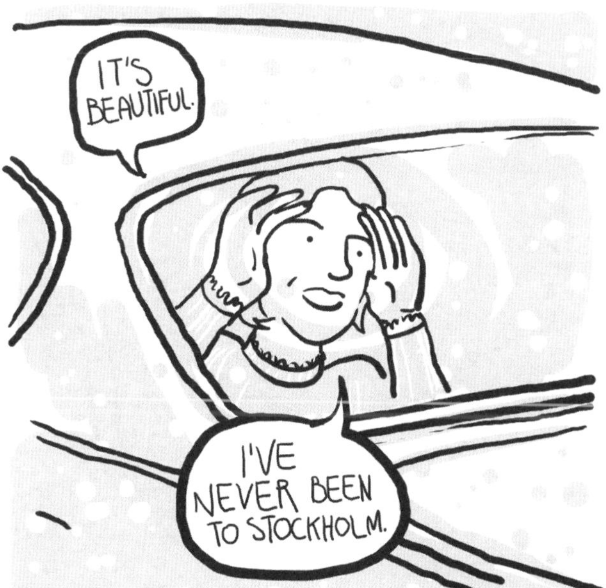
IT'S BEAUTIFUL.
I'VE NEVER BEEN TO STOCKHOLM.

MY GREAT-GRANDMA NEVER TRAVELLED.
THE FARTHEST SHE HAD BEEN WAS WARSAW.

IN THE
SPRING
OF 1910,
SHE PACKED
HER SUITCASE.

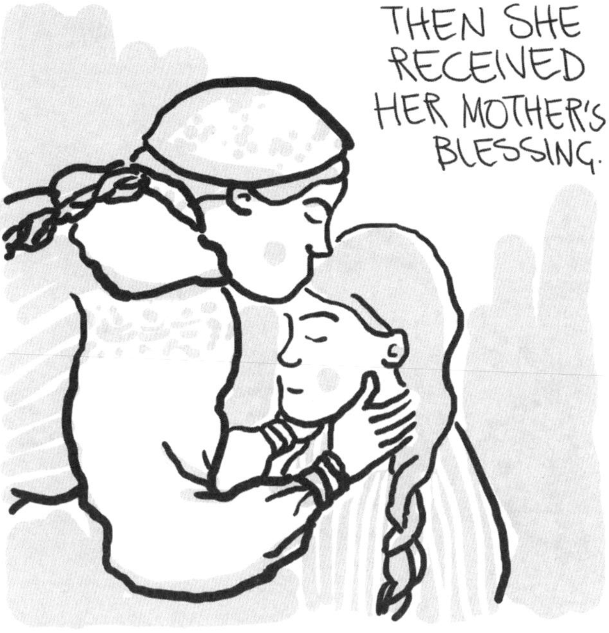
THEN SHE RECEIVED HER MOTHER'S BLESSING.

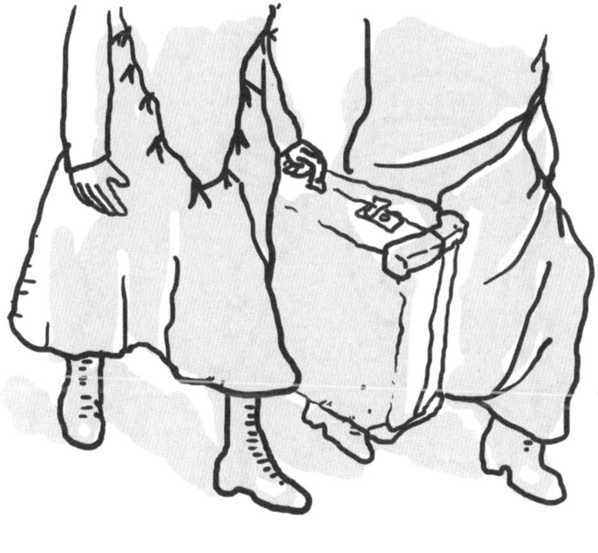
WHILE WALKING TO THE STATION THEY SAW AN OMEN.

A DEAD OWL – A BAD OMEN.

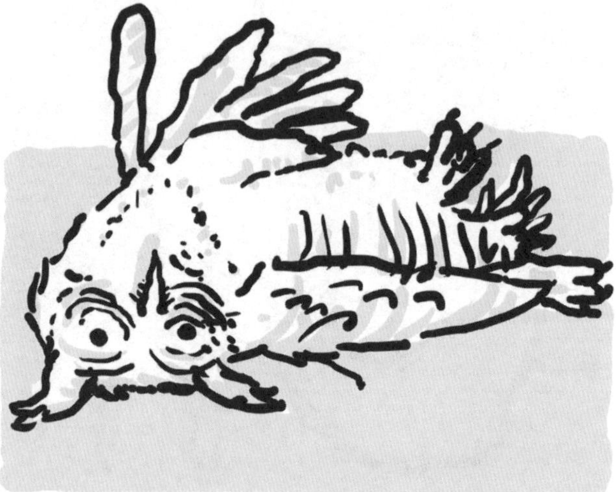

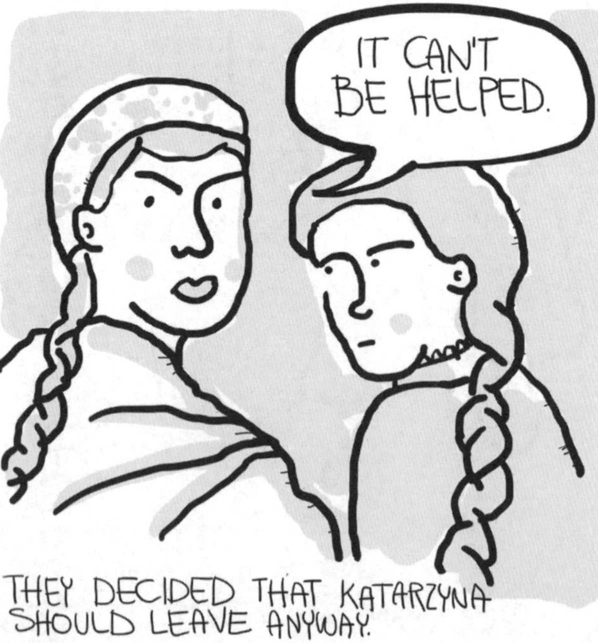
IT CAN'T BE HELPED.

THEY DECIDED THAT KATARZYNA SHOULD LEAVE ANYWAY.

SHE WAS PREPARED TO MEET HER DESTINY.

THE ONLY THING THAT BOTHERED HER WAS HER SHOES.

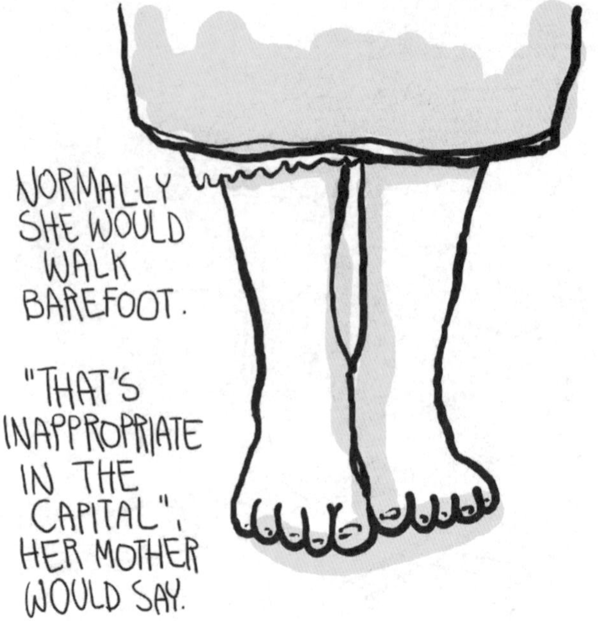
NORMALLY SHE WOULD WALK BAREFOOT.
"THAT'S INAPPROPRIATE IN THE CAPITAL", HER MOTHER WOULD SAY.

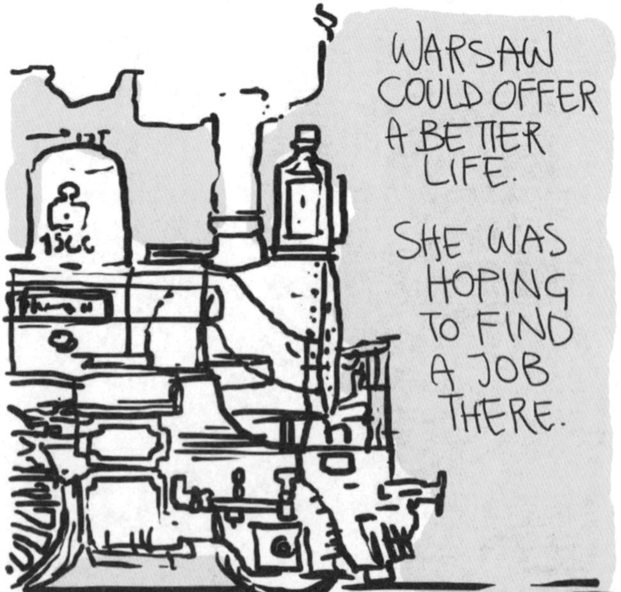
WARSAW COULD OFFER A BETTER LIFE.
SHE WAS HOPING TO FIND A JOB THERE.

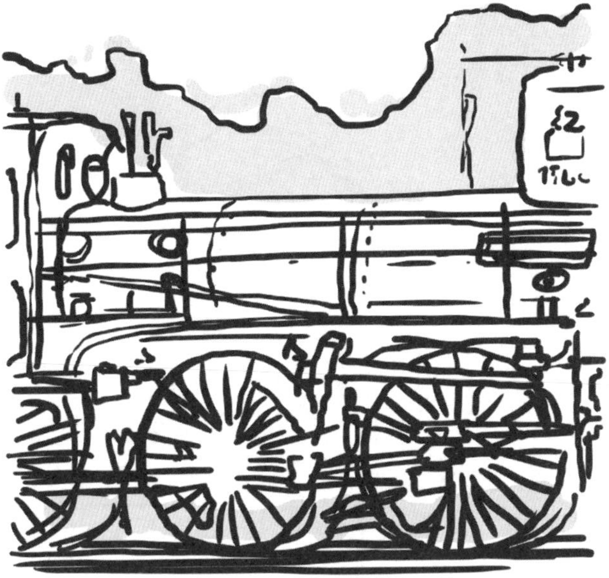

AS A MIDWIFE OR AS A NURSE.

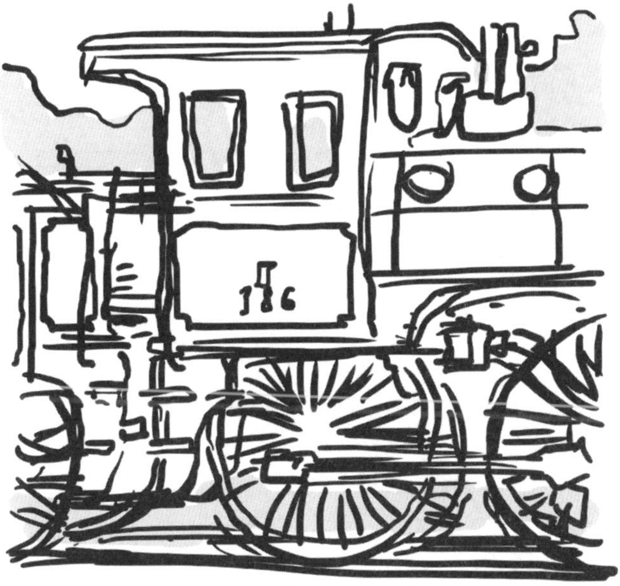

IN HER POCKET SHE HAD THE ADDRESS OF A FAMILY FROM WHOM SHE WOULD RENT A ROOM.

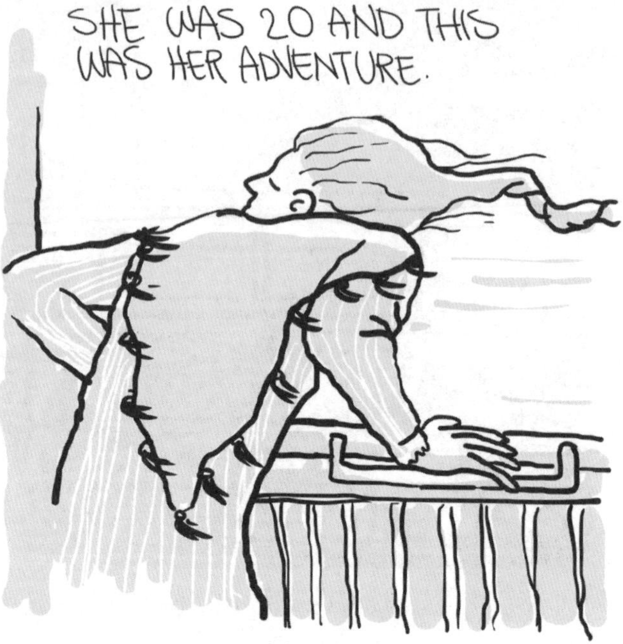
SHE WAS 20 AND THIS WAS HER ADVENTURE.

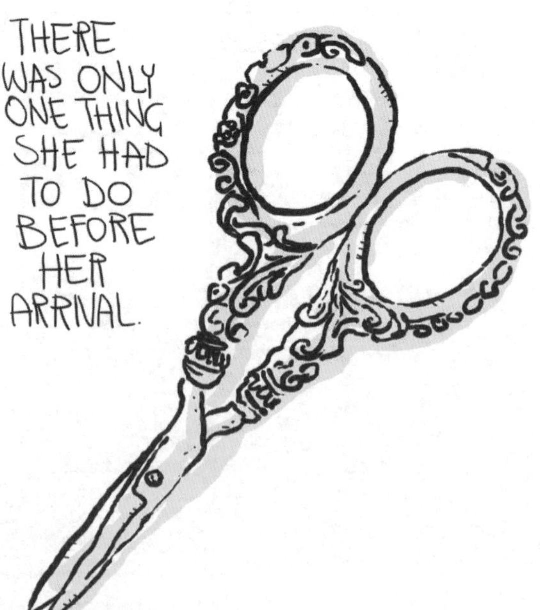
THERE WAS ONLY ONE THING SHE HAD TO DO BEFORE HER ARRIVAL.

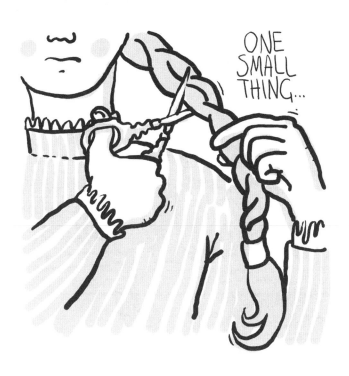

ONE SMALL THING...

...TO MAKE HER FEEL FREE.

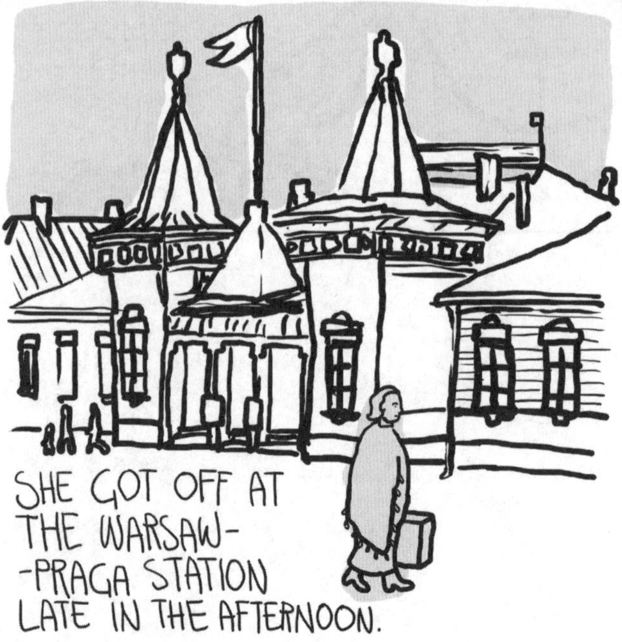
SHE GOT OFF AT THE WARSAW--PRAGA STATION LATE IN THE AFTERNOON.

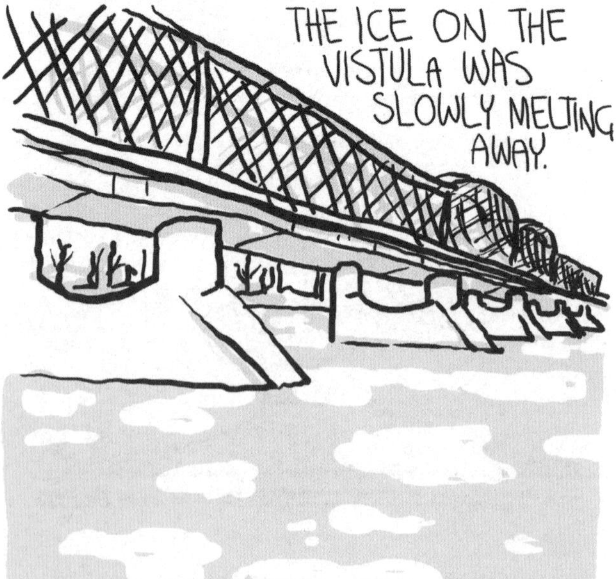
THE ICE ON THE VISTULA WAS SLOWLY MELTING AWAY.

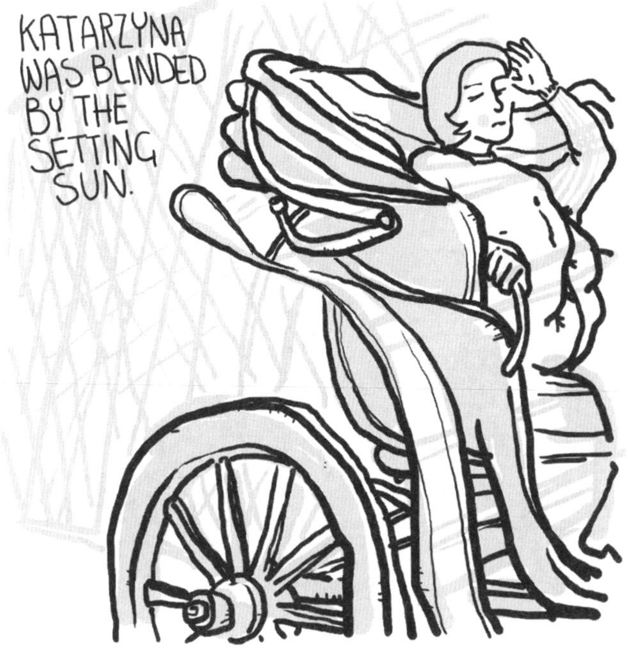
KATARZYNA WAS BLINDED BY THE SETTING SUN.

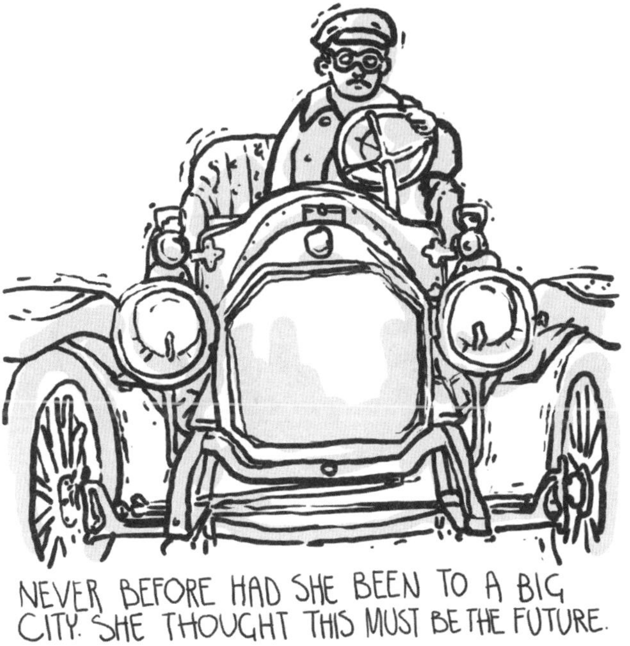

NEVER BEFORE HAD SHE BEEN TO A BIG CITY. SHE THOUGHT THIS MUST BE THE FUTURE.

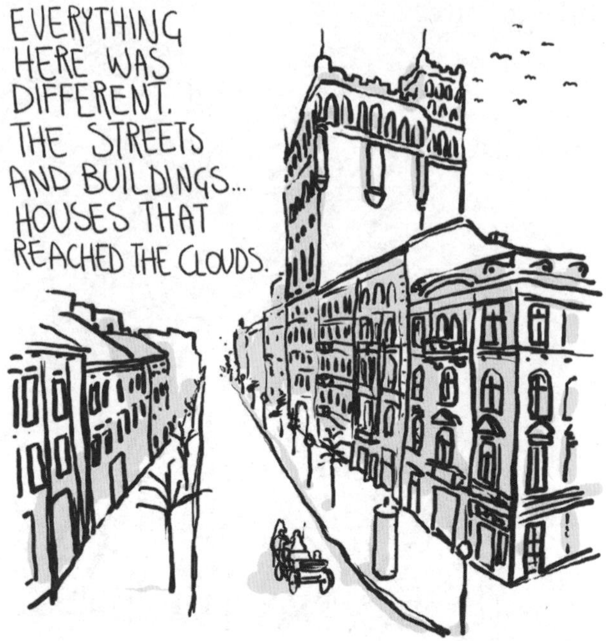
EVERYTHING HERE WAS DIFFERENT. THE STREETS AND BUILDINGS... HOUSES THAT REACHED THE CLOUDS.

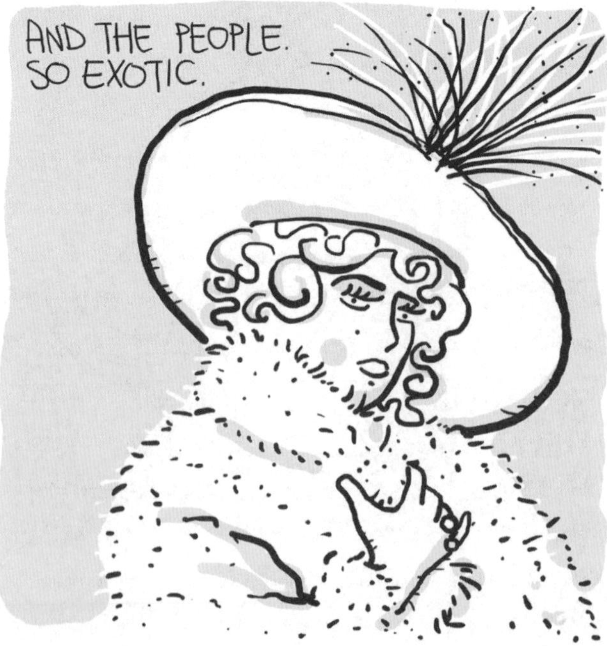
AND THE PEOPLE. SO EXOTIC.

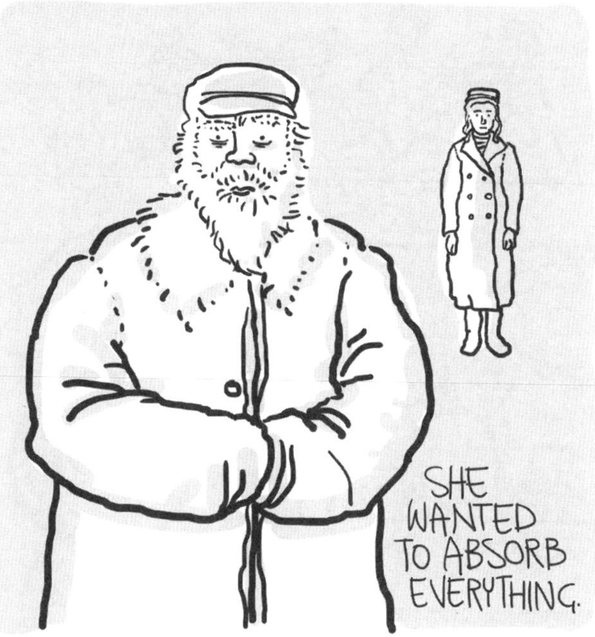
SHE WANTED TO ABSORB EVERYTHING.

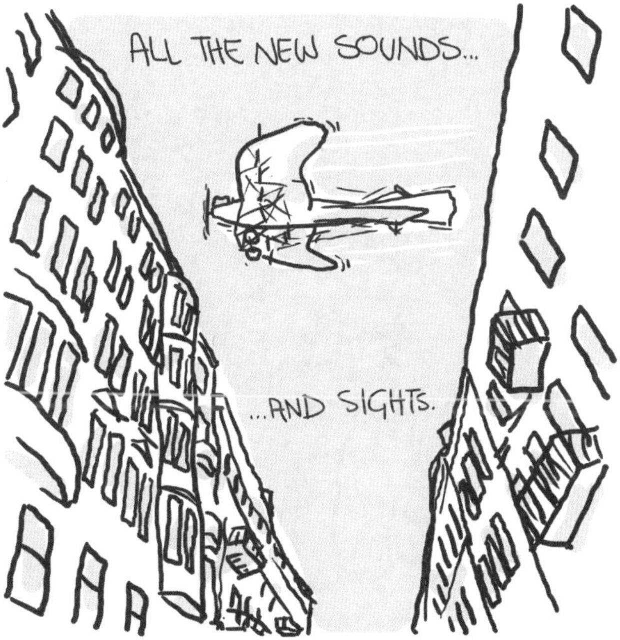
ALL THE NEW SOUNDS...
...AND SIGHTS.

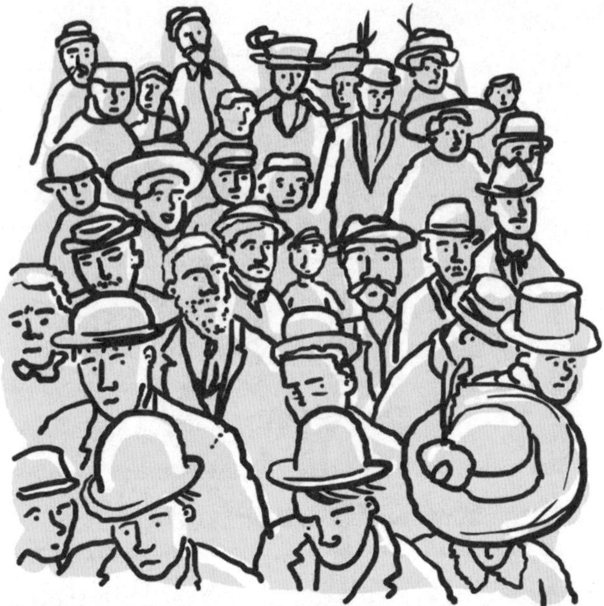

WHEREVER SHE LOOKED, A FRIGHTENING SEA OF HUMANS.

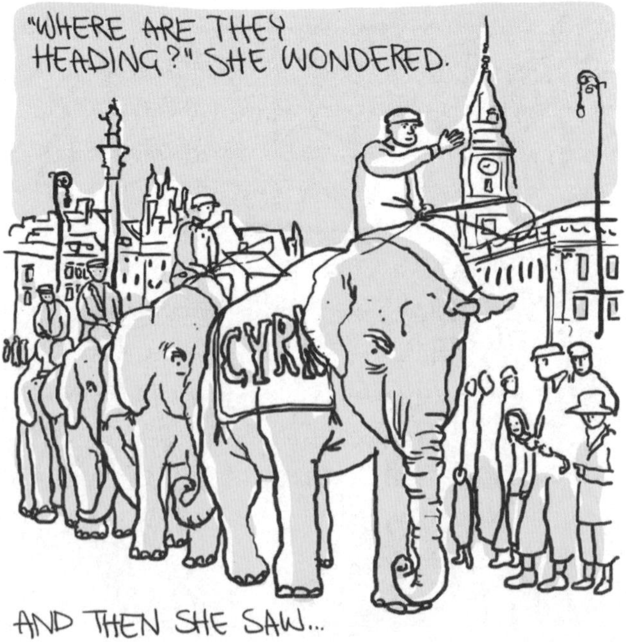
"WHERE ARE THEY HEADING?" SHE WONDERED.
CYRK

AND THEN SHE SAW...

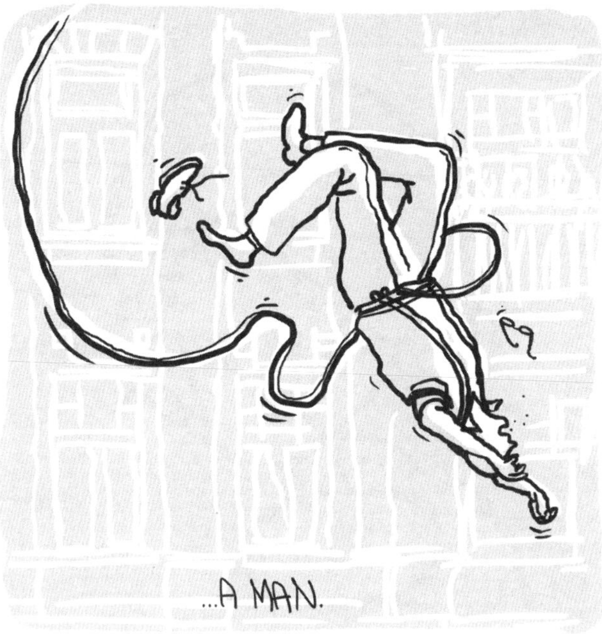
...A MAN.

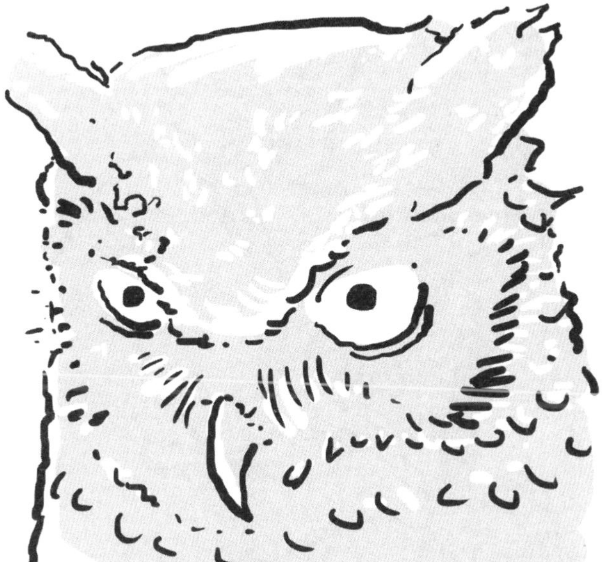

AN OWL HOOTED SOMEWHERE.

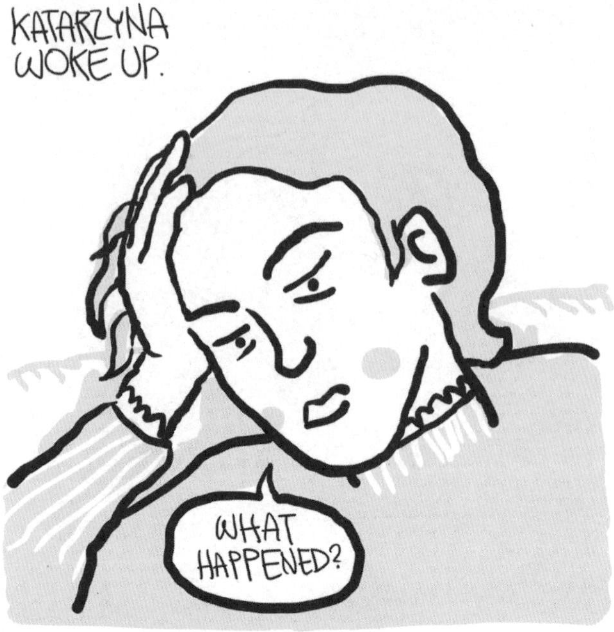
KATARZYNA WOKE UP.
WHAT HAPPENED?

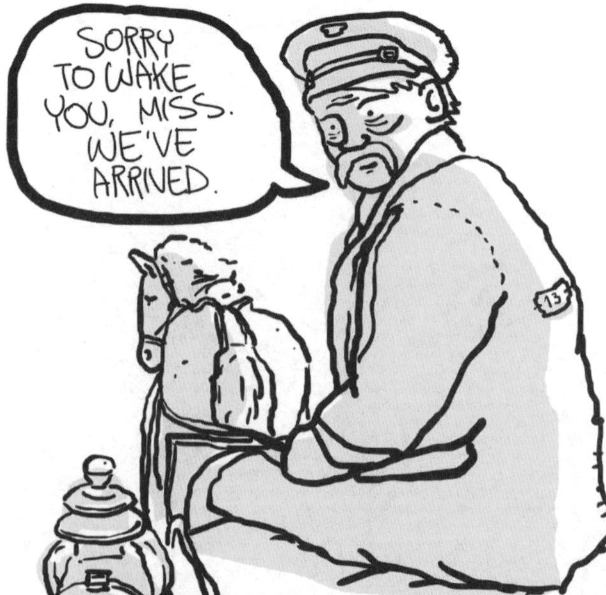
SORRY TO WAKE YOU, MISS. WE'VE ARRIVED.
13

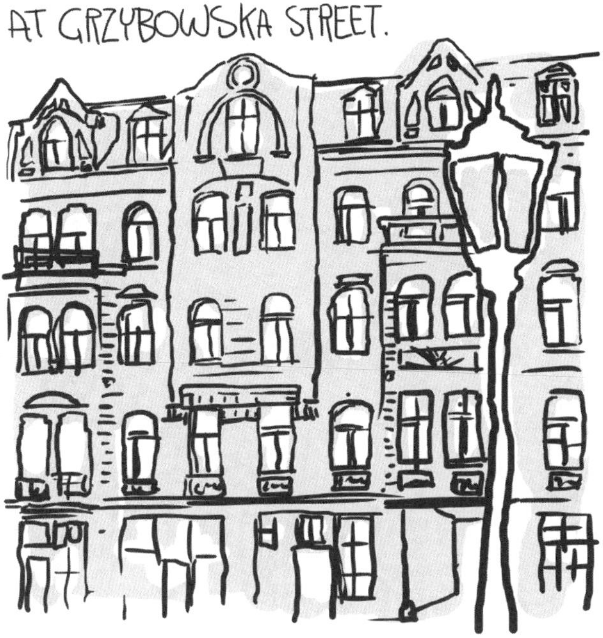
AT GRZYBOWSKA STREET.

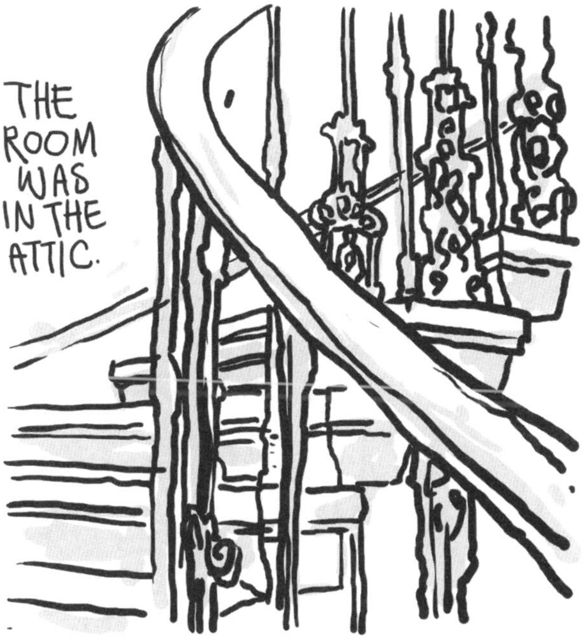
THE ROOM WAS IN THE ATTIC.

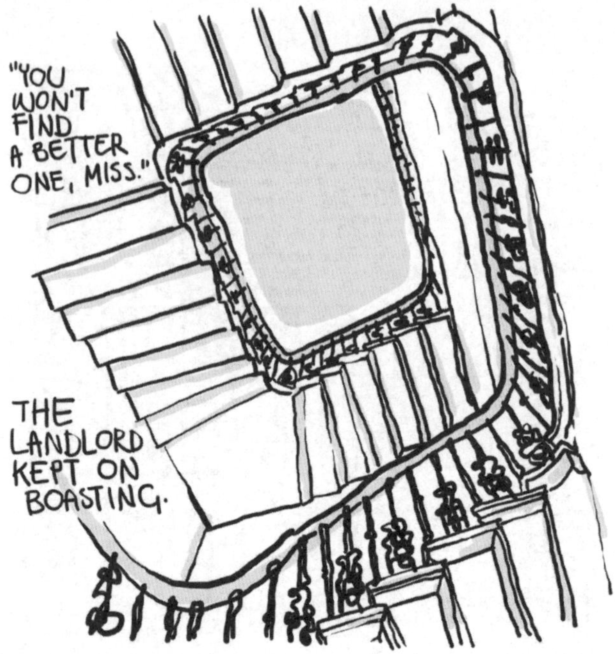
"YOU WON'T FIND A BETTER ONE, MISS."
THE LANDLORD KEPT ON BOASTING.

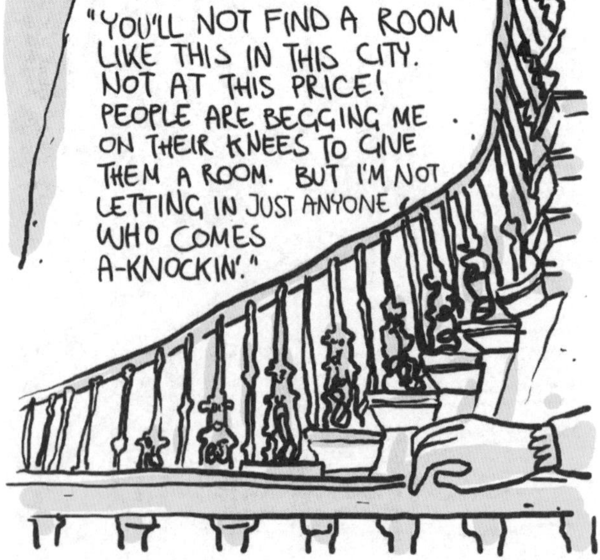
"YOU'LL NOT FIND A ROOM LIKE THIS IN THIS CITY. NOT AT THIS PRICE! PEOPLE ARE BEGGING ME ON THEIR KNEES TO GIVE THEM A ROOM. BUT I'M NOT LETTING IN JUST ANYONE WHO COMES A-KNOCKIN'."

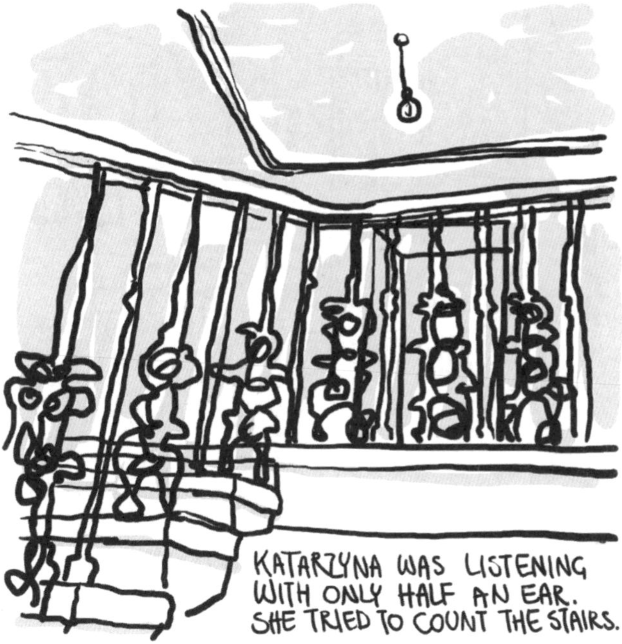
KATARZYNA WAS LISTENING WITH ONLY HALF AN EAR. SHE TRIED TO COUNT THE STAIRS.

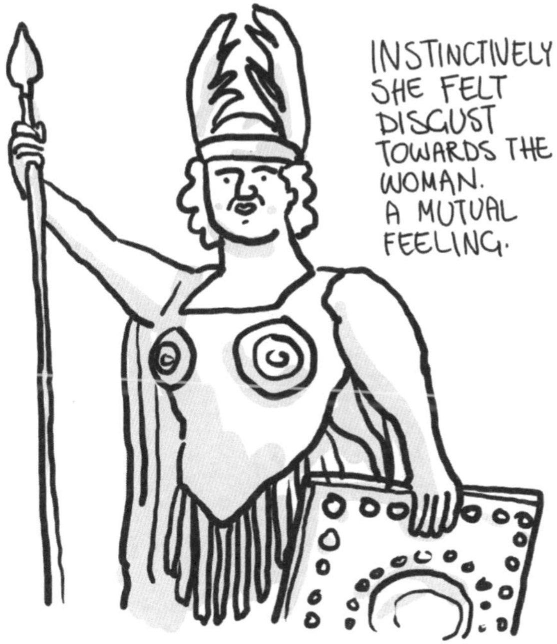
INSTINCTIVELY SHE FELT DISGUST TOWARDS THE WOMAN. A MUTUAL FEELING.

WITH THE ROOM, HOWEVER, SHE FELL IN LOVE AT FIRST SIGHT.

SHE GOT THE FEELING THIS PLACE WAS GOING TO CHANGE HER LIFE.

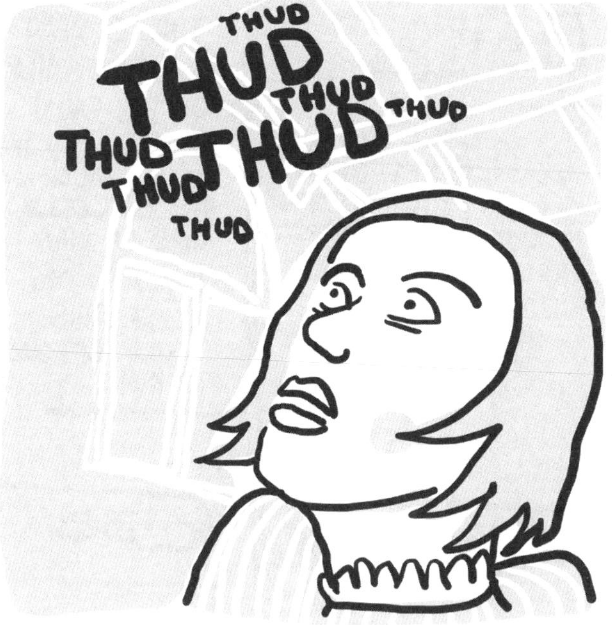
THUD
THUD
THUD
THUD
THUD
THUD
THUD
THUD

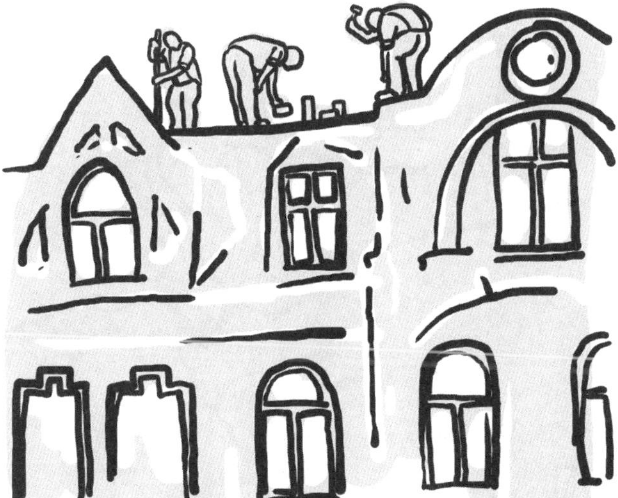

THE LANDLORD HAD THREE GROWNUP SONS.

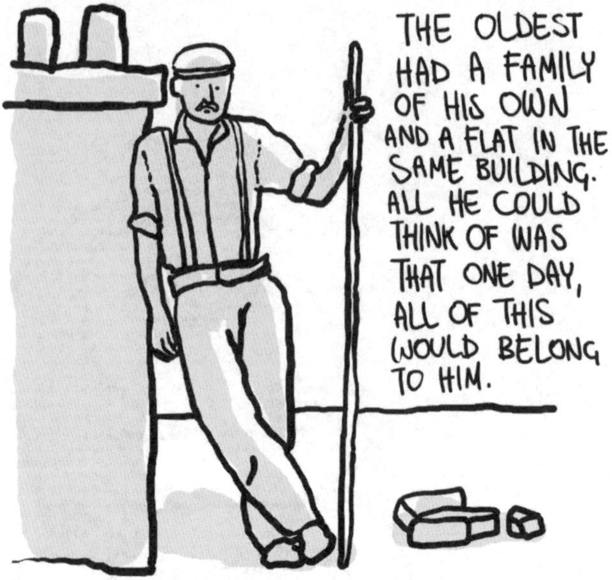
THE OLDEST HAD A FAMILY OF HIS OWN AND A FLAT IN THE SAME BUILDING. ALL HE COULD THINK OF WAS THAT ONE DAY, ALL OF THIS WOULD BELONG TO HIM.

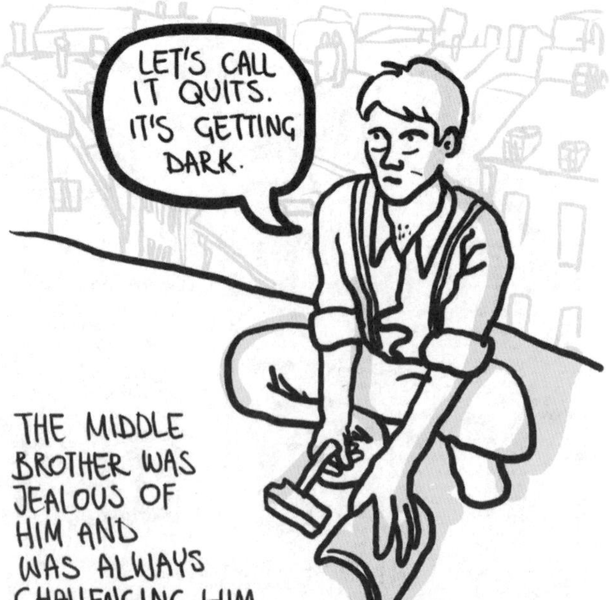
LET'S CALL IT QUITS. IT'S GETTING DARK.
THE MIDDLE BROTHER WAS JEALOUS OF HIM AND WAS ALWAYS CHALLENGING HIM.

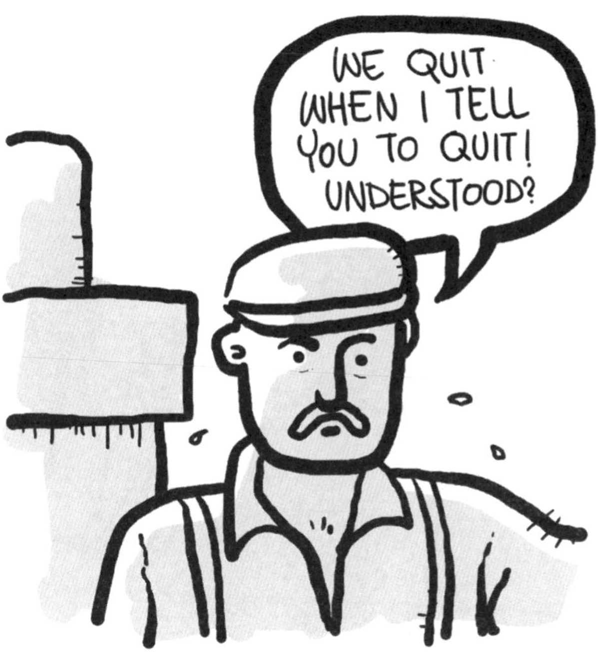
WE QUIT WHEN I TELL YOU TO QUIT! UNDERSTOOD?

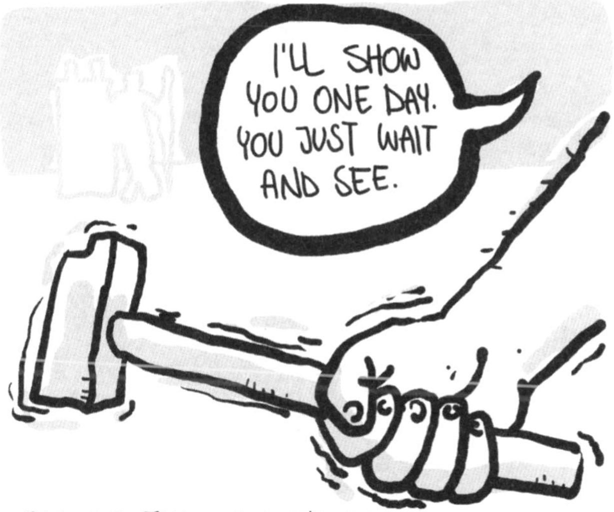
I'LL SHOW YOU ONE DAY. YOU JUST WAIT AND SEE.

BIG BROTHER ALWAYS HAD THE LAST WORD. THE OTHERS ALWAYS HAD TO SUBMIT TO HIM.

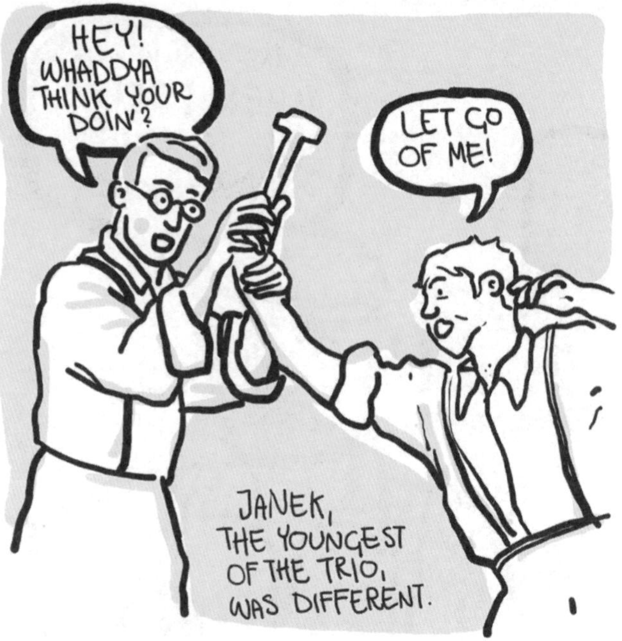
HEY! WHADDYA THINK YOUR DOIN'?
LET GO OF ME!
JANEK, THE YOUNGEST OF THE TRIO, WAS DIFFERENT.

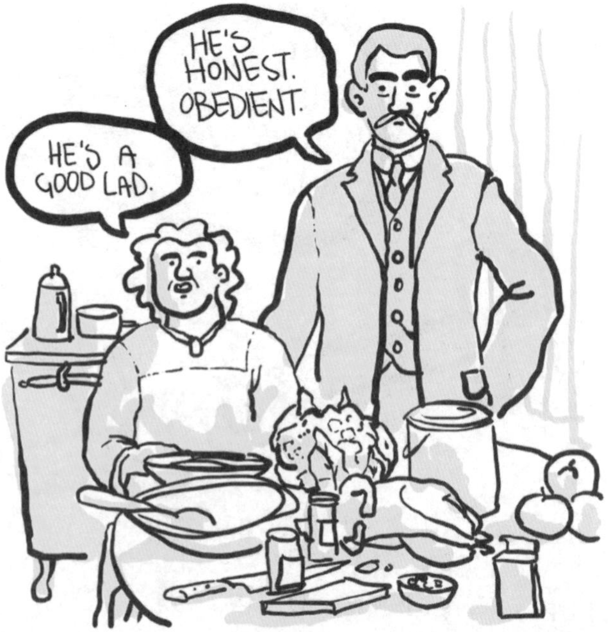
HE'S A GOOD LAD.
HE'S HONEST. OBEDIENT.

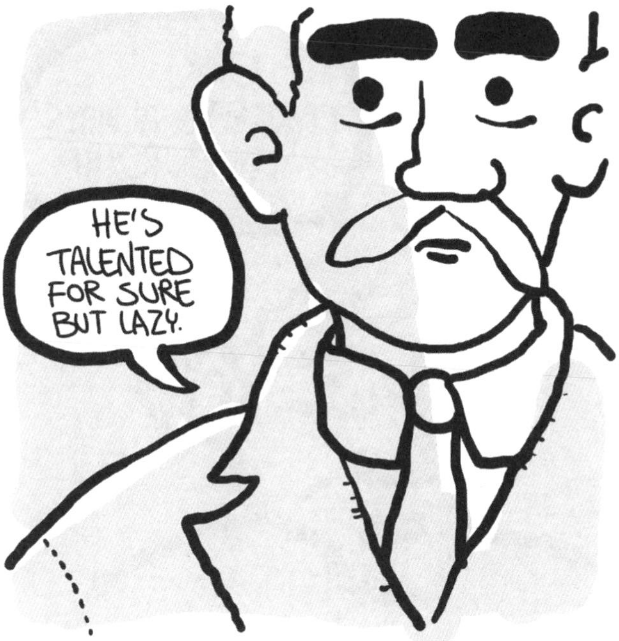
HE'S TALENTED FOR SURE BUT LAZY.

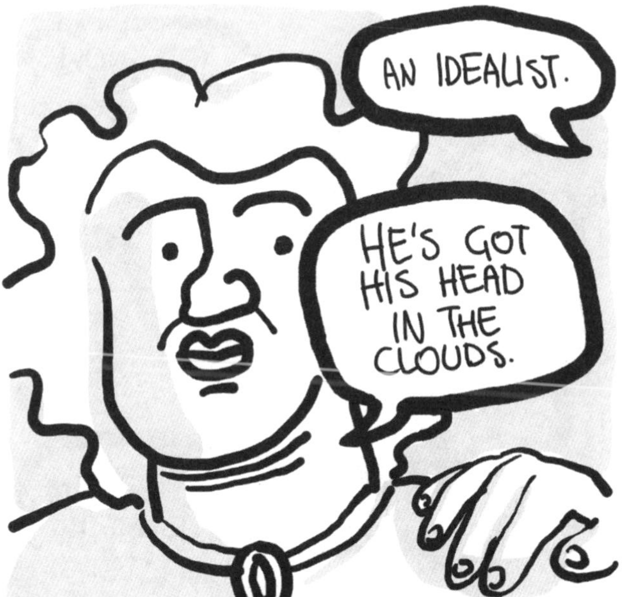
AN IDEALIST.
HE'S GOT HIS HEAD IN THE CLOUDS.

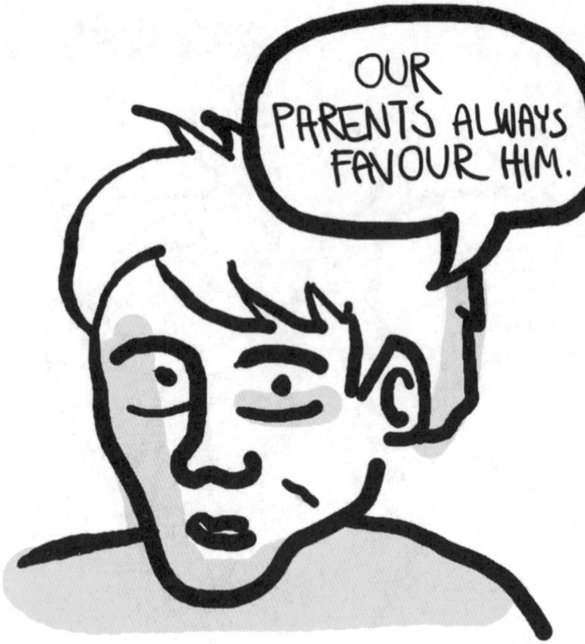
OUR PARENTS ALWAYS FAVOUR HIM.

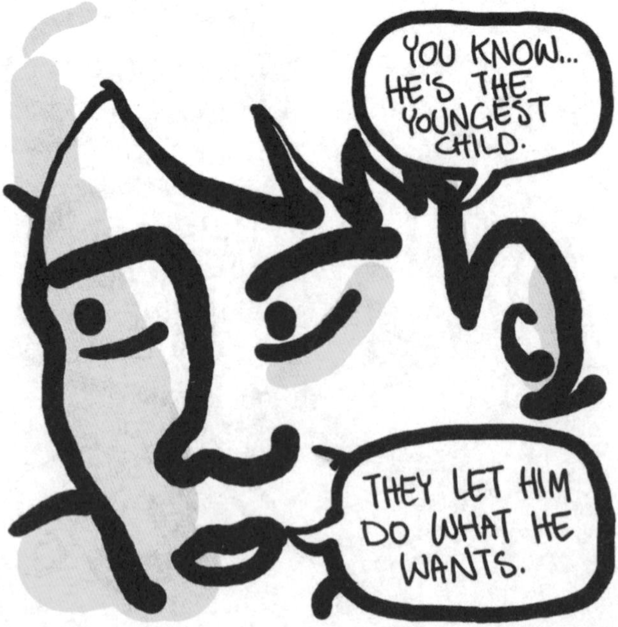
YOU KNOW... HE'S THE YOUNGEST CHILD.
THEY LET HIM DO WHAT HE WANTS.

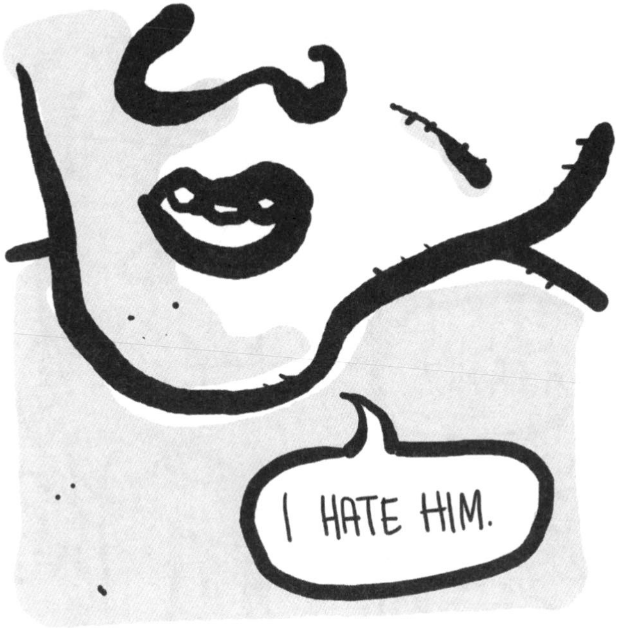
I HATE HIM.

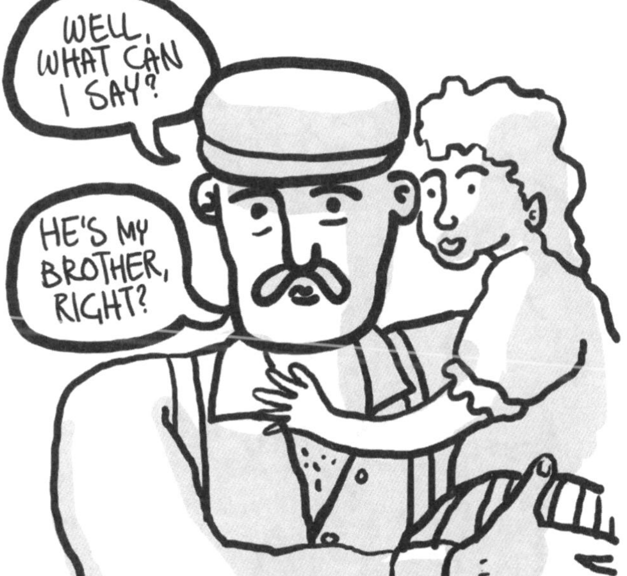
WELL, WHAT CAN I SAY?
HE'S MY BROTHER, RIGHT?

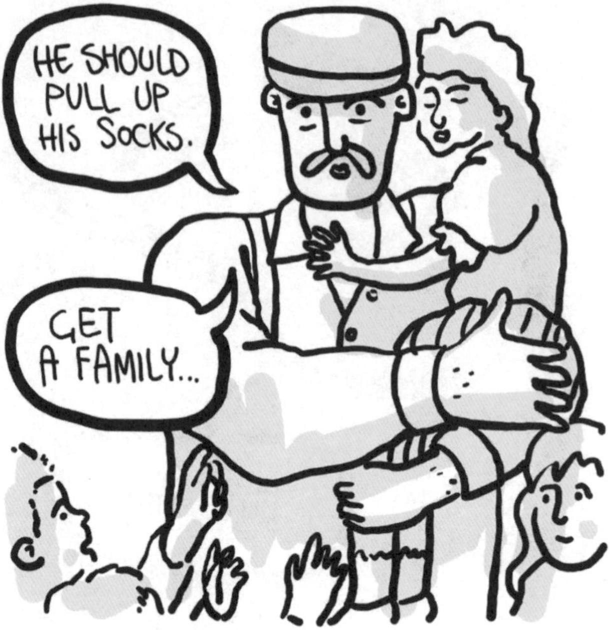
HE SHOULD PULL UP HIS SOCKS.
GET A FAMILY...

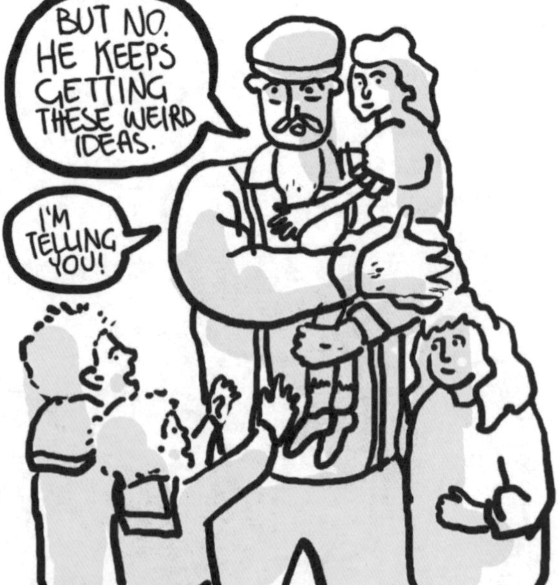
BUT NO. HE KEEPS GETTING THESE WEIRD IDEAS.
I'M TELLING YOU!

FIRST HE WANTED
TO BECOME A CYCLIST.

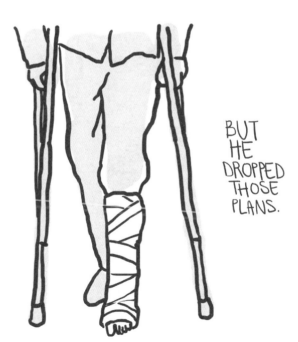

BUT
HE
DROPPED
THOSE
PLANS.

LAST SUMMER HE WENT TO THE SEA.

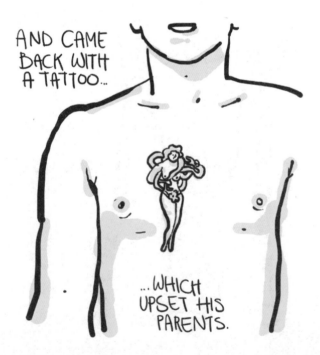

AND CAME BACK WITH A TATTOO...

...WHICH UPSET HIS PARENTS.

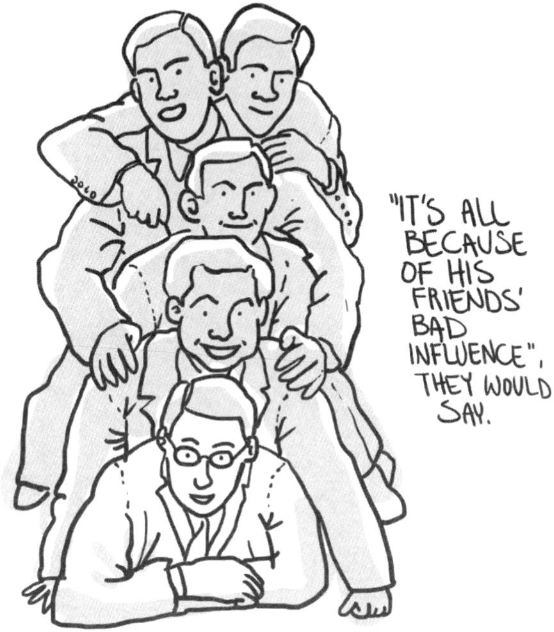
"IT'S ALL BECAUSE OF HIS FRIENDS' BAD INFLUENCE", THEY WOULD SAY.

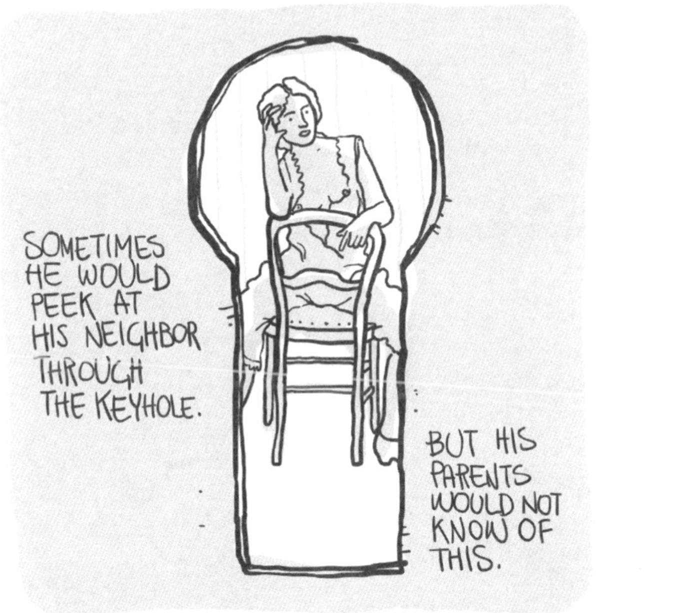
SOMETIMES HE WOULD PEEK AT HIS NEIGHBOR THROUGH THE KEYHOLE.
BUT HIS PARENTS WOULD NOT KNOW OF THIS.

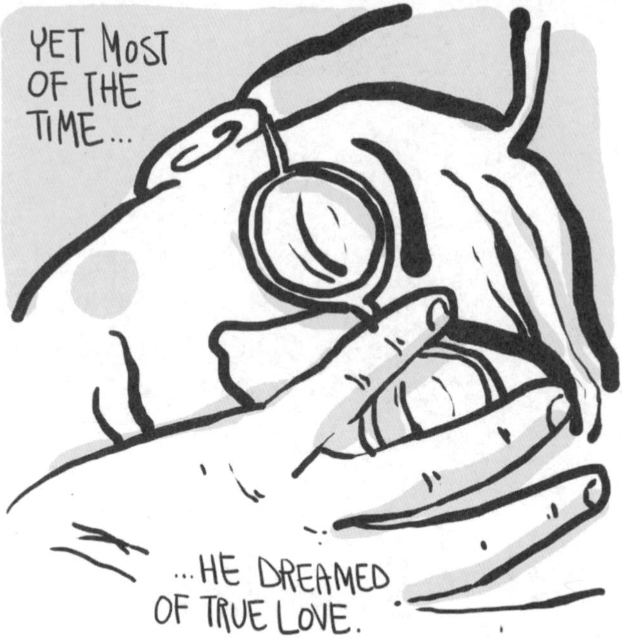
YET MOST OF THE TIME...
...HE DREAMED OF TRUE LOVE.

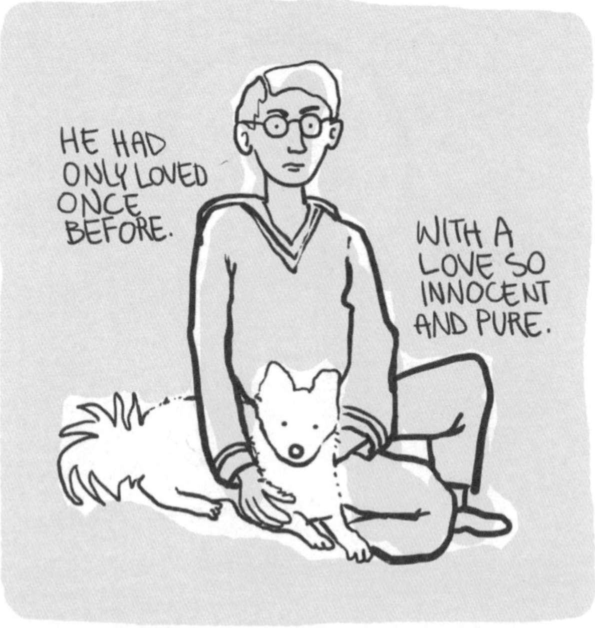
HE HAD ONLY LOVED ONCE BEFORE.
WITH A LOVE SO INNOCENT AND PURE.

LIKE A
LADYBUG
ON THE
TIP OF A
FINGER.

OR LIKE
A SNOWFLAKE...

...ON THE TONGUE WHEN HE WAS 3.

NOT OFTEN, BUT SOMETIMES, HIS FATHER WOULD PICK HIM UP.

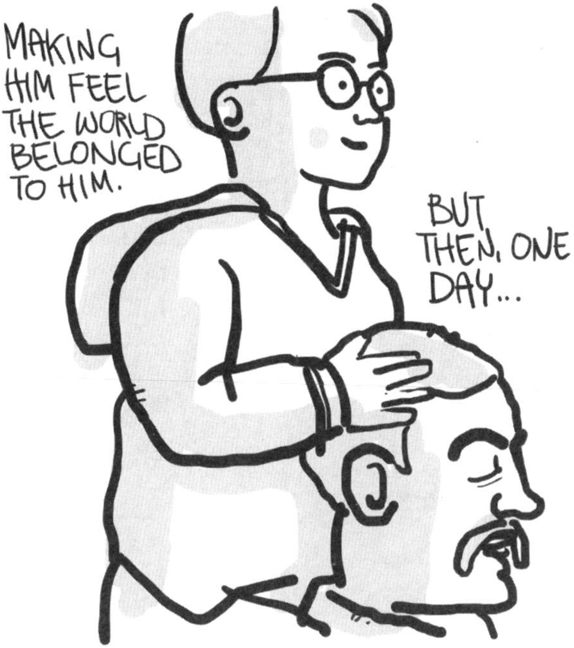
MAKING HIM FEEL THE WORLD BELONGED TO HIM.
BUT THEN, ONE DAY...

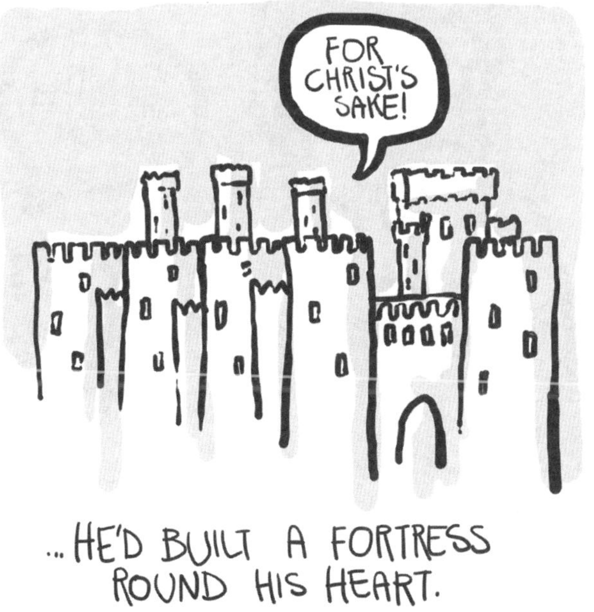
FOR CHRIST'S SAKE!
...HE'D BUILT A FORTRESS ROUND HIS HEART.

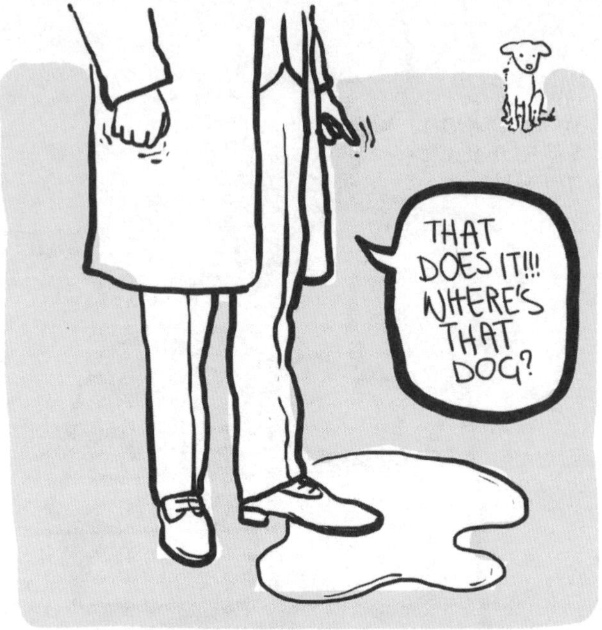
THAT DOES IT!!! WHERE'S THAT DOG?

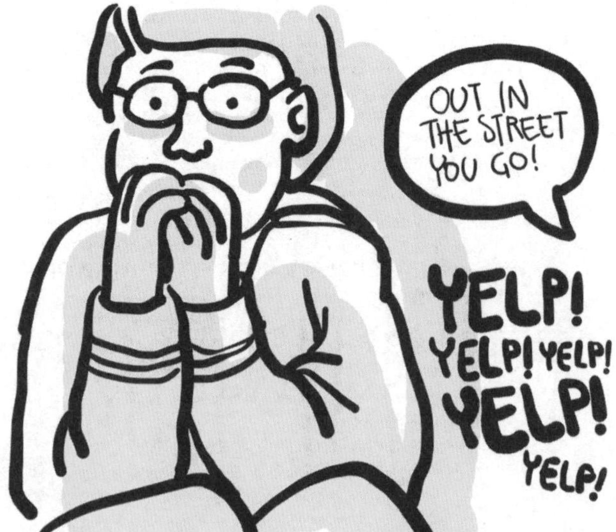
OUT IN THE STREET YOU GO!
YELP!
YELP! YELP!
YELP!
YELP!

WHO WOULD HAVE THOUGHT THAT IT TAKES LESS TO BREAK A CHILD'S HEART.

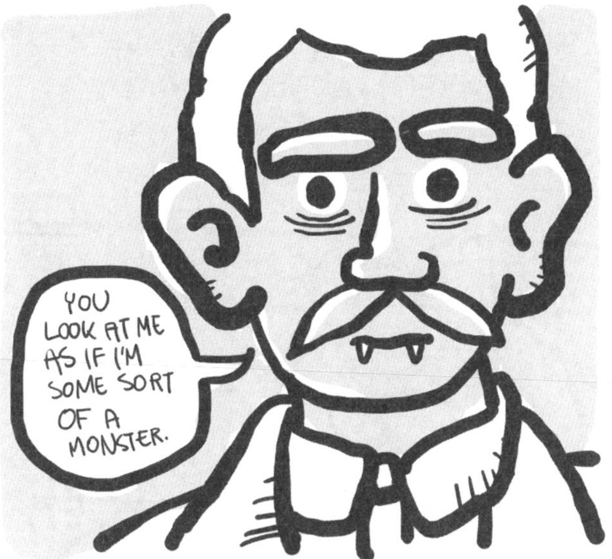
YOU LOOK AT ME AS IF I'M SOME SORT OF A MONSTER.

OVERNIGHT HIS FATHER BECAME A COMPLETE STRANGER TO HIM.

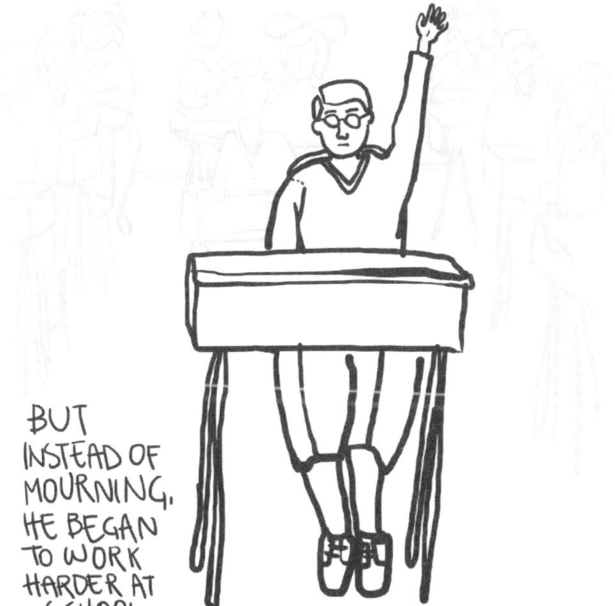

BUT INSTEAD OF MOURNING, HE BEGAN TO WORK HARDER AT SCHOOL.

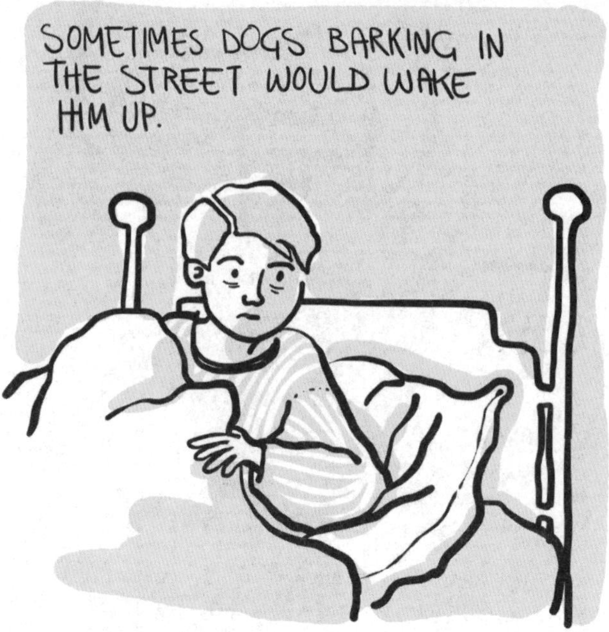
SOMETIMES DOGS BARKING IN THE STREET WOULD WAKE HIM UP.

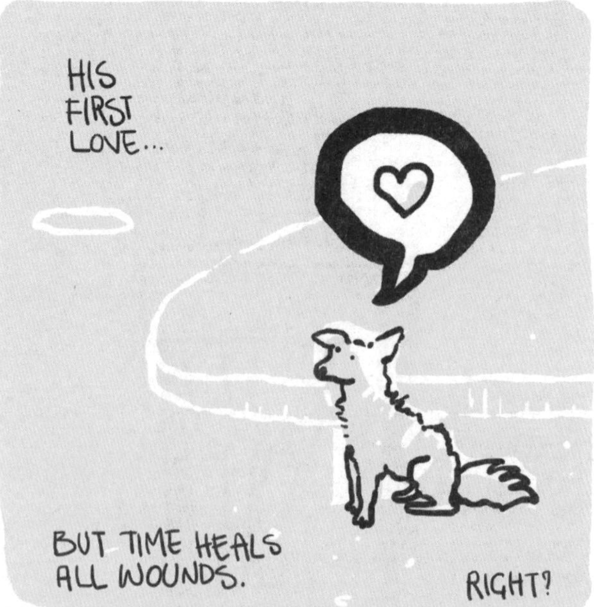
HIS FIRST LOVE...
BUT TIME HEALS ALL WOUNDS.
RIGHT?

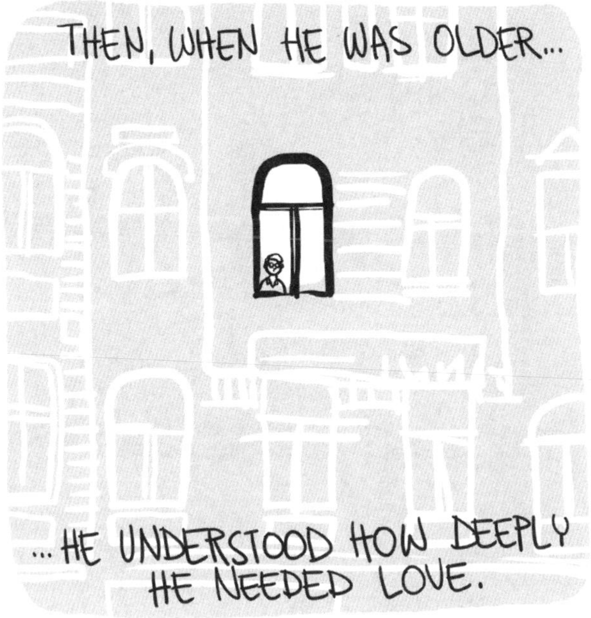
THEN, WHEN HE WAS OLDER...
...HE UNDERSTOOD HOW DEEPLY HE NEEDED LOVE.

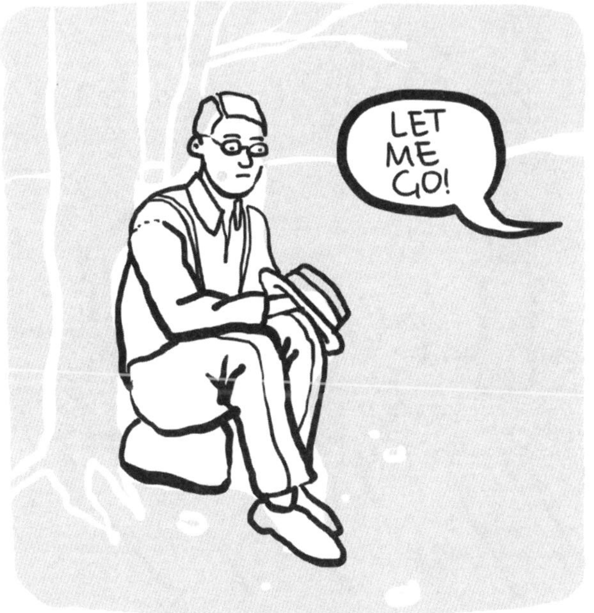
LET ME GO!

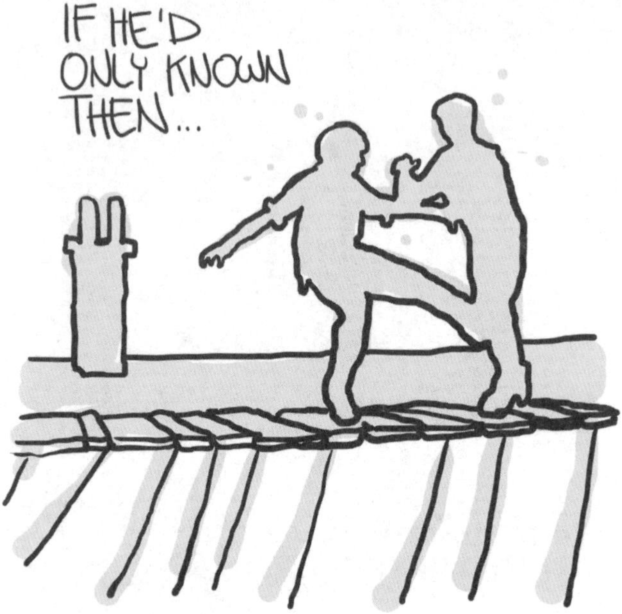
IF HE'D ONLY KNOWN THEN...

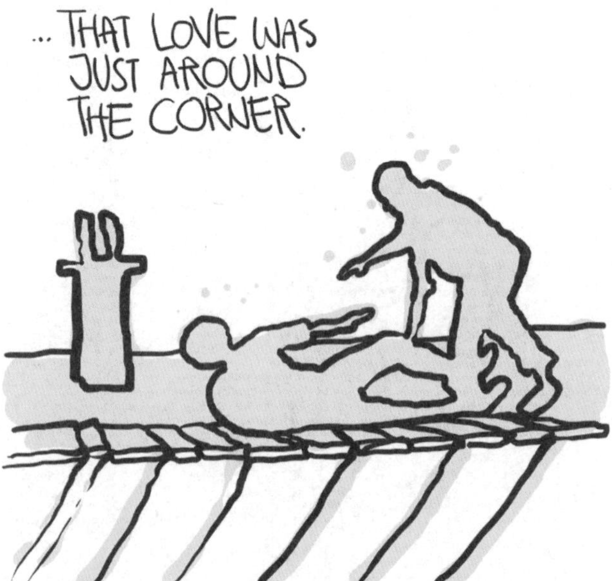
...THAT LOVE WAS JUST AROUND THE CORNER.

WOULD HE
HAVE ACTED
DIFFERENTLY?

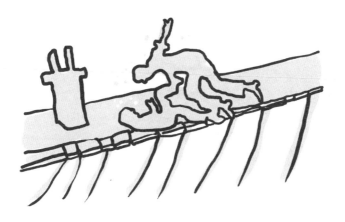

PROBABLY
NOT.

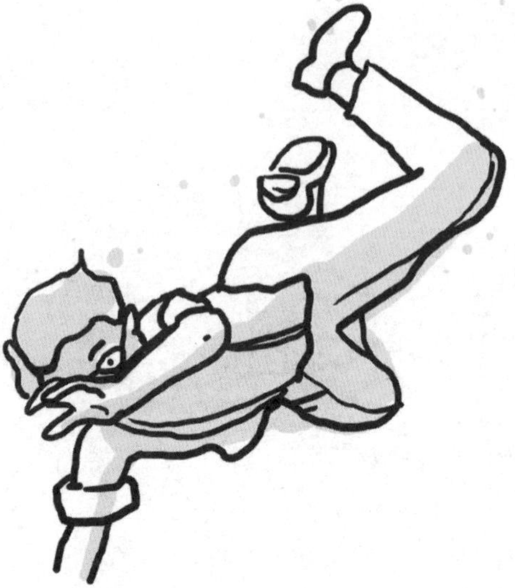

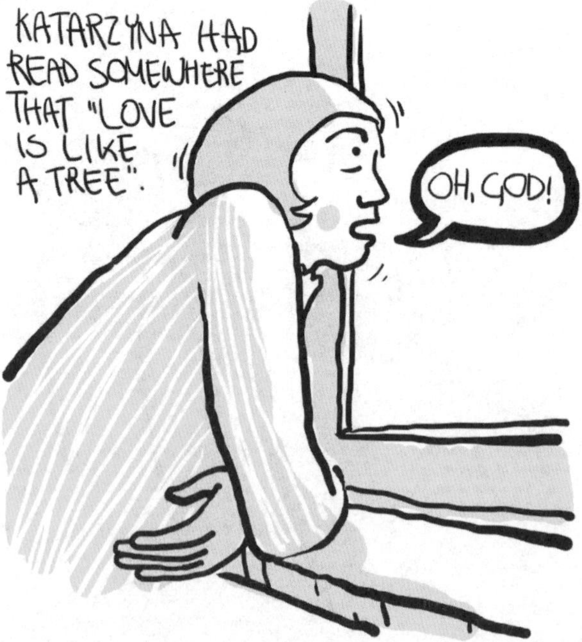
KATARZYNA HAD READ SOMEWHERE THAT "LOVE IS LIKE A TREE".
OH, GOD!

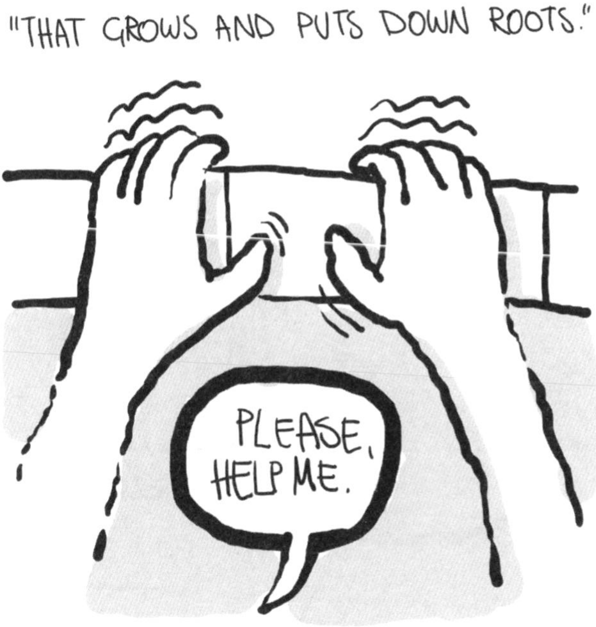
"THAT GROWS AND PUTS DOWN ROOTS."
PLEASE, HELP ME.

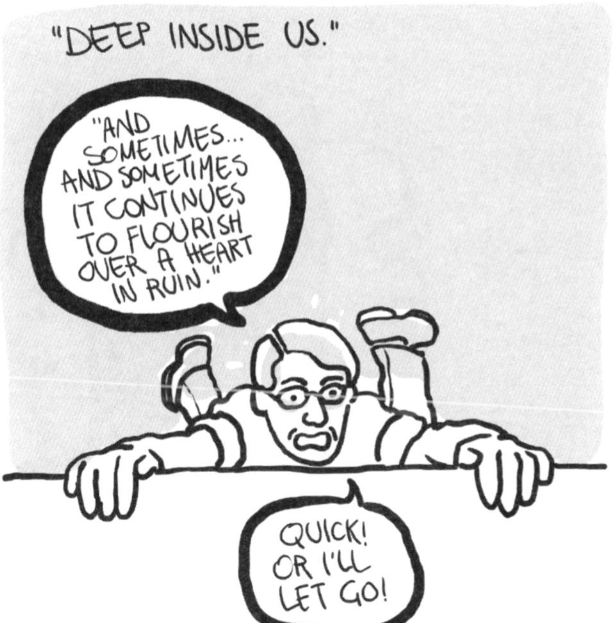
"DEEP INSIDE US."
"AND SOMETIMES... AND SOMETIMES IT CONTINUES TO FLOURISH OVER A HEART IN RUIN."
QUICK! OR I'LL LET GO!

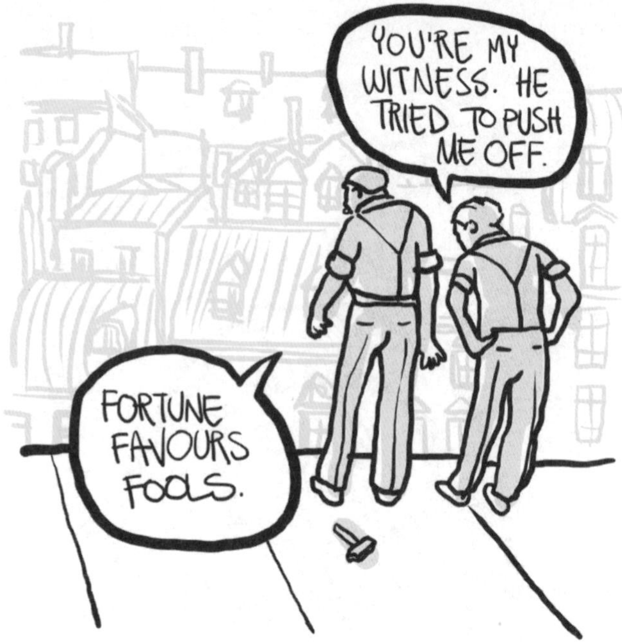
YOU'RE MY WITNESS. HE TRIED TO PUSH ME OFF.
FORTUNE FAVOURS FOOLS.

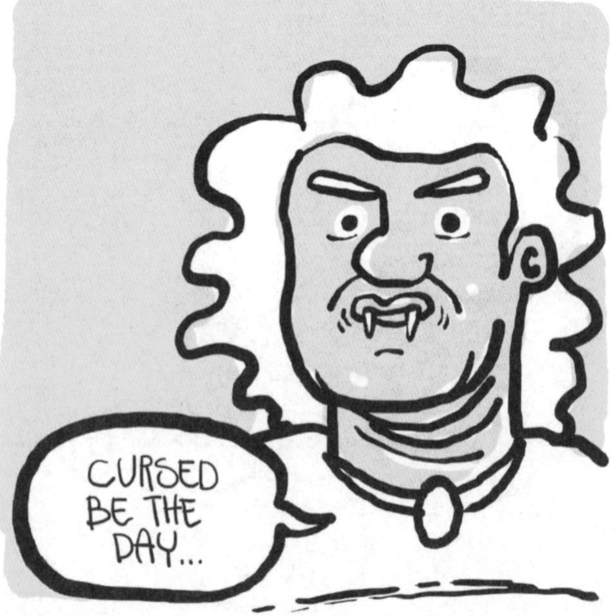
CURSED BE THE DAY...

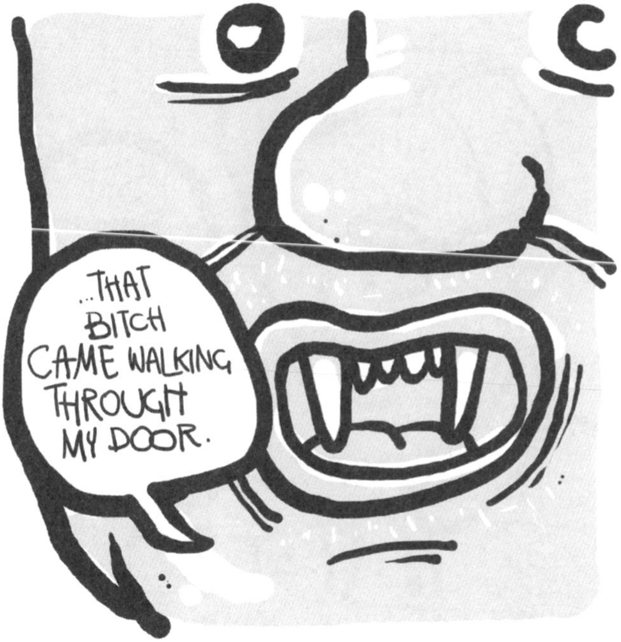
...THAT BITCH CAME WALKING THROUGH MY DOOR.

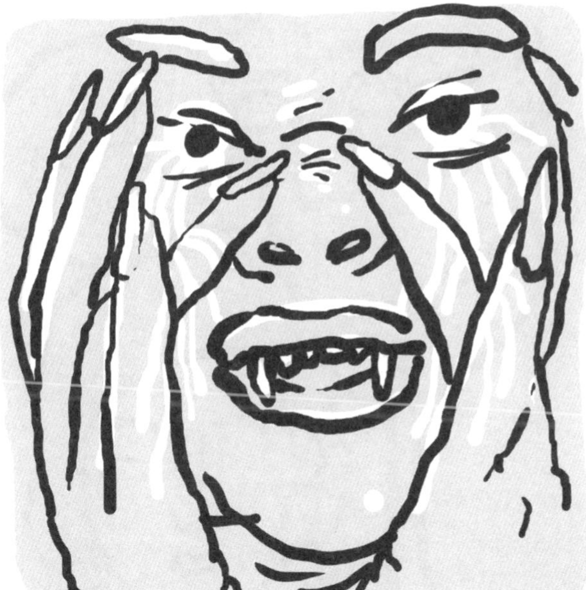

BUT HIS PARENTS' WAILING DIDN'T CHANGE A THING.

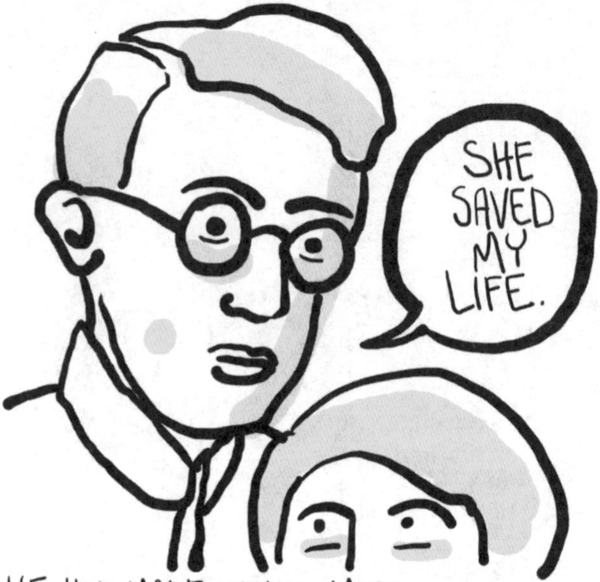
SHE SAVED MY LIFE.

HE HAD MADE UP HIS MIND.

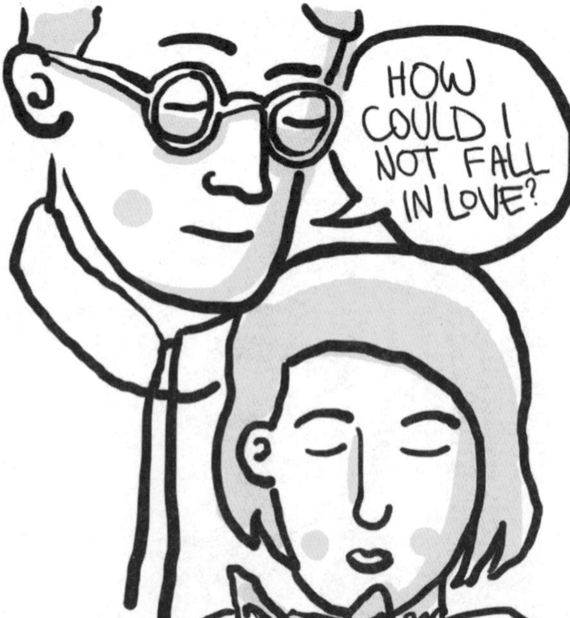
HOW COULD I NOT FALL IN LOVE?

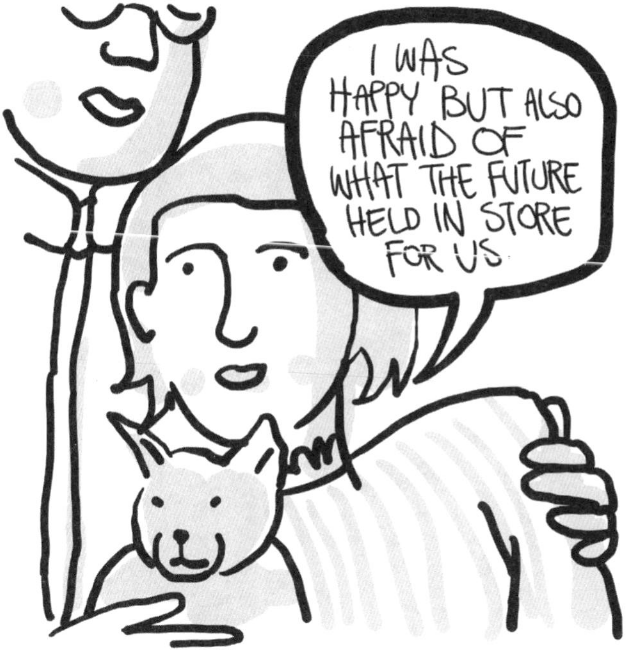
I WAS HAPPY BUT ALSO AFRAID OF WHAT THE FUTURE HELD IN STORE FOR US.

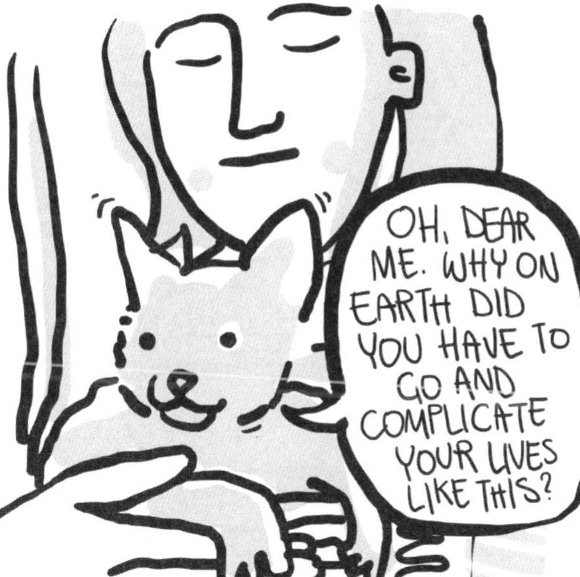
OH, DEAR ME. WHY ON EARTH DID YOU HAVE TO GO AND COMPLICATE YOUR LIVES LIKE THIS?

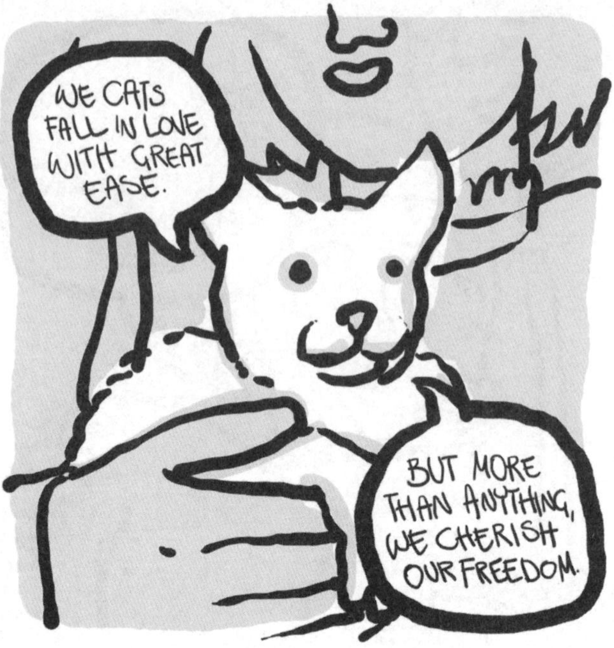
WE CATS FALL IN LOVE WITH GREAT EASE.
BUT MORE THAN ANYTHING, WE CHERISH OUR FREEDOM.

THE NEXT DAY HE TOOK HER TO A CAFÉ. IT FELT LIKE HEAVEN COMPARED TO HER MOTHER'S COUNTRY INN.

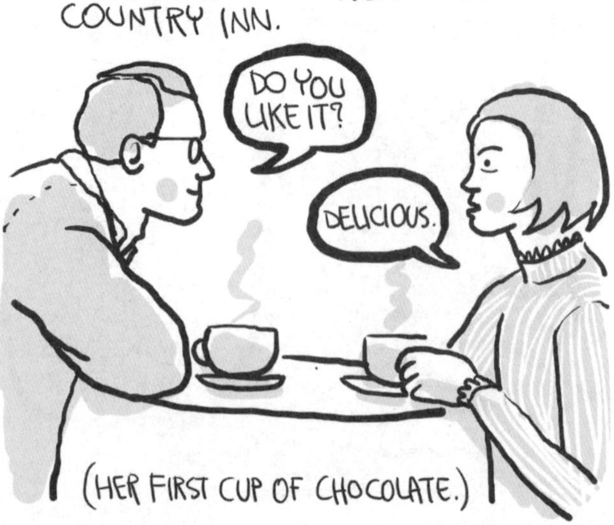
DO YOU LIKE IT?
DELICIOUS.
(HER FIRST CUP OF CHOCOLATE.)

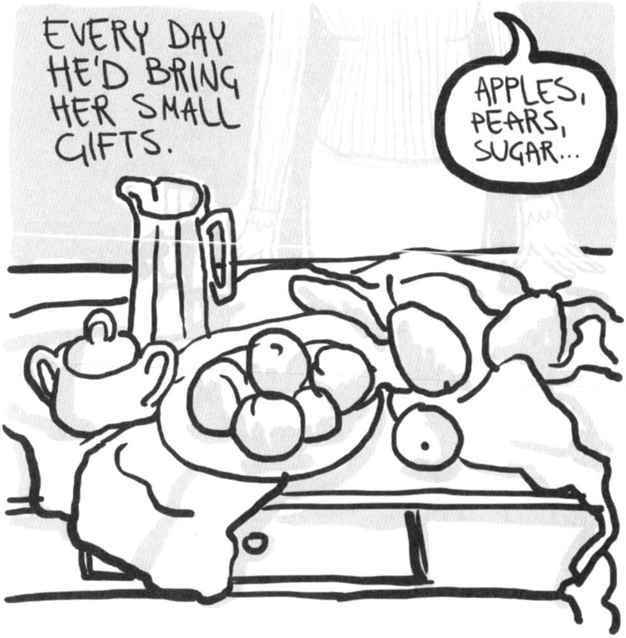
EVERY DAY HE'D BRING HER SMALL GIFTS.
APPLES, PEARS, SUGAR...

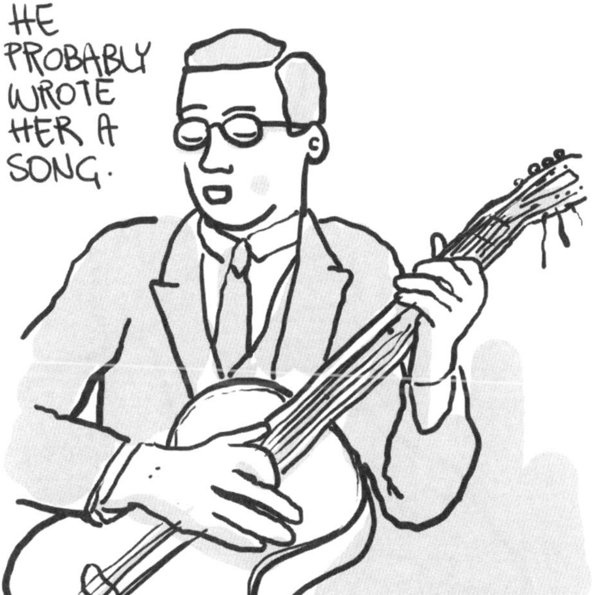
HE PROBABLY WROTE HER A SONG.

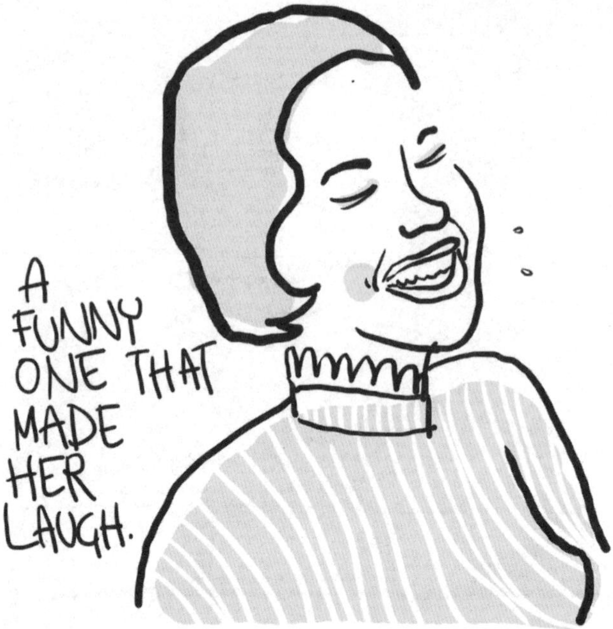
A FUNNY ONE THAT MADE HER LAUGH.

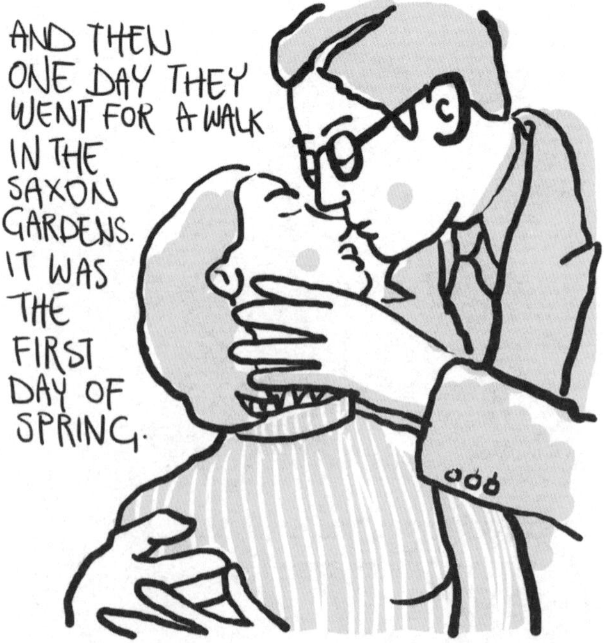
AND THEN ONE DAY THEY WENT FOR A WALK IN THE SAXON GARDENS. IT WAS THE FIRST DAY OF SPRING.

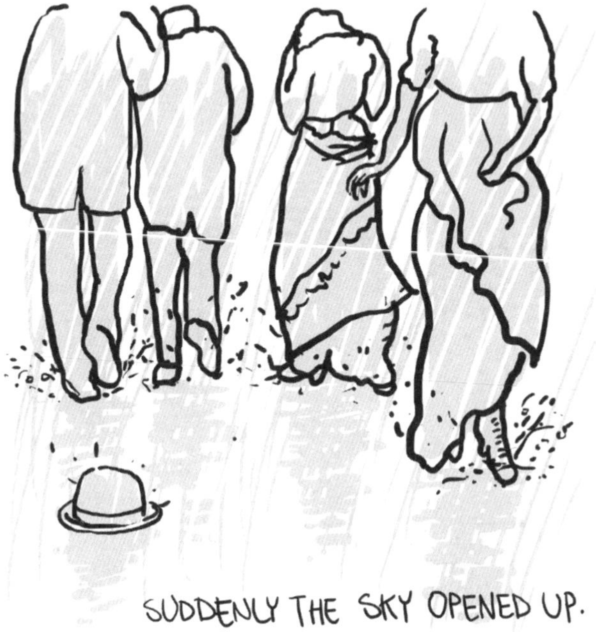
SUDDENLY THE SKY OPENED UP.

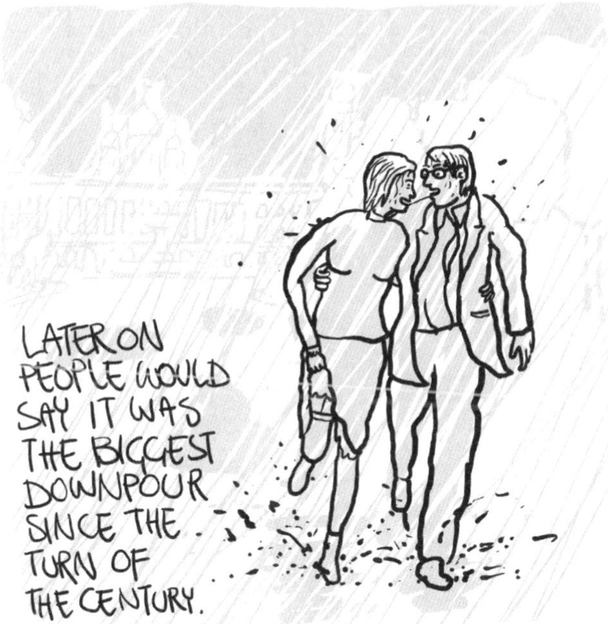
LATER ON PEOPLE WOULD SAY IT WAS THE BIGGEST DOWNPOUR SINCE THE TURN OF THE CENTURY.

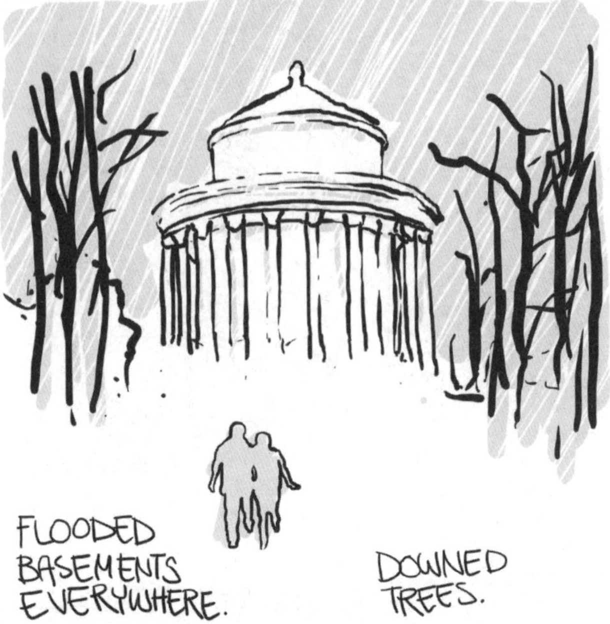
FLOODED BASEMENTS EVERYWHERE.
DOWNED TREES.

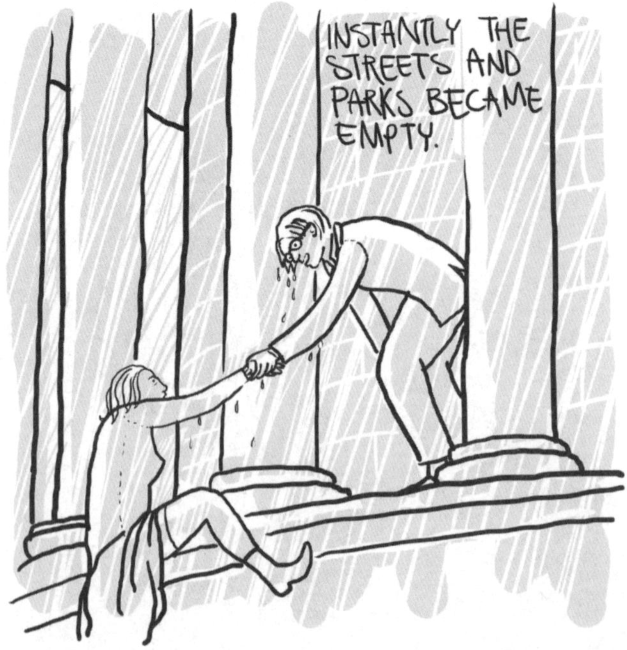
INSTANTLY THE STREETS AND PARKS BECAME EMPTY.

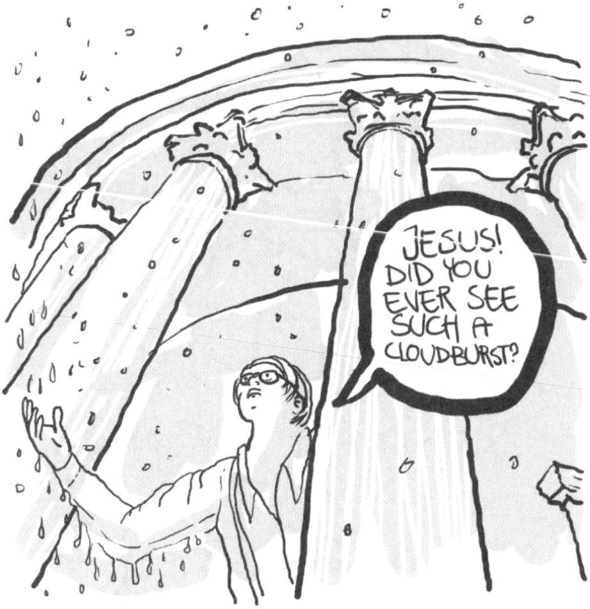
JESUS! DID YOU EVER SEE SUCH A CLOUDBURST?

FOR A MOMENT THE WORLD HAD STOPPED.

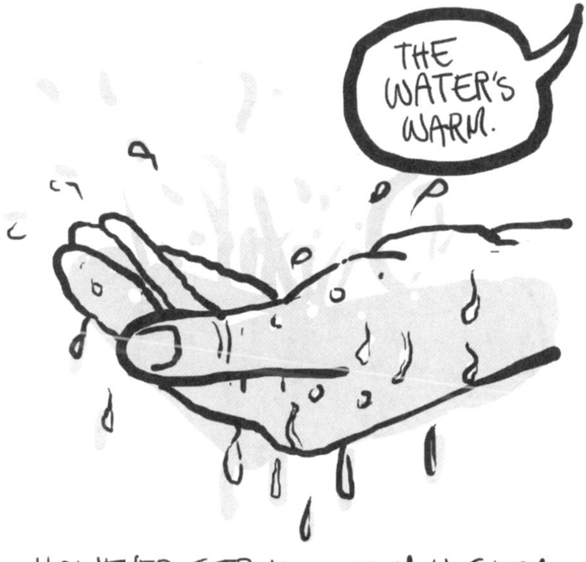
THE WATER'S WARM.

HOWEVER STRANGE IT MAY SEEM, IT WASN'T CHILLY AT ALL.

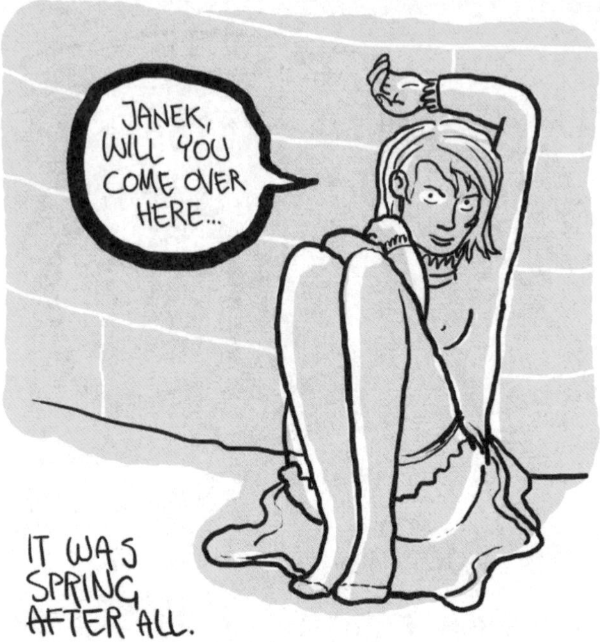
JANEK, WILL YOU COME OVER HERE...
IT WAS SPRING AFTER ALL.

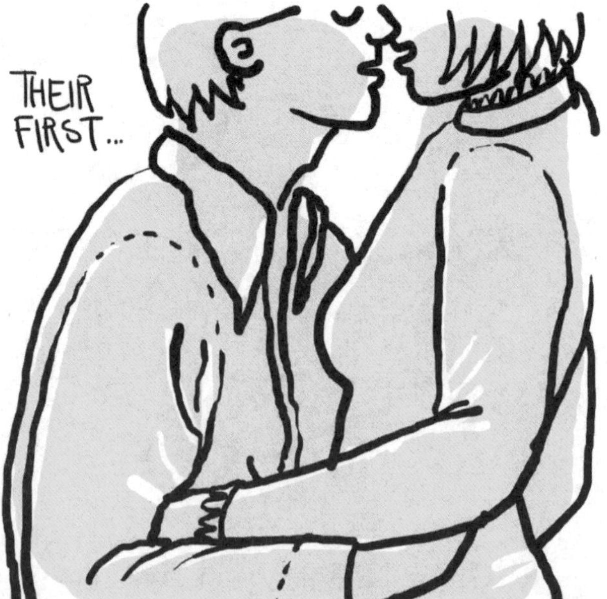
THEIR FIRST...

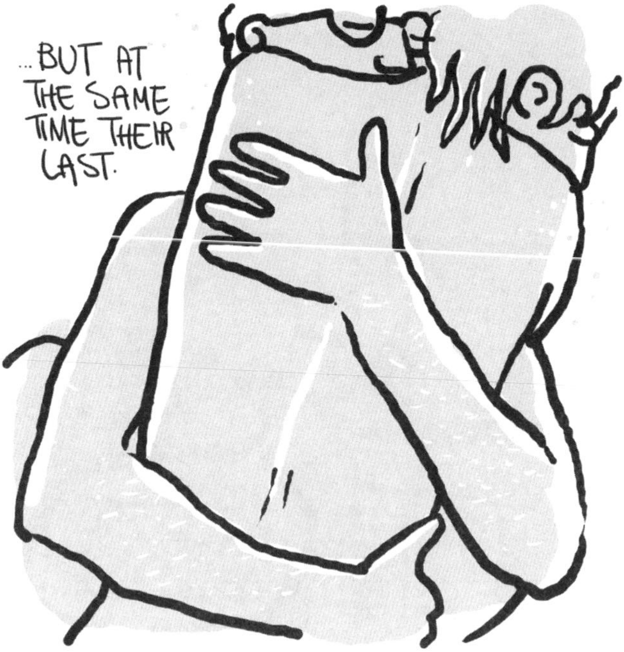
...BUT AT THE SAME TIME THEIR LAST.

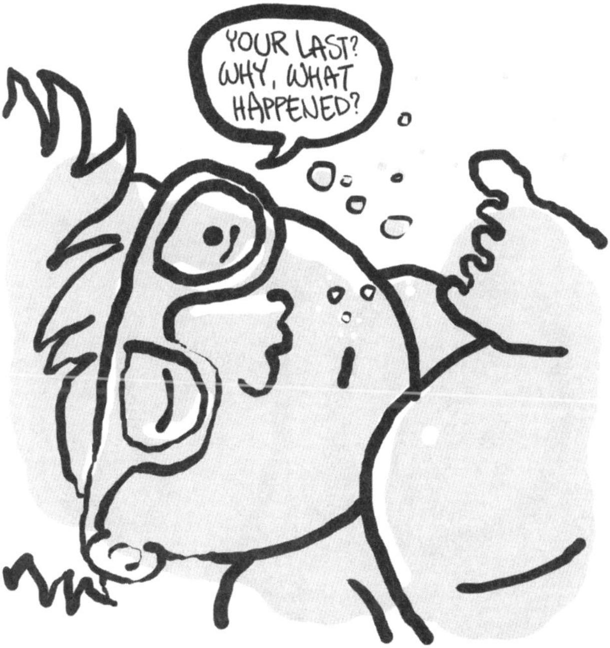
YOUR LAST? WHY, WHAT HAPPENED?

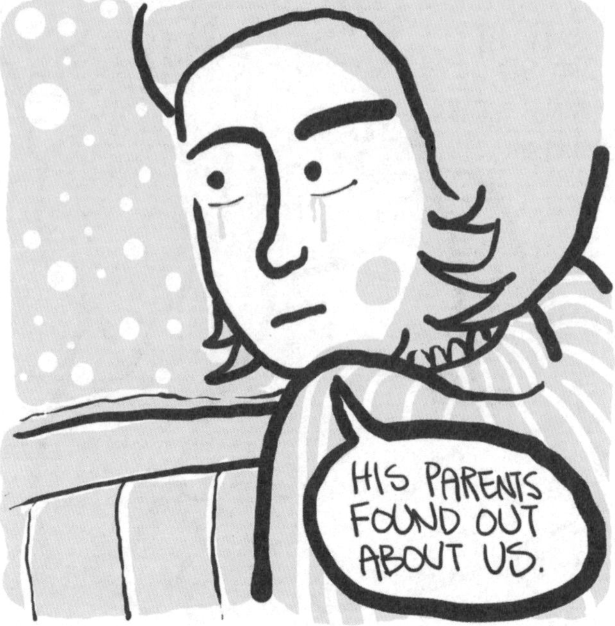
HIS PARENTS FOUND OUT ABOUT US.

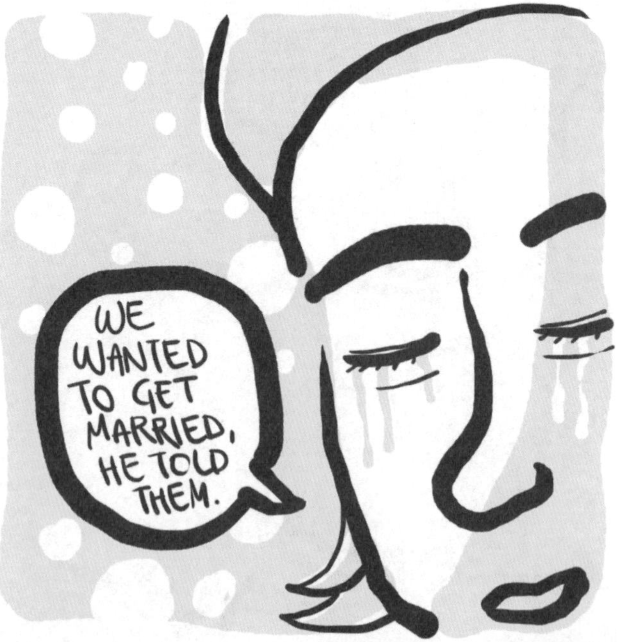
WE WANTED TO GET MARRIED, HE TOLD THEM.

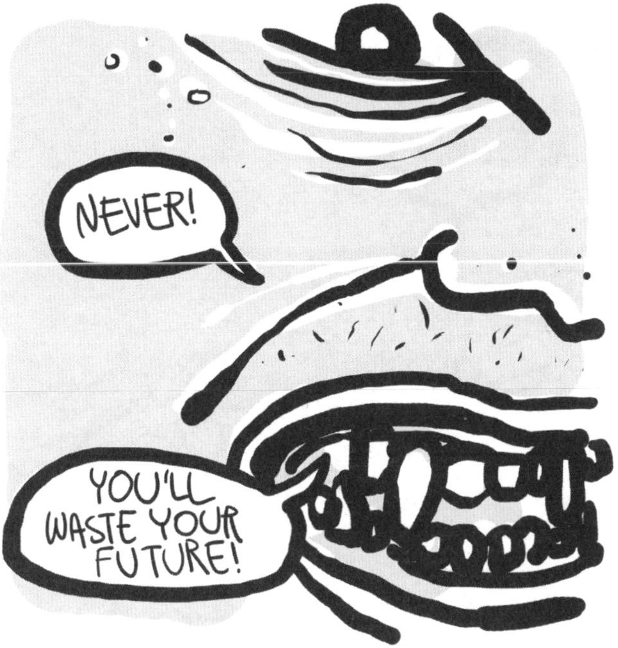
NEVER!
YOU'LL WASTE YOUR FUTURE!

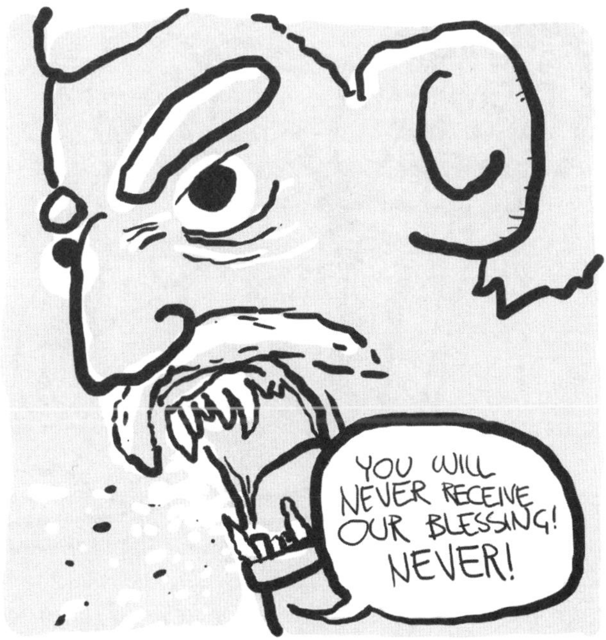
YOU WILL NEVER RECEIVE OUR BLESSING! NEVER!

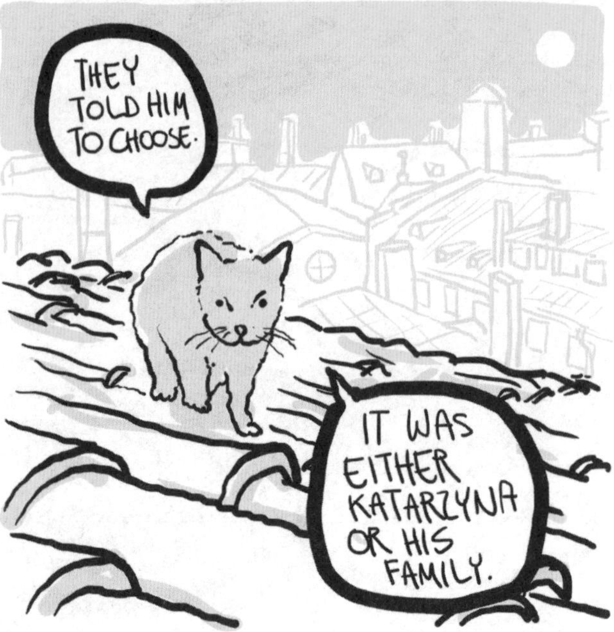
THEY TOLD HIM TO CHOOSE.
IT WAS EITHER KATARZYNA OR HIS FAMILY.

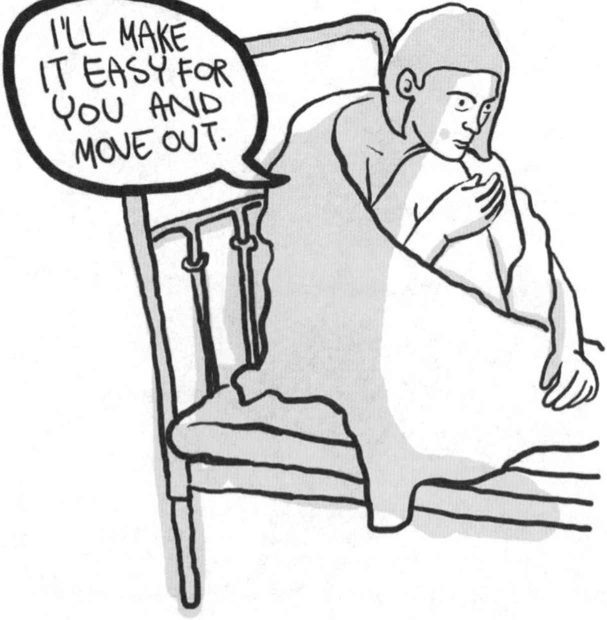
I'LL MAKE IT EASY FOR YOU AND MOVE OUT.

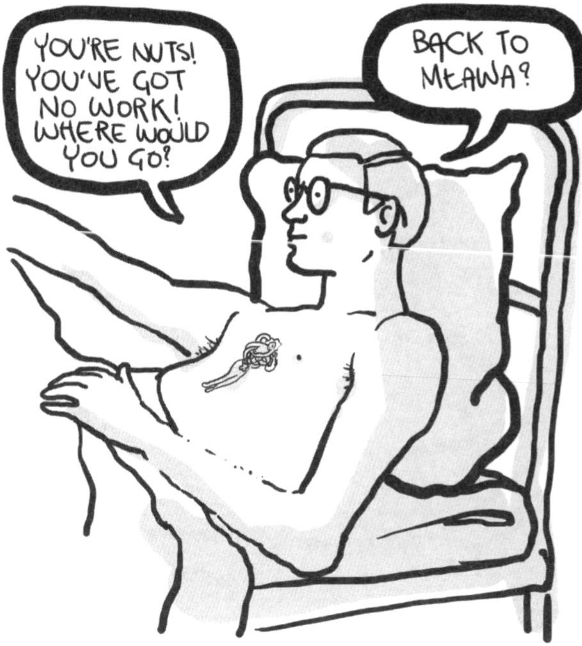
YOU'RE NUTS! YOU'VE GOT NO WORK! WHERE WOULD YOU GO?
BACK TO MŁAWA?

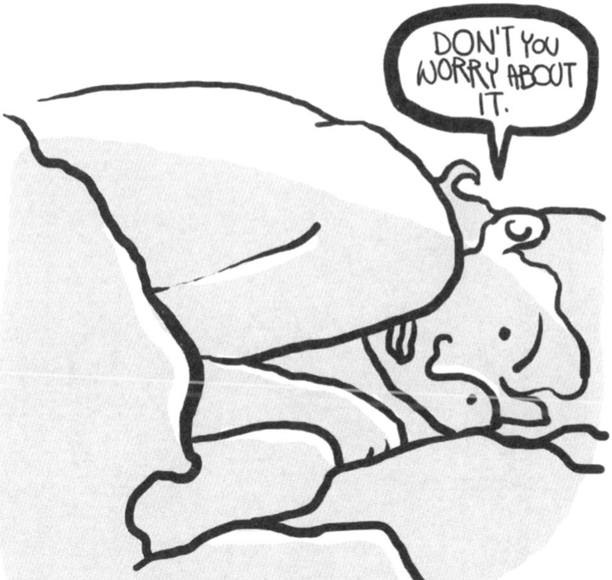
DON'T YOU WORRY ABOUT IT.

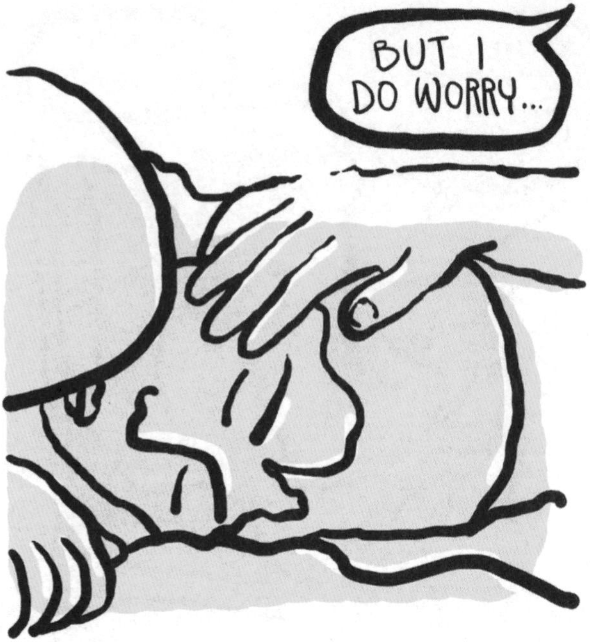
BUT I DO WORRY...

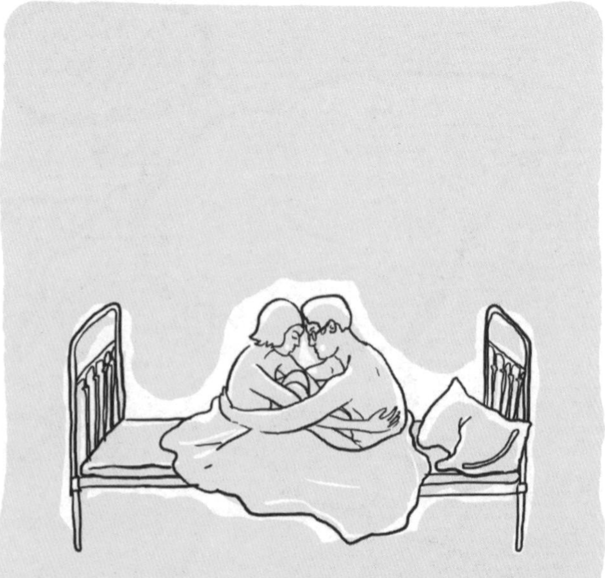

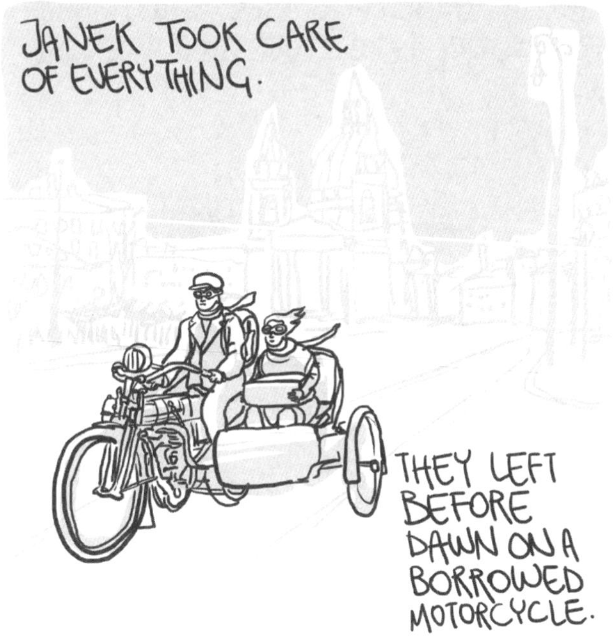
JANEK TOOK CARE OF EVERYTHING.
THEY LEFT BEFORE DAWN ON A BORROWED MOTORCYCLE.

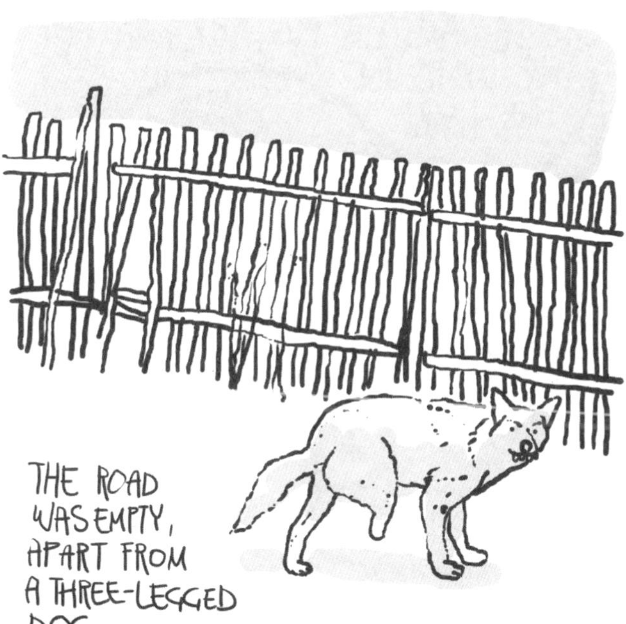
THE ROAD WAS EMPTY, APART FROM A THREE-LEGGED DOG.

THE MORNING FOG WAS STILL HANGING LOW OVER THE FIELDS.

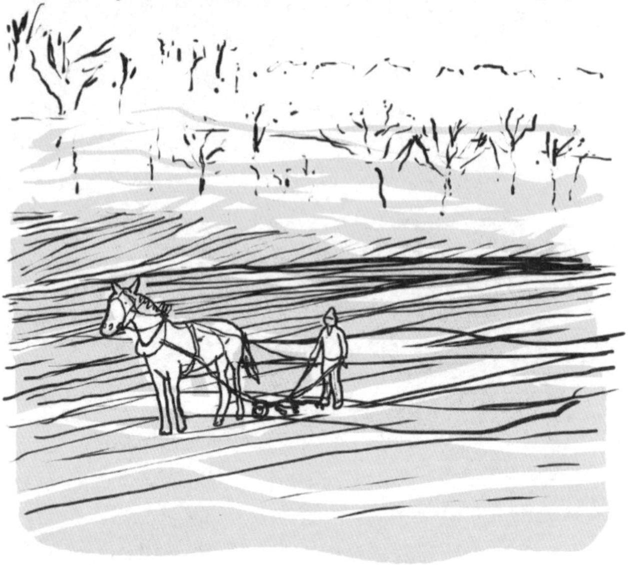

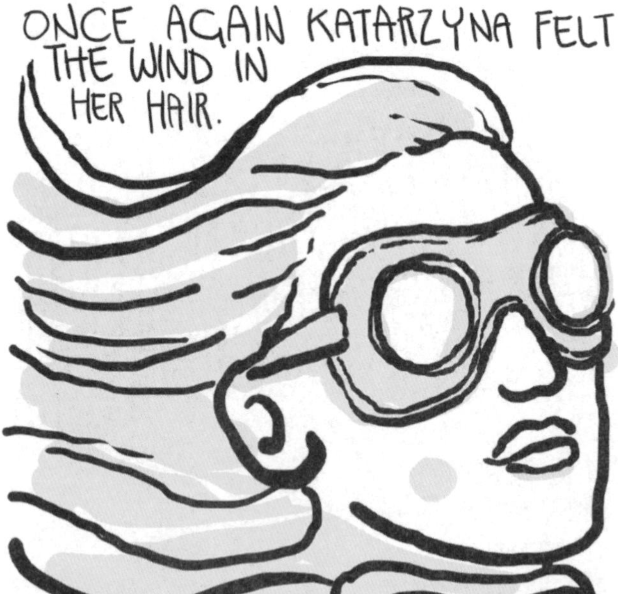
ONCE AGAIN KATARZYNA FELT THE WIND IN HER HAIR.

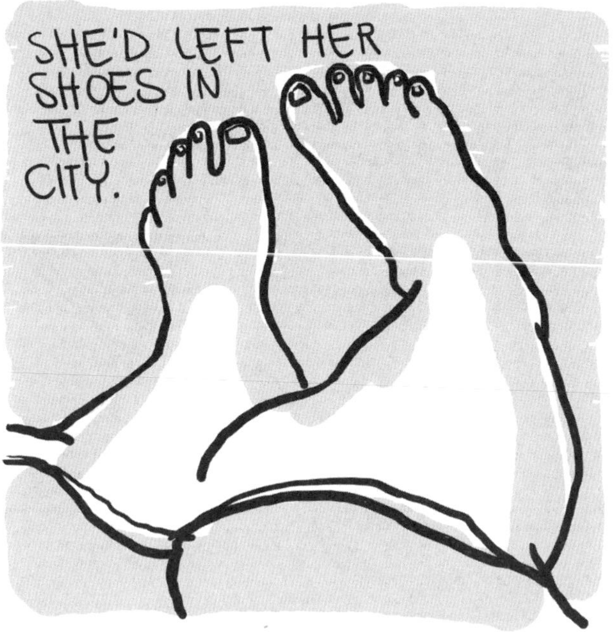
SHE'D LEFT HER SHOES IN THE CITY.

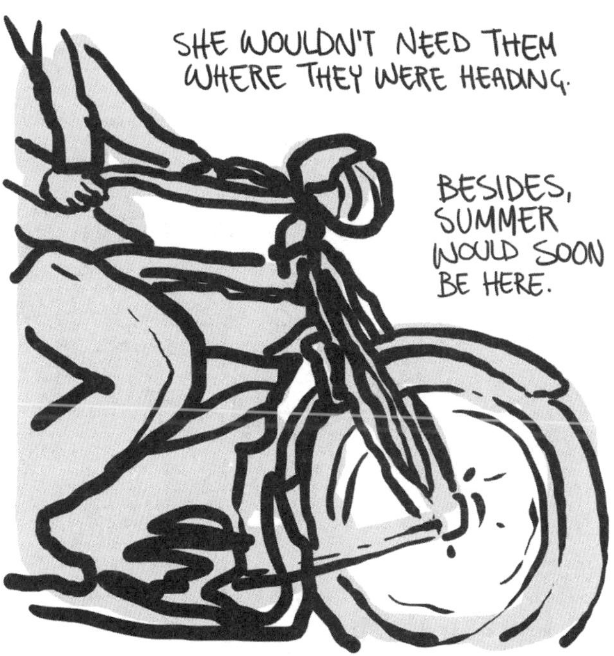
SHE WOULDN'T NEED THEM WHERE THEY WERE HEADING.
BESIDES, SUMMER WOULD SOON BE HERE.

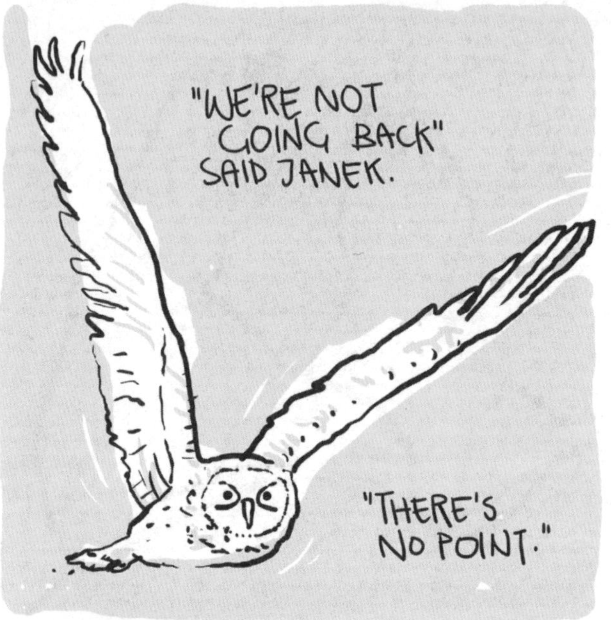
"WE'RE NOT GOING BACK" SAID JANEK.
"THERE'S NO POINT."

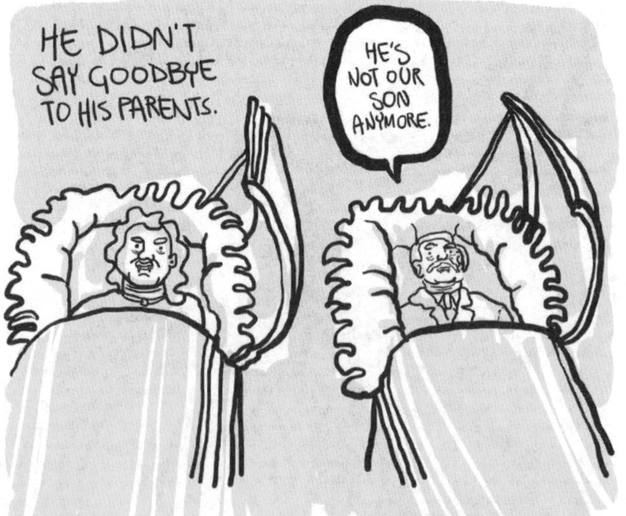
HE DIDN'T SAY GOODBYE TO HIS PARENTS.
HE'S NOT OUR SON ANYMORE.

IT WAS HIS WAY OF PUNISHING THEM.
HE WANTED THEM TO FEEL AS BAD AS HE DID.

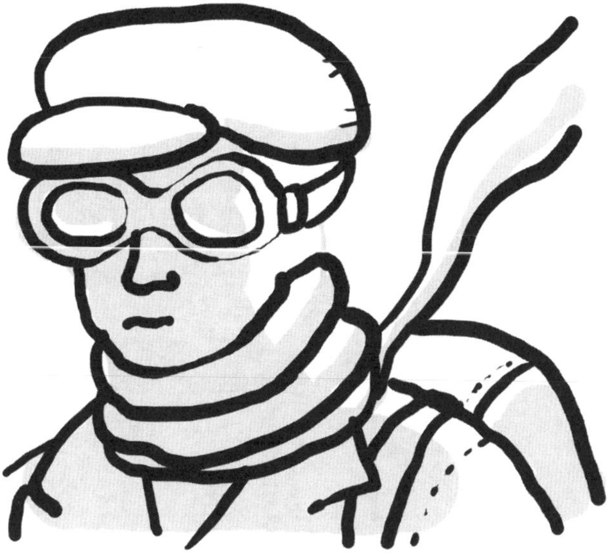

HE NEVER FORGAVE THEM.

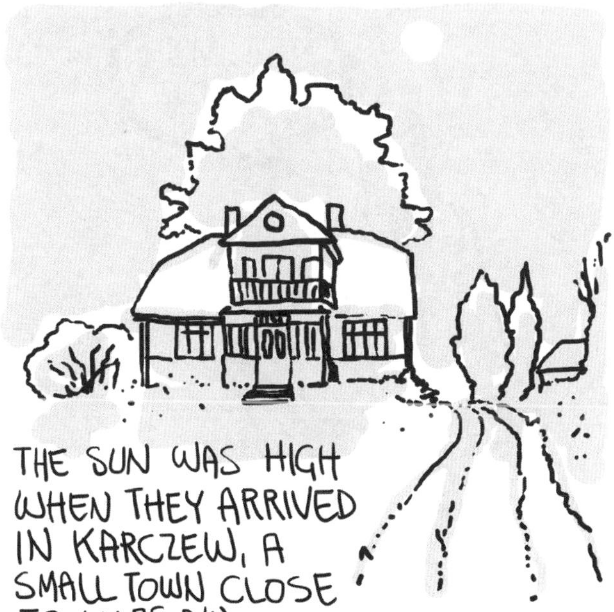
THE SUN WAS HIGH WHEN THEY ARRIVED IN KARCZEW, A SMALL TOWN CLOSE TO WARSAW.

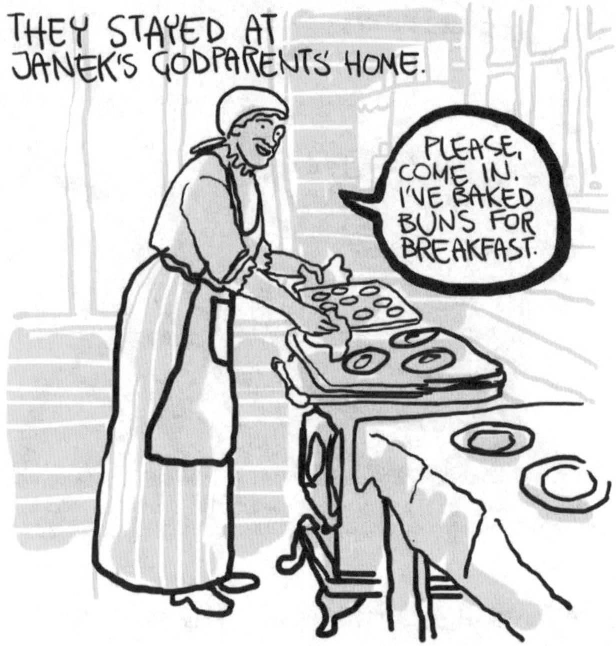
THEY STAYED AT JANEK'S GODPARENTS' HOME.
PLEASE, COME IN. I'VE BAKED BUNS FOR BREAKFAST.

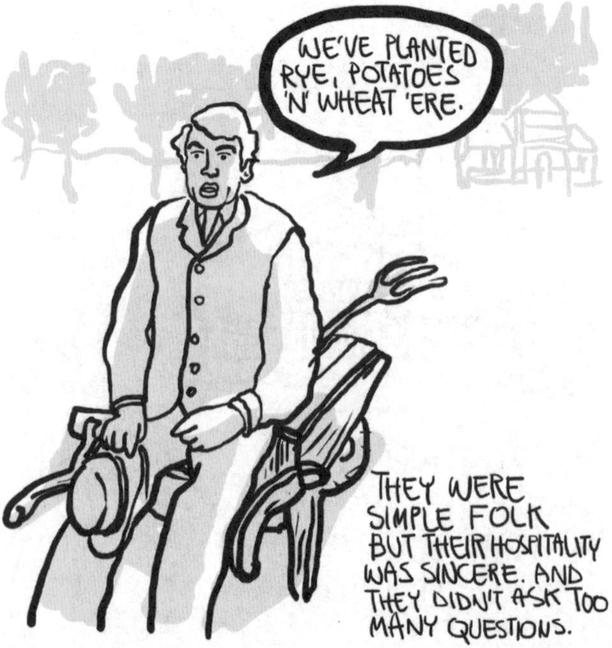
WE'VE PLANTED RYE, POTATOES 'N' WHEAT 'ERE.
THEY WERE SIMPLE FOLK BUT THEIR HOSPITALITY WAS SINCERE. AND THEY DIDN'T ASK TOO MANY QUESTIONS.

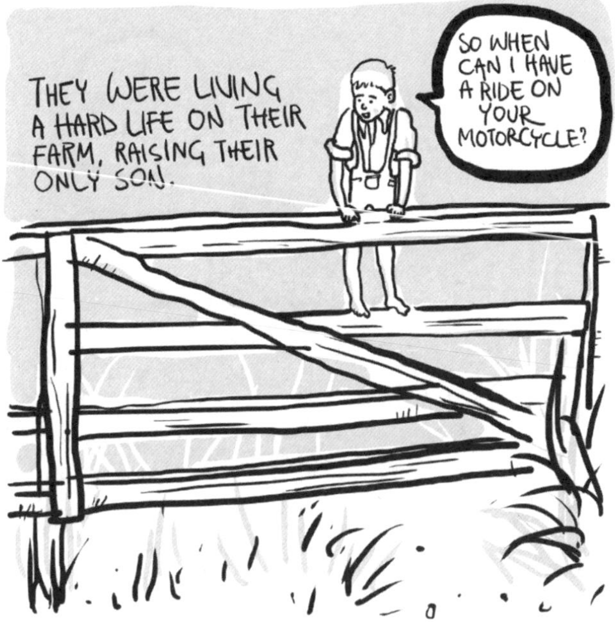
THEY WERE LIVING A HARD LIFE ON THEIR FARM, RAISING THEIR ONLY SON.
SO WHEN CAN I HAVE A RIDE ON YOUR MOTORCYCLE?

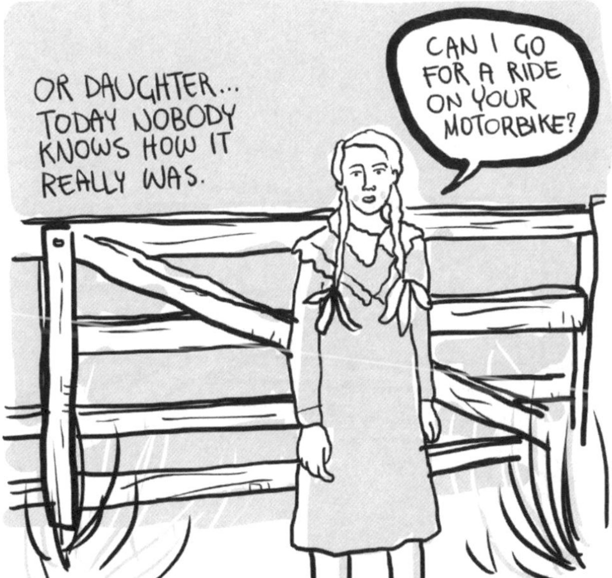
OR DAUGHTER... TODAY NOBODY KNOWS HOW IT REALLY WAS.
CAN I GO FOR A RIDE ON YOUR MOTORBIKE?

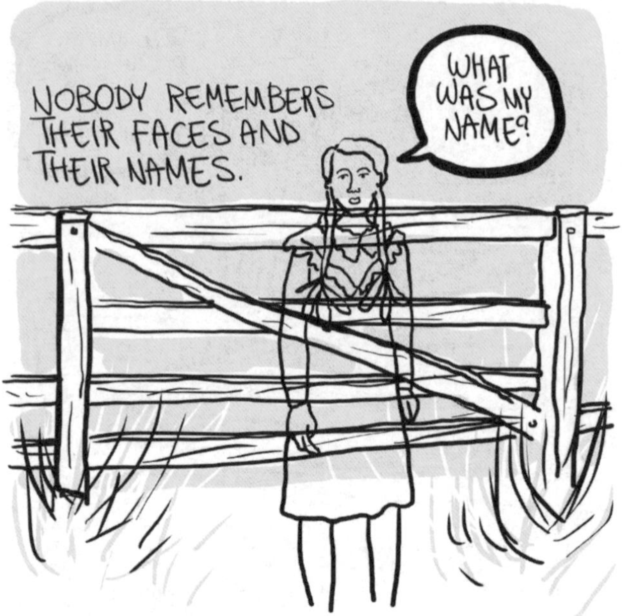
NOBODY REMEMBERS THEIR FACES AND THEIR NAMES.
WHAT WAS MY NAME?

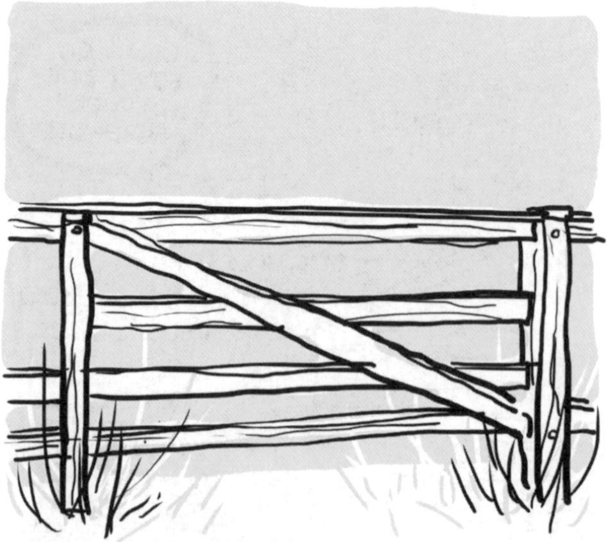
LIKE GHOSTS FADING IN THE MORNING SUN.

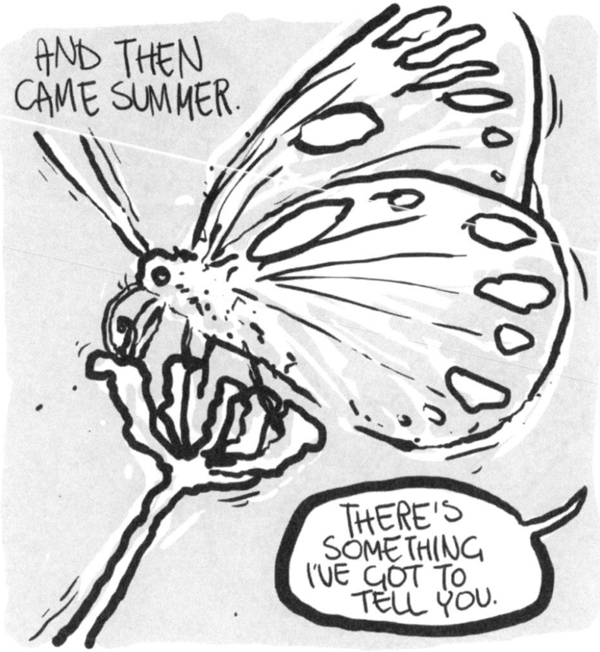
AND THEN CAME SUMMER.
THERE'S SOMETHING I'VE GOT TO TELL YOU.

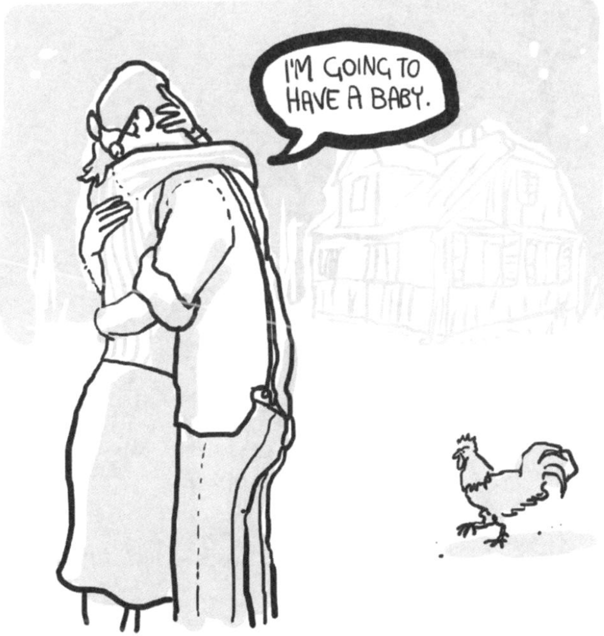
I'M GOING TO HAVE A BABY.

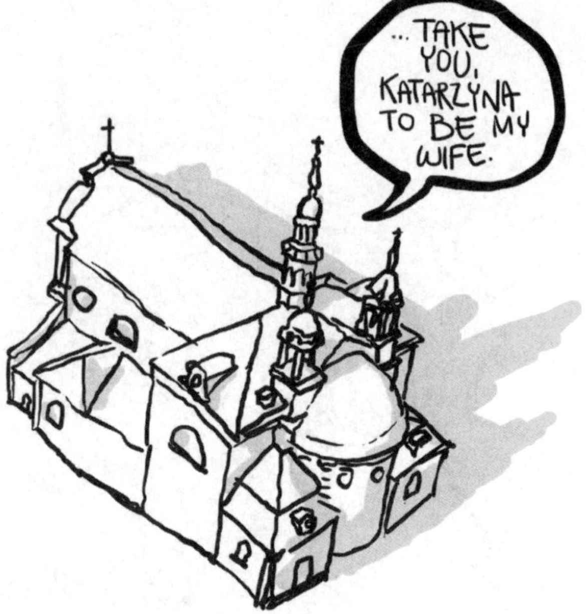
...TAKE YOU, KATARZYNA TO BE MY WIFE.

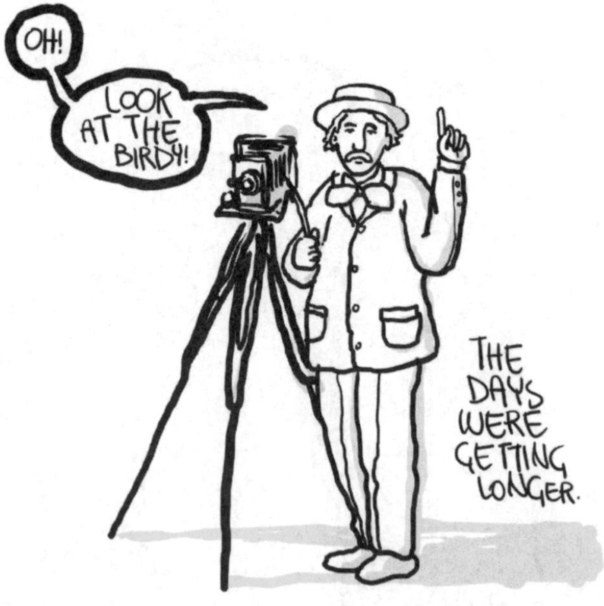
OH!
LOOK AT THE BIRDY!
THE DAYS WERE GETTING LONGER.

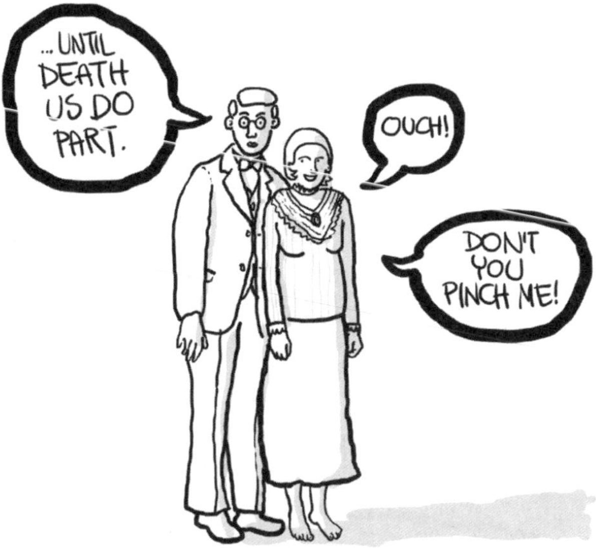
...UNTIL DEATH US DO PART.
OUCH!
DON'T YOU PINCH ME!

...AND THE NIGHTS SHORTER.

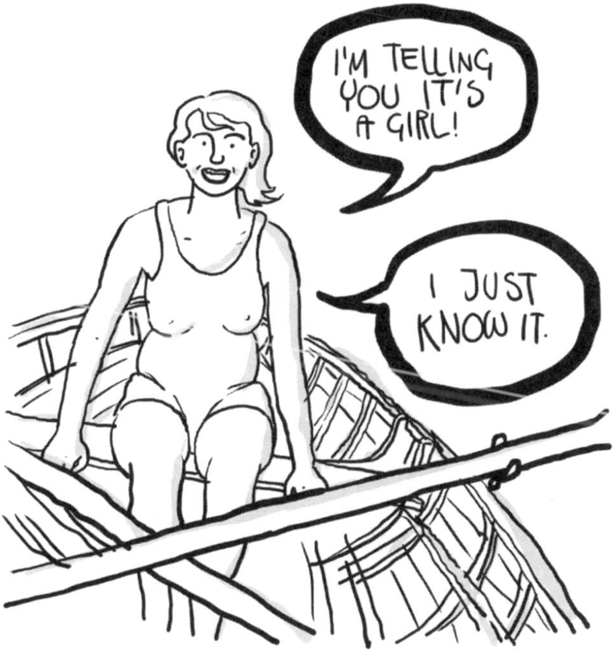
I'M TELLING YOU IT'S A GIRL!
I JUST KNOW IT.

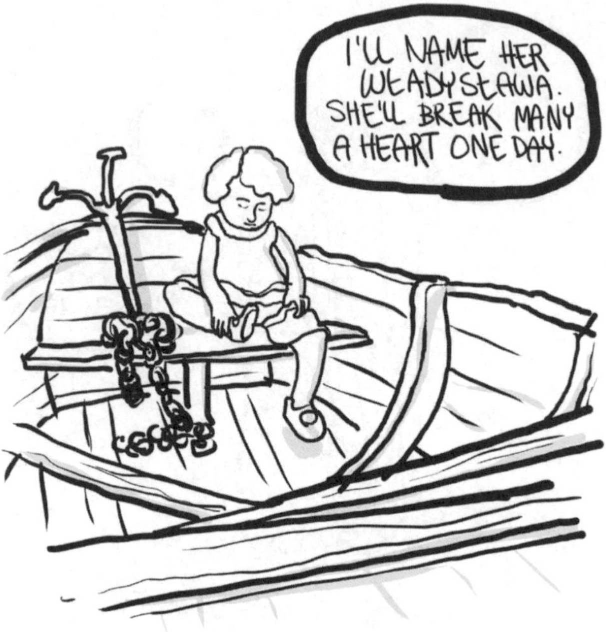
I'LL NAME HER WŁADYSŁAWA. SHE'LL BREAK MANY A HEART ONE DAY.

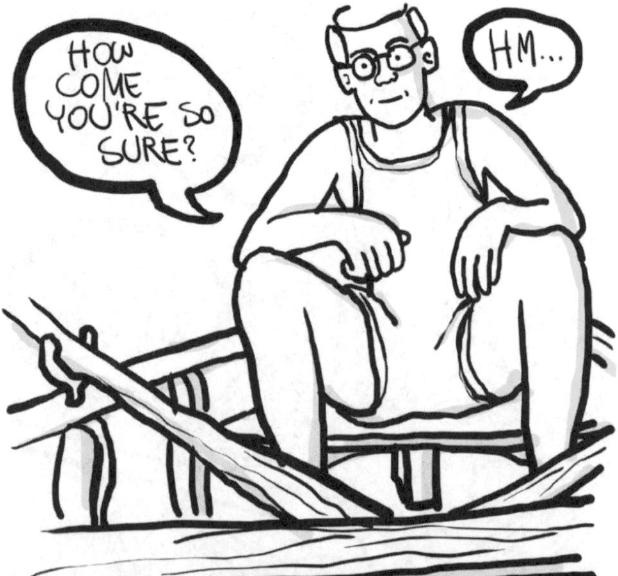
HOW COME YOU'RE SO SURE?
HM...

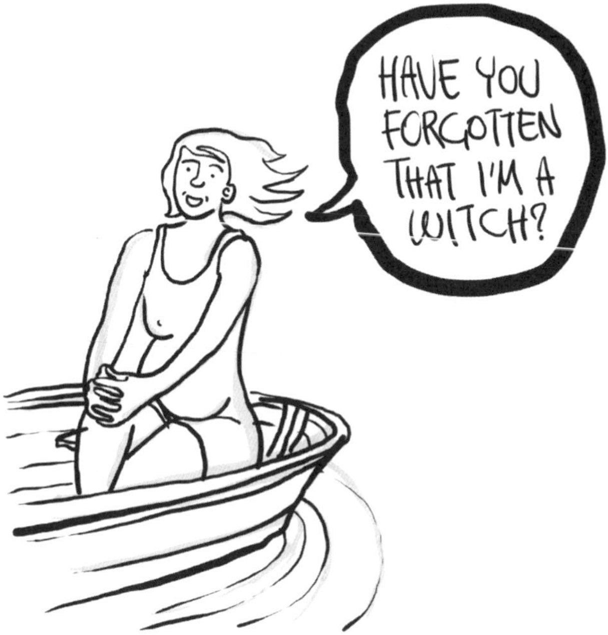
HAVE YOU FORGOTTEN THAT I'M A WITCH?

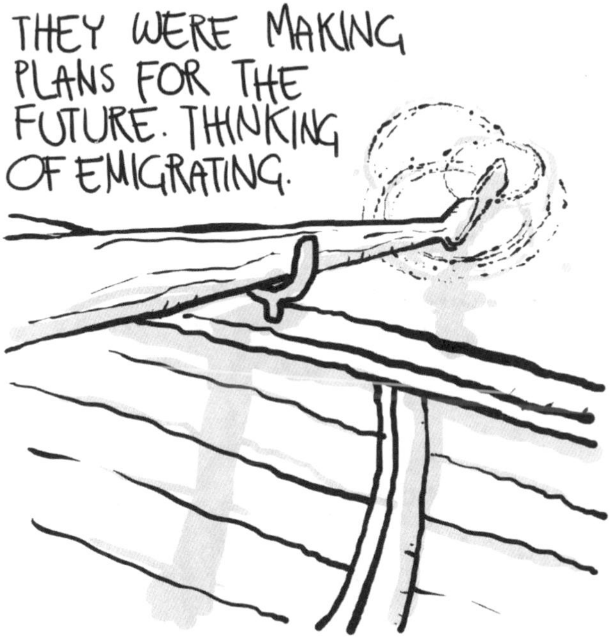
THEY WERE MAKING PLANS FOR THE FUTURE. THINKING OF EMIGRATING.

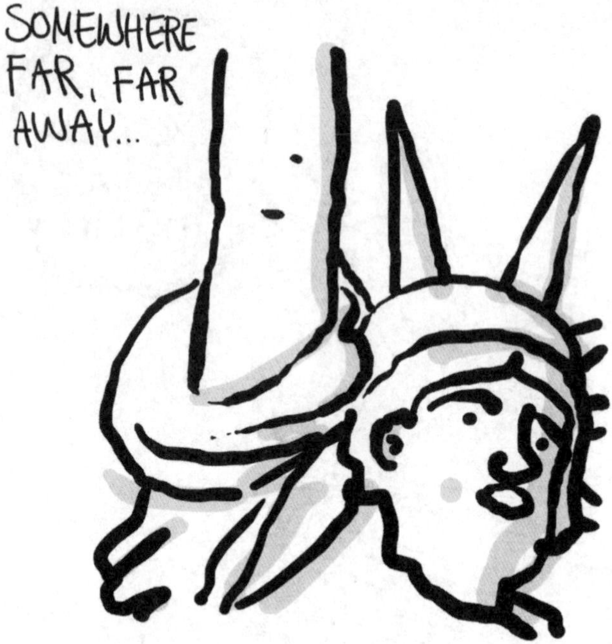
SOMEWHERE FAR, FAR AWAY...

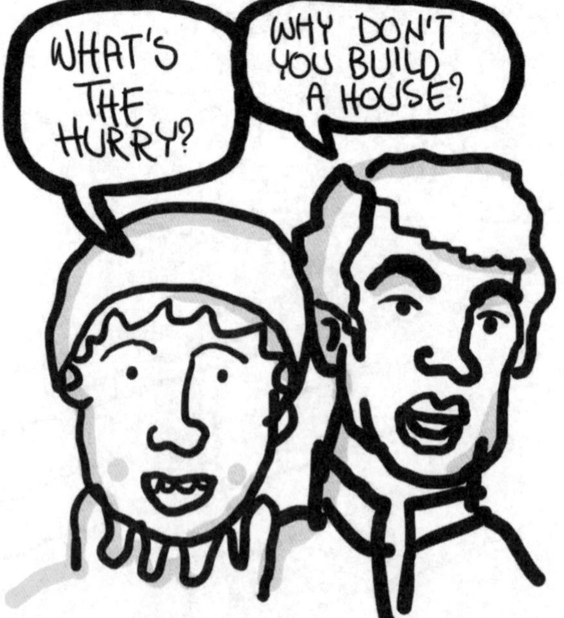
WHAT'S THE HURRY?
WHY DON'T YOU BUILD A HOUSE?

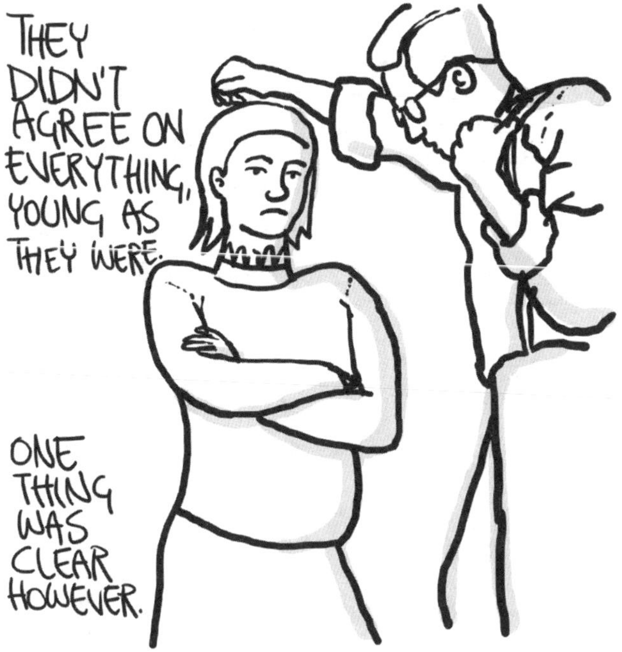
THEY DIDN'T AGREE ON EVERYTHING, YOUNG AS THEY WERE.
ONE THING WAS CLEAR HOWEVER.

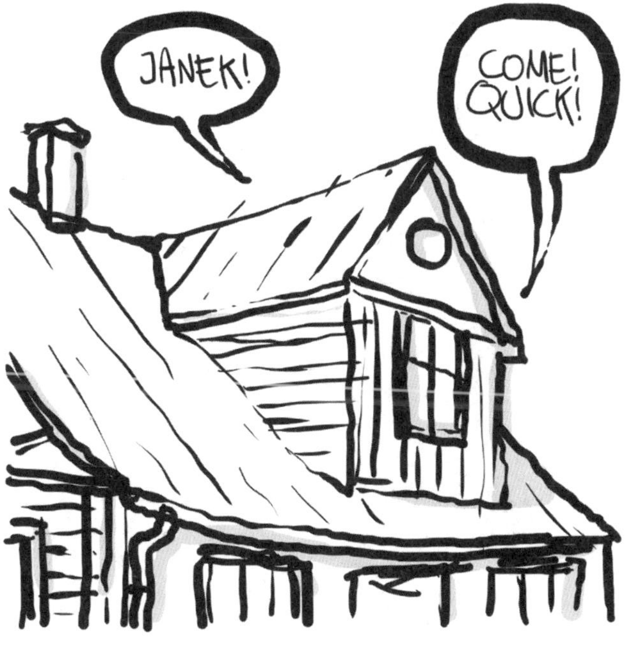
JANEK!
COME! QUICK!

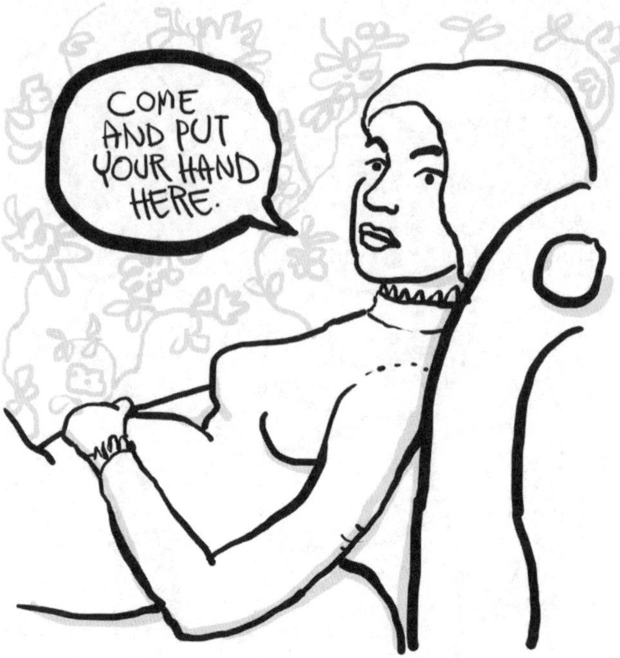
COME AND PUT YOUR HAND HERE.

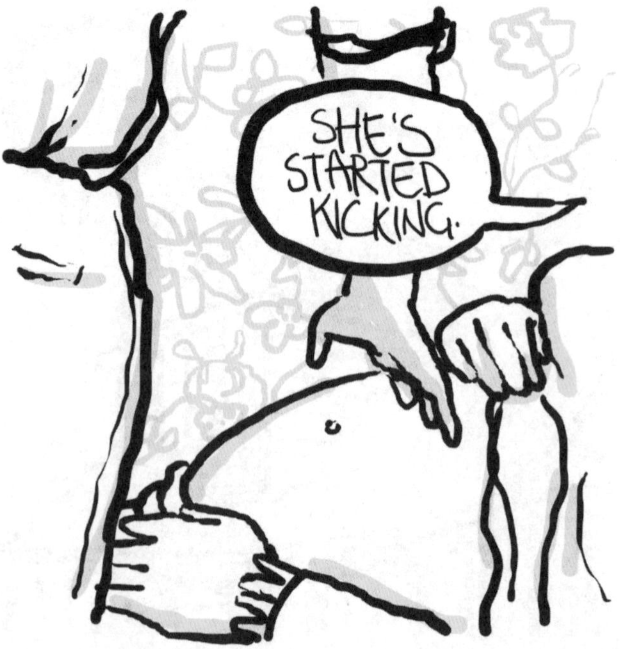
SHE'S STARTED KICKING.

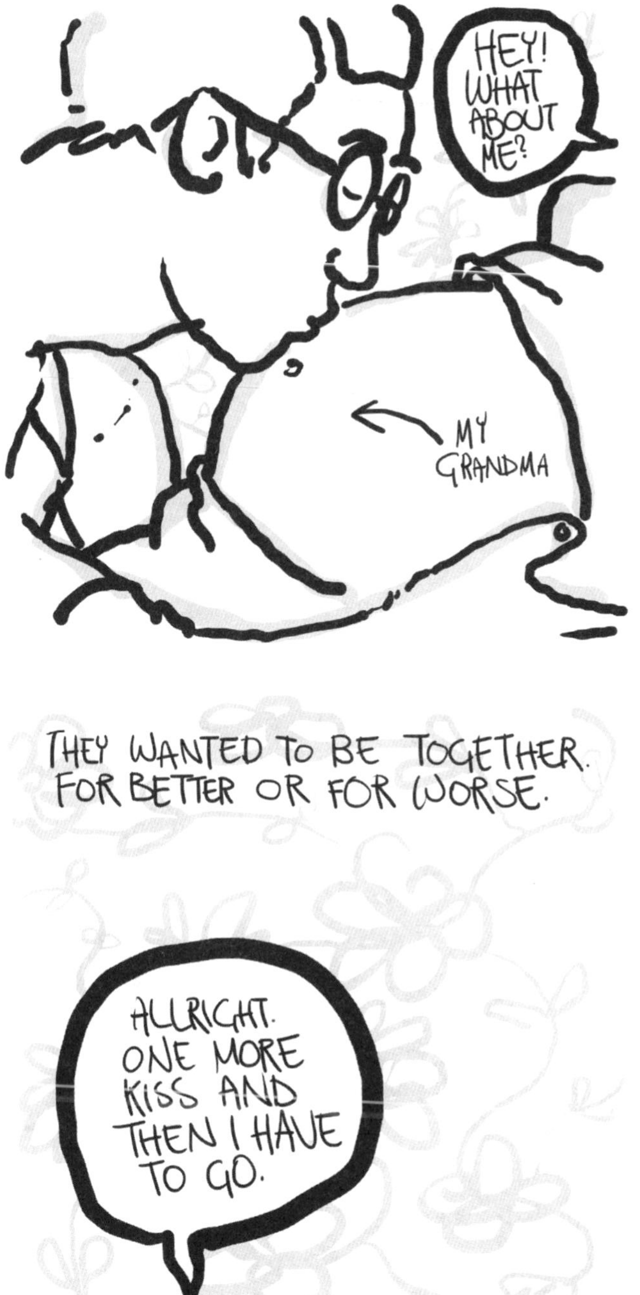
HEY! WHAT ABOUT ME?
MY GRANDMA
THEY WANTED TO BE TOGETHER. FOR BETTER OR FOR WORSE.
ALLRIGHT. ONE MORE KISS AND THEN I HAVE TO GO.

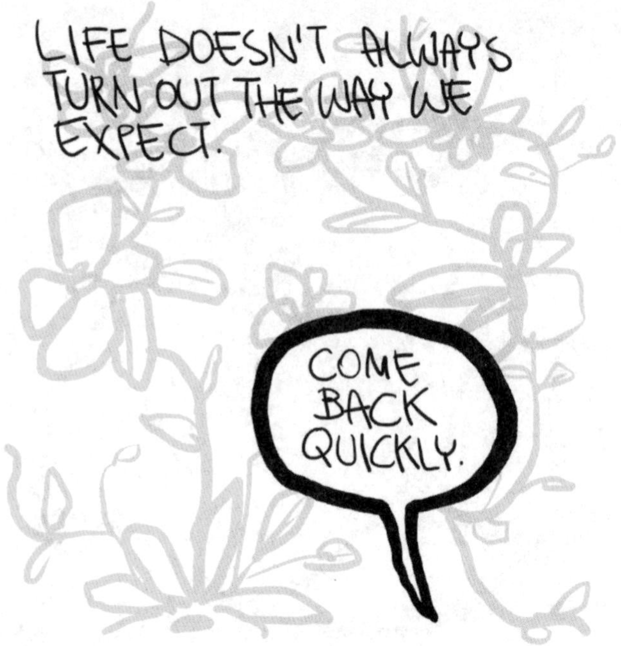
LIFE DOESN'T ALWAYS TURN OUT THE WAY WE EXPECT.
COME BACK QUICKLY.

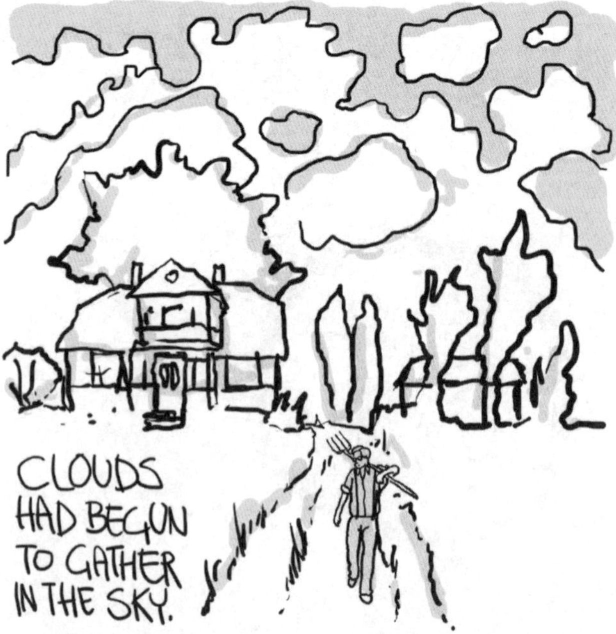
CLOUDS HAD BEGUN TO GATHER IN THE SKY.

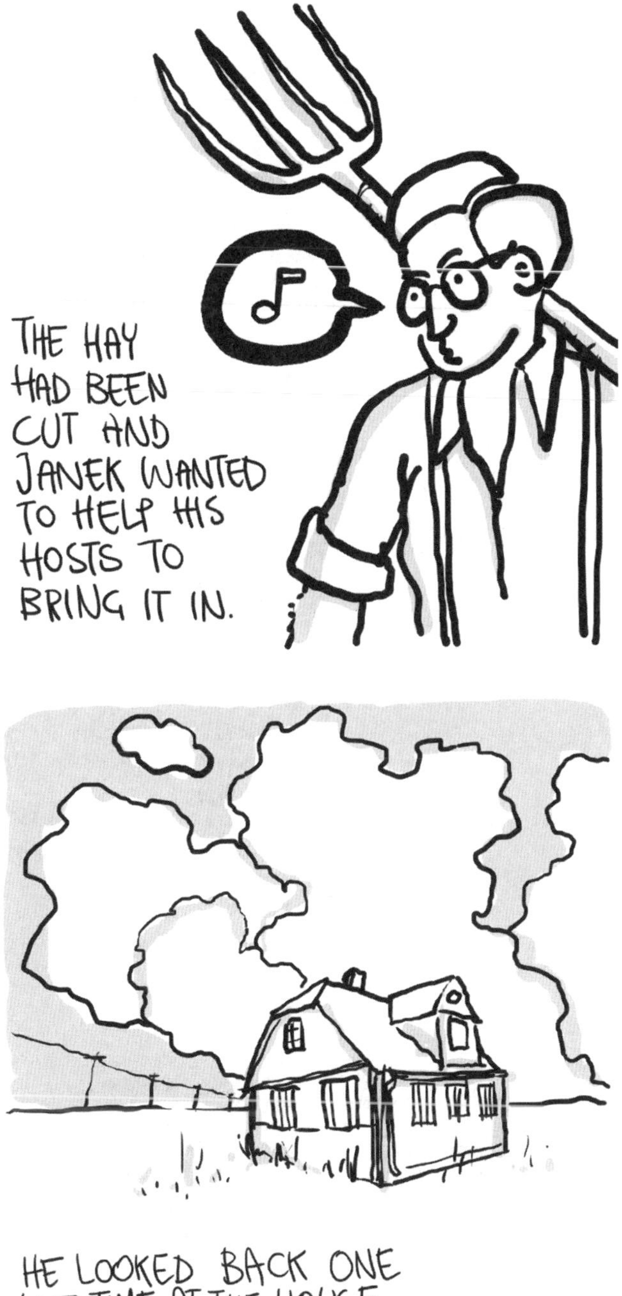
THE HAY HAD BEEN CUT AND JANEK WANTED TO HELP HIS HOSTS TO BRING IT IN.
HE LOOKED BACK ONE LAST TIME AT THE HOUSE.

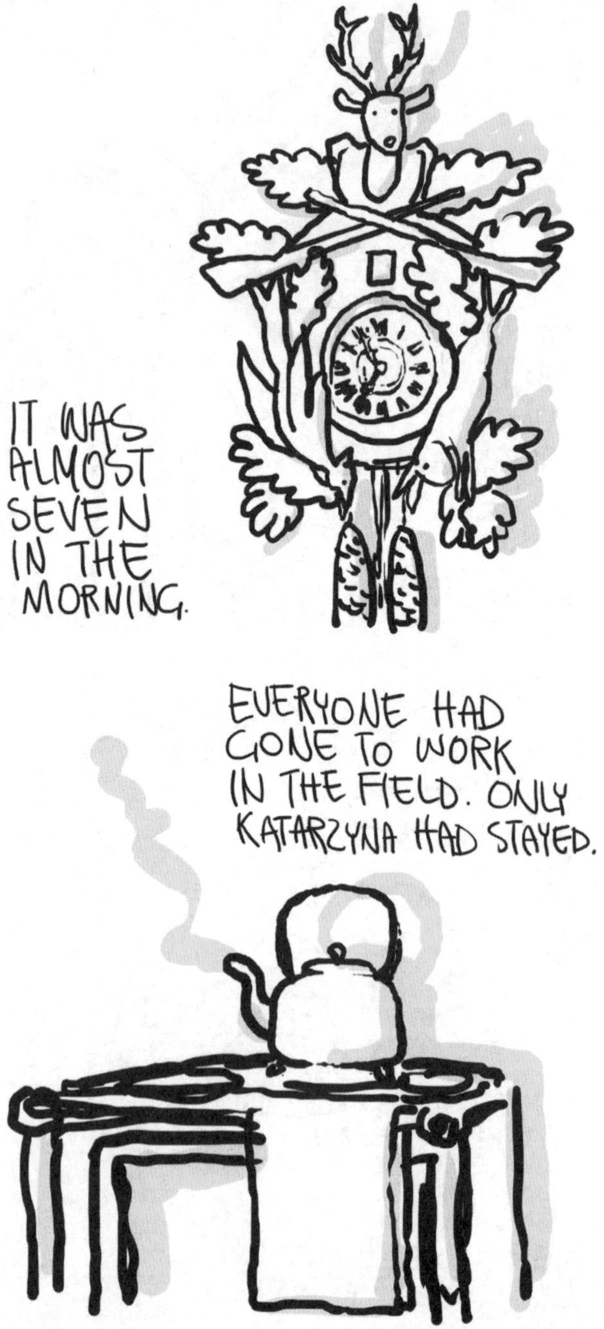
IT WAS ALMOST SEVEN IN THE MORNING.
EVERYONE HAD GONE TO WORK IN THE FIELD. ONLY KATARZYNA HAD STAYED.

AND
THAT WAS
THE LAST
TIME...

...AN OWL
HOOTED.

KATARZYNA?

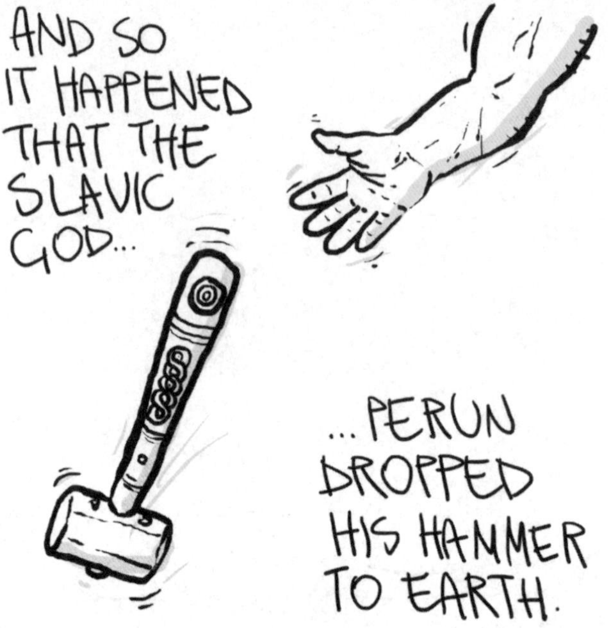
AND SO IT HAPPENED THAT THE SLAVIC GOD...
...PERUN DROPPED HIS HAMMER TO EARTH.

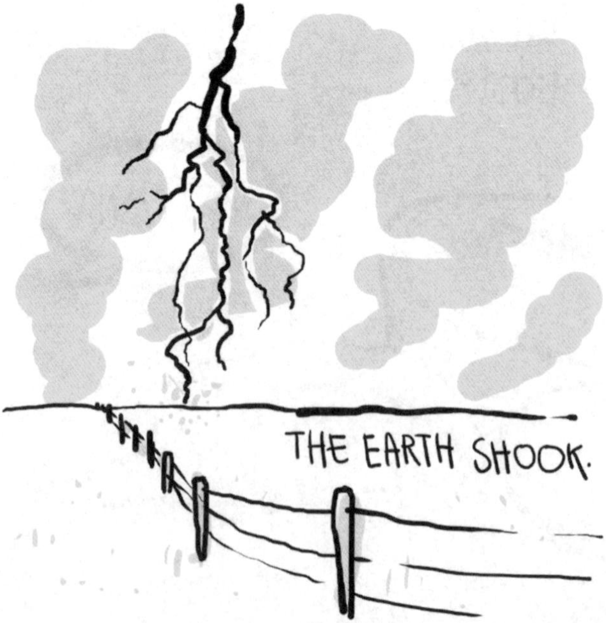
THE EARTH SHOOK.

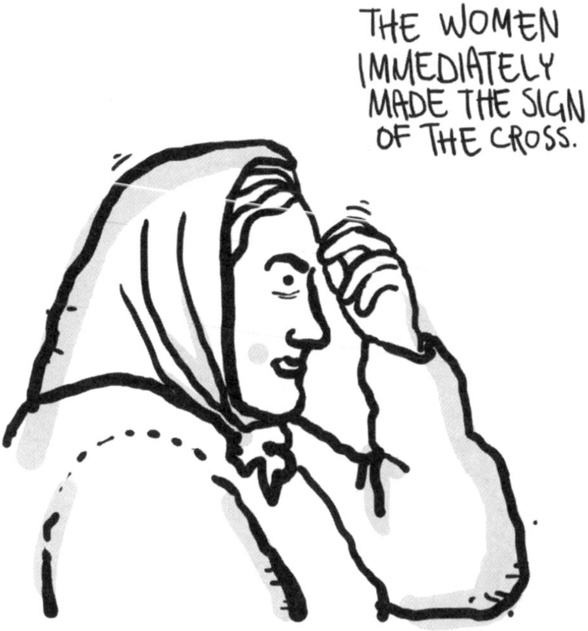
THE WOMEN IMMEDIATELY MADE THE SIGN OF THE CROSS.

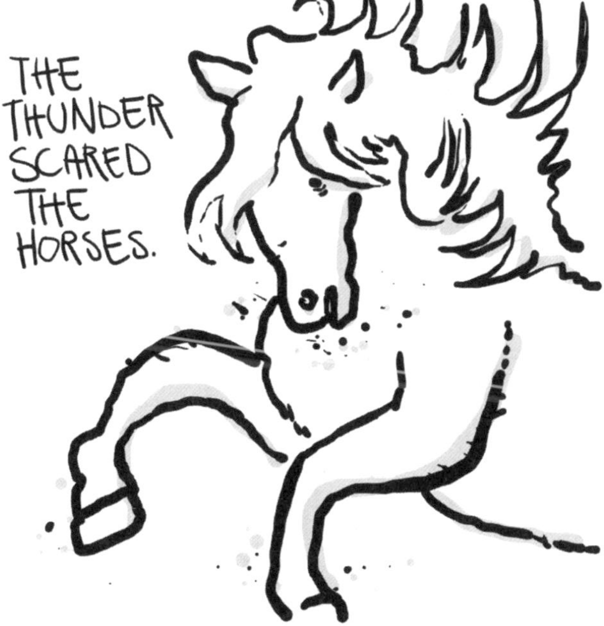
THE THUNDER SCARED THE HORSES.

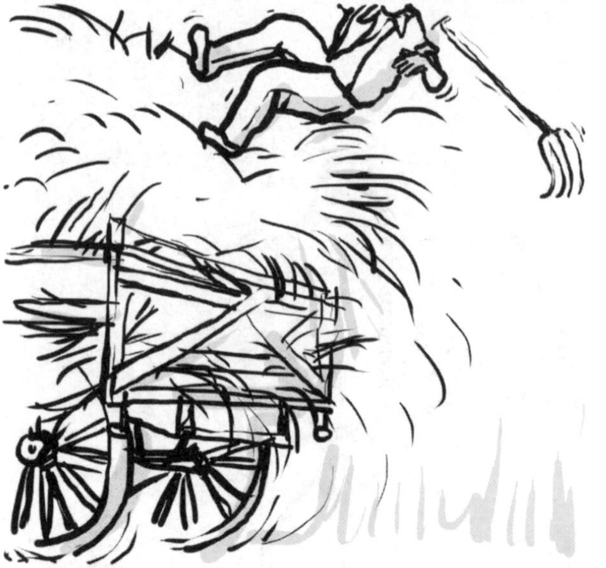

WHEN THEY SUDDENLY MOVED FORWARD, JAN FELL FROM THE WAGON.

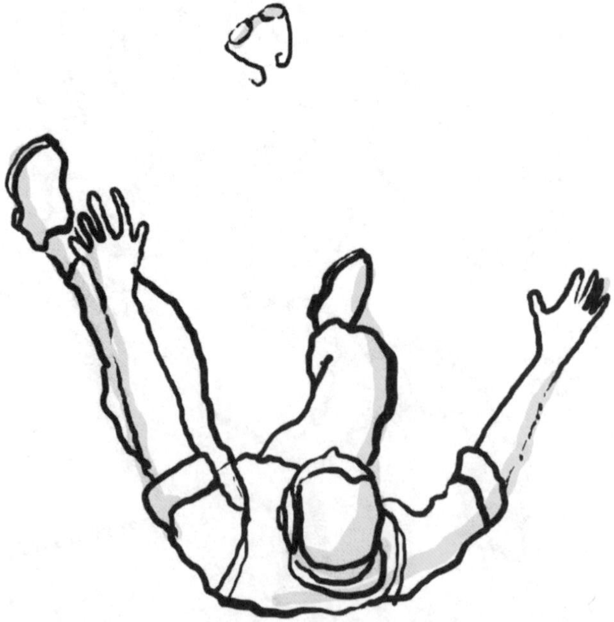

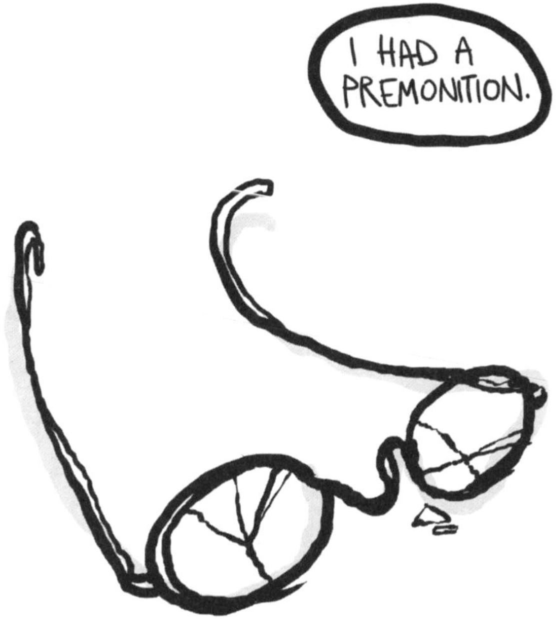
I HAD A PREMONITION.

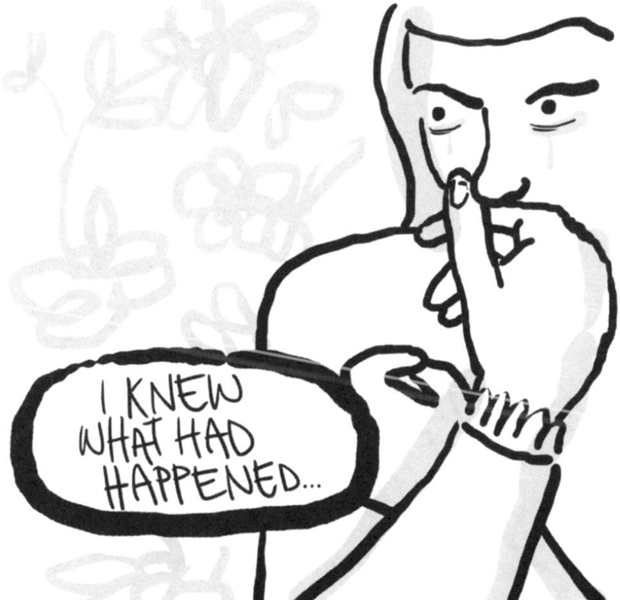
I KNEW WHAT HAD HAPPENED...

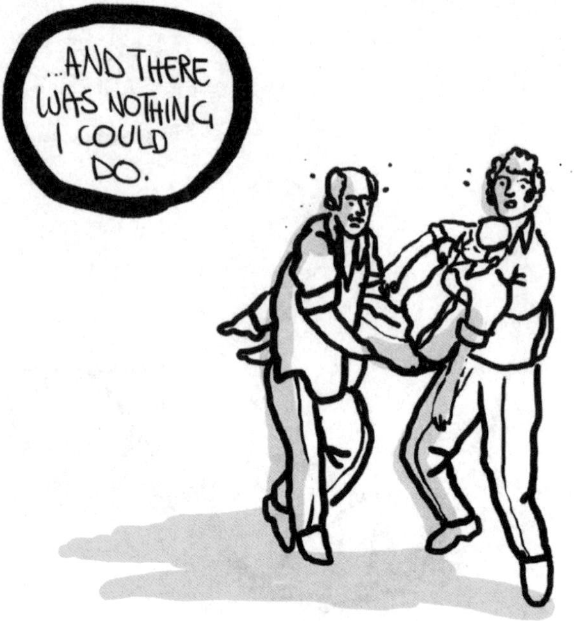
...AND THERE WAS NOTHING I COULD DO.

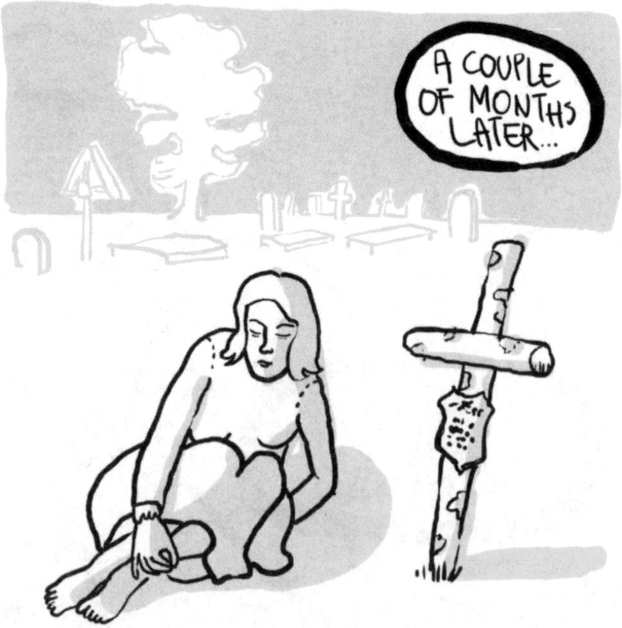
A COUPLE OF MONTHS LATER...

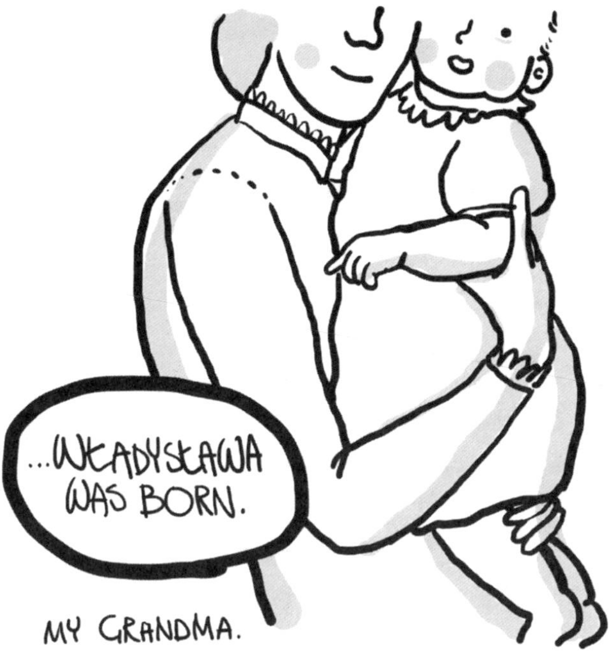
...WŁADYSŁAWA WAS BORN.
MY GRANDMA.

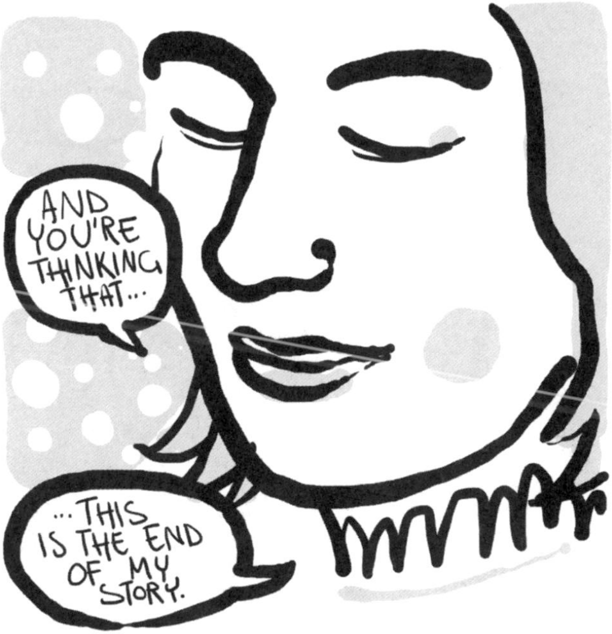
AND YOU'RE THINKING THAT...
...THIS IS THE END OF MY STORY.

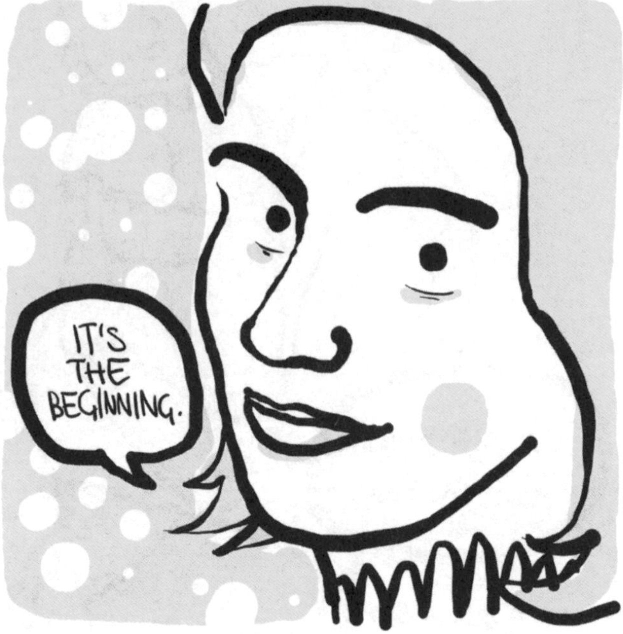
IT'S THE BEGINNING.

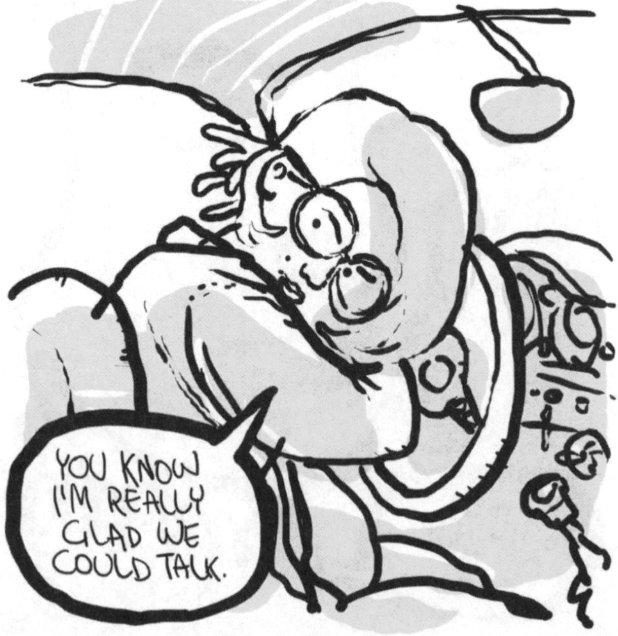
YOU KNOW I'M REALLY GLAD WE COULD TALK.

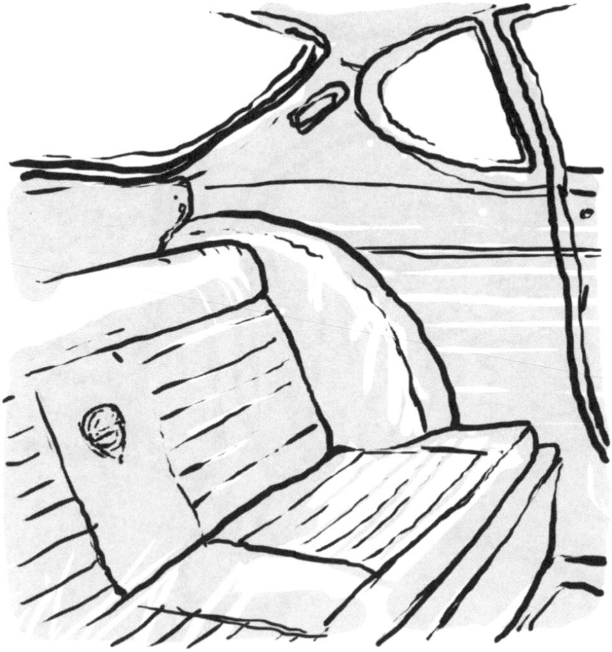

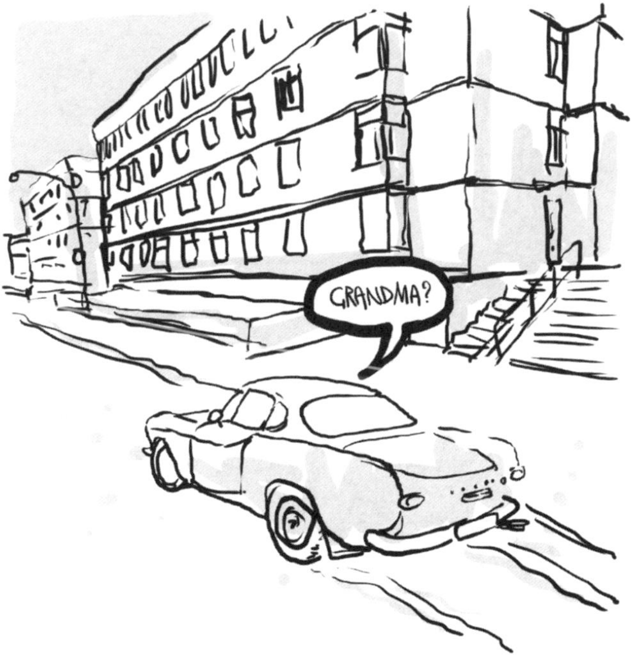
GRANDMA?

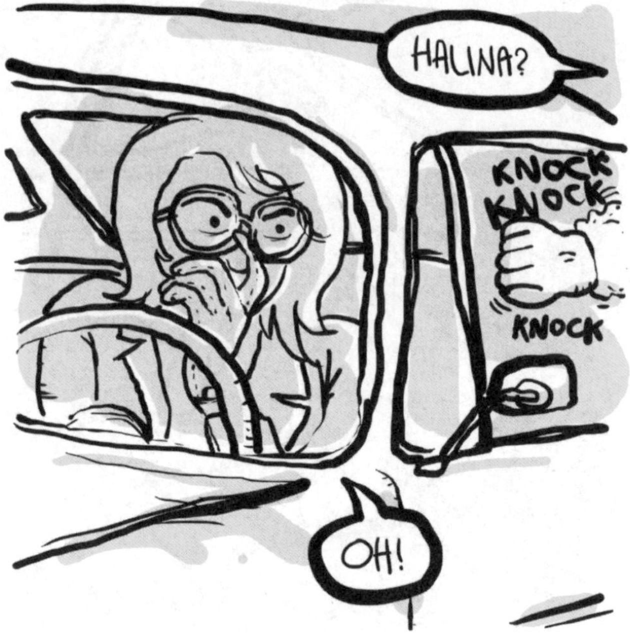
HALINA?
KNOCK
KNOCK
KNOCK
OH!

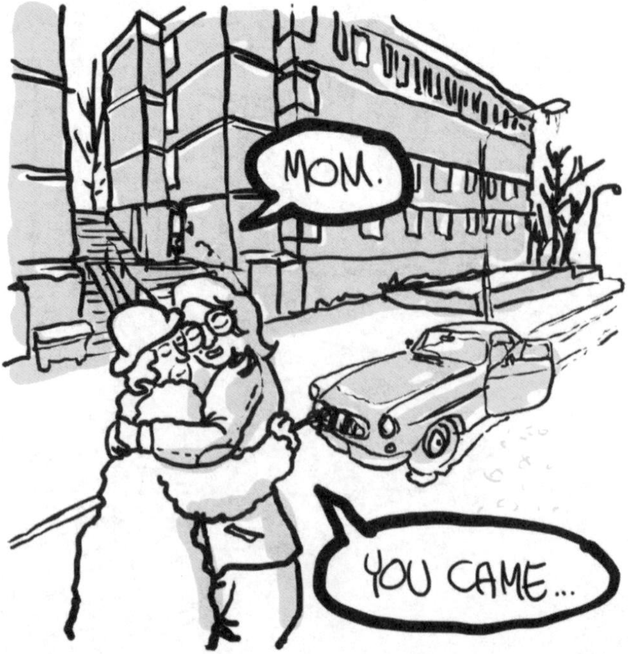
MOM.
YOU CAME...

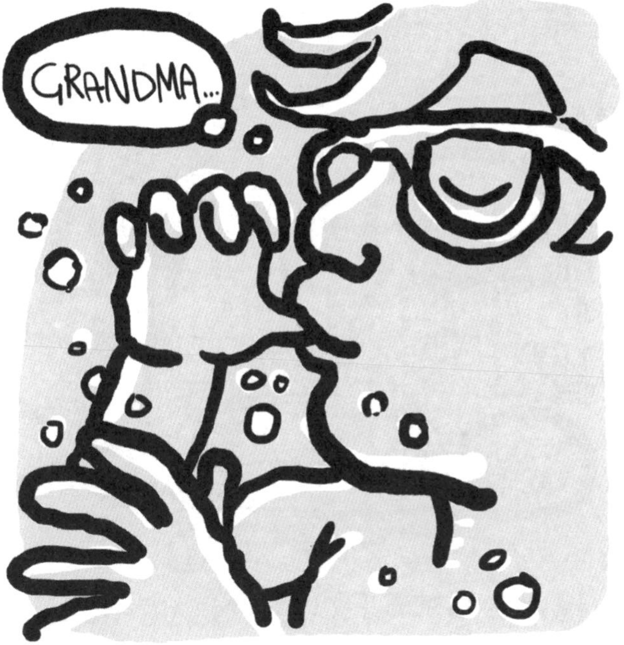
GRANDMA...

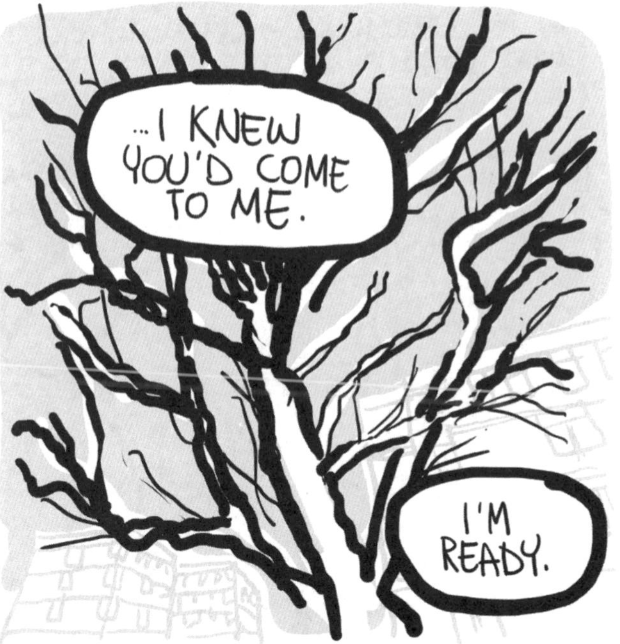
...I KNEW YOU'D COME TO ME.
I'M READY.

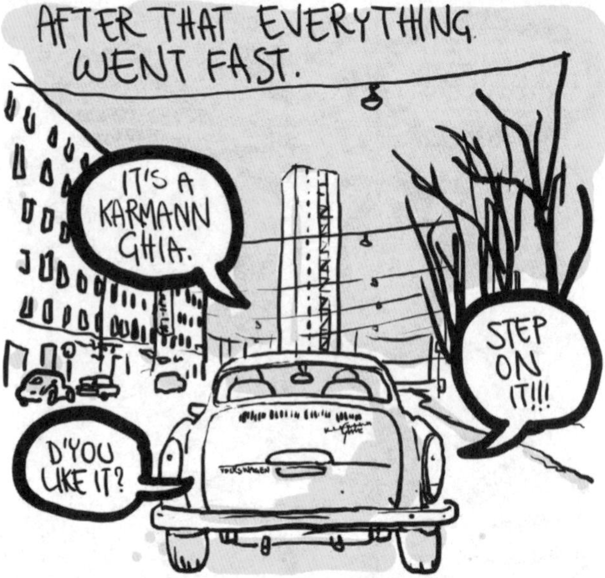
AFTER THAT EVERYTHING WENT FAST.
IT'S A KARMANN GHIA.
STEP ON IT!!!
D'YOU LIKE IT?

MUM'S GOOD FRIEND DROVE HER...

...TO THE KAROLINSKA HOSPITAL WHERE I WAS BORN IN THE PRESENCE OF A LARGE GROUP OF MEDICAL STUDENTS.

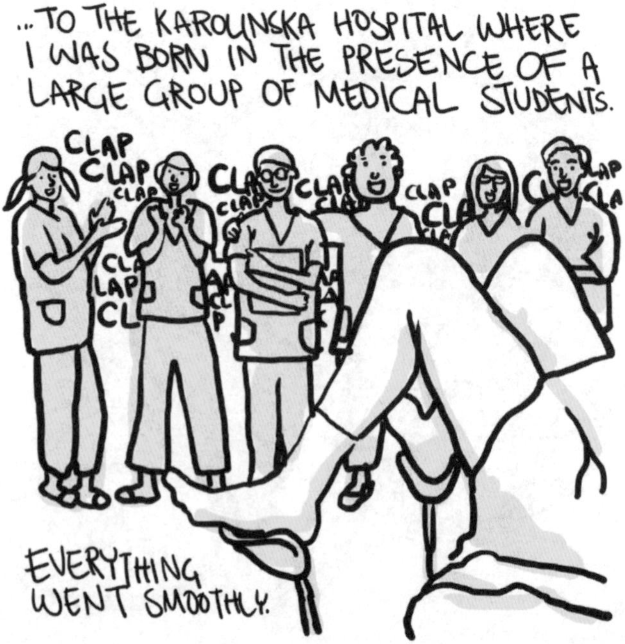
CLAP
CLAP
CLAP
CLAP
EVERYTHING WENT SMOOTHLY.

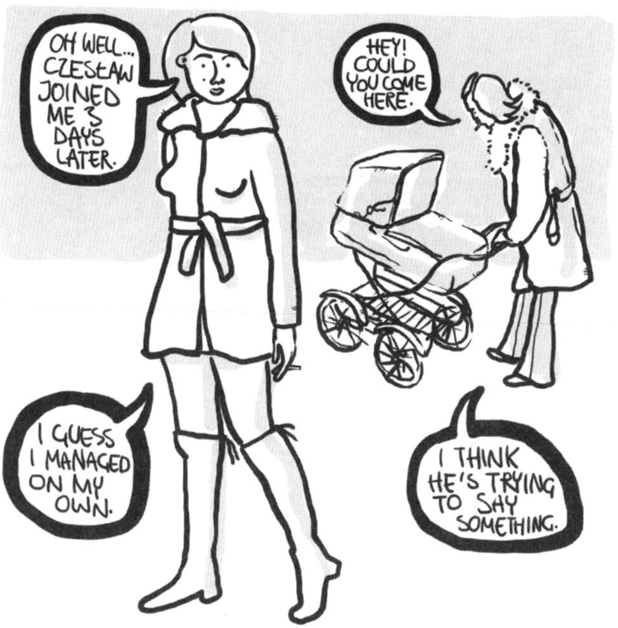
OH WELL... CZESŁAW JOINED ME 3 DAYS LATER.
HEY! COULD YOU COME HERE.
I GUESS I MANAGED ON MY OWN.
I THINK HE'S TRYING TO SAY SOMETHING.

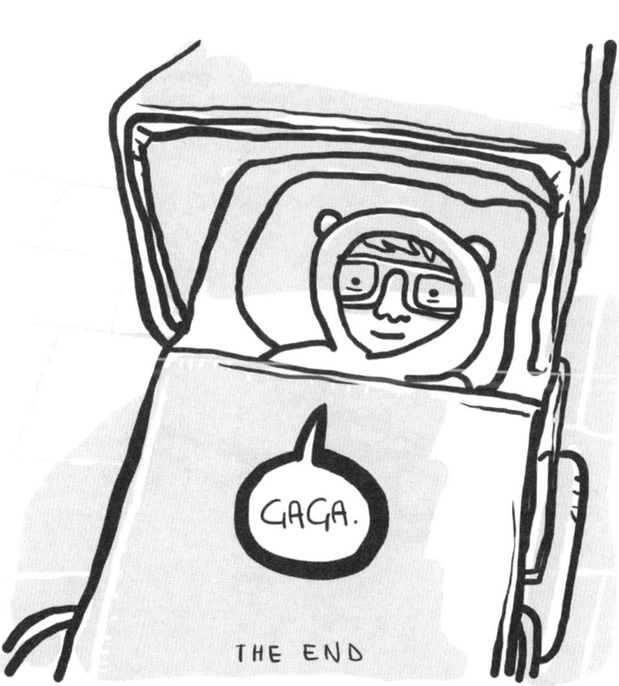
GAGA.
THE END

BORDERLINE PRESS
45 FULLINGDALE ROAD
NORTHAMPTON, NORTHANTS NN3 2PZ
WWW.BORDERLINE-PRESS.COM

FIRST PUBLISHED IN POLAND IN 2013 BY
GRUPA WYDAWNICZA FOKSAL SP. Z O.O.

FIRST PUBLISHED IN THE UNITED KINGDOM
IN 2013 BY BORDERLINE PRESS

1ST EDITION — © DENNIS WOJDA

ISBN 978-0-9926972-0-4 566 FRAMES PAPERBACK

EDITED BY PHIL HALL
WITH THE HELP OF BETTY AND ERIC BEDNARSKI

FIND OUT MORE ABOUT DENNIS WOJDA:
WWW.DENNISSIMO.COM

PRINTED BY BERFORTS

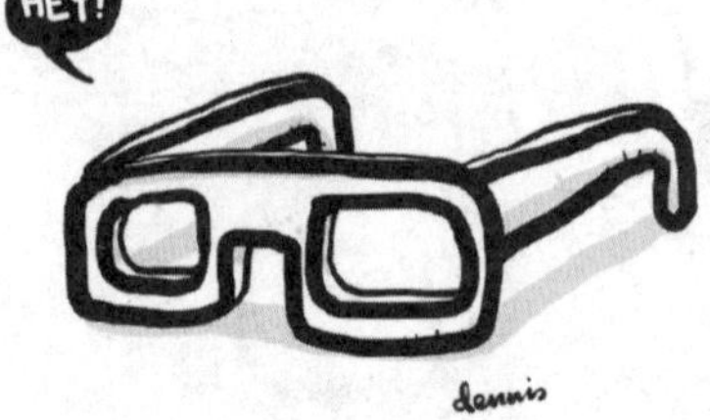
HEY!
dennis